CLIFFORD ODETS
AND AMERICAN POLITICAL THEATRE

CLIFFORD ODETS
AND AMERICAN POLITICAL THEATRE

Christopher J. Herr

Contributions in Drama and Theatre Studies, Number 103
Lives of the Theatre
Josh Beer, Christopher Innes, and Simon Williams, Series Advisers

Westport, Connecticut
London

Library of Congress Cataloging-in-Publication Data

Herr, Christopher J., 1966–
    Clifford Odets and American political theatre / Christopher J. Herr.
       p.   cm.—(Contributions in drama and theatre studies, ISSN 0163-3821 ; no. 103)
    Includes bibliographical references and index.
    ISBN 0-313-31594-9 (alk. paper)
    1. Odets, Clifford, 1906–1963—Criticism and interpretation. 2. Politics and
literature—United States—History—20th century. 3. Odets, Clifford, 1906–1963—Political
and social views. 4. Political plays, American—History—20th century. 5. Theater—Political
aspects—United States. I. Title. II. Series.
PS3529.D46Z69   2003
812′.52—dc21   2003046329

British Library Cataloguing in Publication Data is available.

Library of Congress Catalog Card Number: 2003046329
ISBN: 0-313-31594-9
ISSN: 0163-3821

First published in 2003

Praeger Publishers, 88 Post Road West, Westport, CT 06881
An imprint of Greenwood Publishing Group, Inc.
www.praeger.com

Printed in the United States of America

The paper used in this book complies with the
Permanent Paper Standard issued by the National
Information Standards Organization (Z39.48–1984).

10 9 8 7 6 5 4 3 2 1

Copyright Acknowledgments

The author and publisher gratefully acknowledge permission for use of the following material:

Excerpts from the *The Fervent Years* by Harold Clurman, copyright © 1957 by Harold Clurman.
Used by permission of Alfred A. Knopf, a division of Random House, Inc.

Excerpts reprinted with the permission of Scribner, an imprint of Simon & Schuster Adult
Publishing Group from *Clifford Odets, American Playwright, 1906–1940* by Margaret
Brenman-Gibson. Copyright © 1981 Margaret Brenman-Gibson.

Excerpts from the works of Clifford Odets as cited within the text are courtesy of Robert A.
Freedman Dramatic Agency, Inc.

To my parents, William and Joanne

Contents

Series Foreword

Lives of the Theatre is designed to provide scholarly introductions to important periods and movements in the history of world theatre from the earliest instances of recorded performance through to the twentieth century, viewing the theatre consistently through the lives of representative theatrical practitioners. Although many of the volumes will be centred upon playwrights, other important theatre people, such as actors and directors, will also be prominent in the series. The subjects have been chosen not simply for their individual importance, but because their lives in the theatre can well serve to provide a major perspective on the theatrical trends of their eras. They are therefore either representative of their time, figures whom their contemporaries recognized as vital presences in the theatre, or they are people whose work was to have a fundamental influence on the development of theatre, not only in their lifetimes but after their deaths as well. While the discussion of verbal and written scripts will inevitably be a central concern in any volume that is about an artist who wrote for the theatre, these scripts will always be considered in their function as a basis for performance.

The rubric "Lives of the Theatre" is therefore intended to suggest both biographies of people who created theatre as an institution and as a medium of performance and of the life of the theatre itself. This dual focus will be illustrated through the titles of the individual volumes, such as *Christopher Marlowe and the Renaissance of Tragedy*, *George Bernard Shaw and the Socialist Theatre*, and *Richard Wagner and Festival Theatre*, to name just a few. At the same time, although the focus of each volume will be different, depending on the particular subject, appropriate emphasis will be given to the cultural and political context within which the theatre of any given time is set. Theatre itself can be seen to have a palpable effect upon the social world around it, as it both reflects the life of its time and helps to form that life by feeding it images, epitomes, and alternative versions of itself. Hence, we hope that this series will also contribute to an understanding of the broader social life of the period of which the theatre that is the subject of each volume was a part.

Lives of the Theatre grew out of an idea that Josh Beer put to Christopher Innes and Peter Arnott. Sadly, Peter Arnott did not live to see the inauguration of the series. Simon Williams kindly agreed to replace him as one of the series editors and has played a full part in its preparation. In commemoration, the editors wish to acknowledge Peter's own rich contribution to the life of the theatre.

Josh Beer
Christopher Innes
Simon Williams

Preface

Luther Adler, a friend of Odets' and fellow Group Theatre member, asked the playwright, "Again fruit?" when he heard Odets had made one of his characters a fruit vendor. This book was born from a similar attempt to make sense of the images of abundance in Odets' plays and nurtured by a growing sense that Odets' work still had much to tell us, not only about himself but about the times through which he lived.

My debt to previous scholars cannot be repaid in words. Most particularly, Margaret Brenman-Gibson's fascinating biography offered insights into his character that were invaluable to my work. Many colleagues and teachers have read drafts of this at various stages. Fred and Lise-Lone Marker, Ronald Bryden, David Blostein, and Barrie Hayne all helped shape the early drafts into a recognizable form. Colleagues from the University of Toronto—Nadine Sivak, Marlene Moser, Rebecca Harries, Mark Ceolin, Sharon Reid and others—offered camaraderie and insight. Christopher Innes, Simon Williams, and Josh Beer gave patient encouragement and suggestions during the revision process.

California State University, Los Angeles (CSULA) awarded me a creative leave in 2001 to finish important revisions; Bowling Green State University and Ron Shields secured an opportunity for me to present a paper at the Southeastern Theatre Conference's Theatre Symposium 2000; students in my graduate and undergraduate courses at both universities have challenged me see the period differently, as did the talented actors in CSULA's production of *Waiting for Lefty*.

The City Museum of New York gave me access to its theatre files, and the New York Public Library for the Performing Arts, Billy Rose Collection gave invaluable access to the Odets papers housed there. The Clifford Odets estate graciously granted permission to quote from his plays and archival materials.

My dear friends and teachers Matthew Wikander and Christine Child gave hospitality and good counsel, and deepened my understanding of theatre. For her patience, hard work, and unflagging support, the deepest debt is to my wife, Melissa.

Abbreviations

BFP   John Gassner and Dudley Nichols, *Best Film Plays of 1945*. New York: Garland, 1977.

B-G   Margaret Brenman-Gibson, *Clifford Odets, American Playwright: The Years From 1906-1940*. New York: Atheneum, 1981.

CBN   Clifford Odets, *Clash by Night*. New York: Random House, 1942.

HPT   Clifford Odets, "How a Playwright Triumphs." Based on an Interview with Arthur Wagner. *Harper's Magazine*. September, 1966, 64-74.

LCA   Clifford Odets, Billy Rose Theatre Collection, The New York Public Library for the Performing Arts.

NM   Clifford Odets, *Night Music*. New York: Random House, 1940.

NYT   *New York Times*.

RLD   Wendy Smith, *Real Life Drama: The Group Theatre and America, 1931-1940*. New York: Grove Press, 1990.

SP   Clifford Odets, *Six Plays*. . New York: Methuen, 1982

TBK   Clifford Odets, *The Big Knife*. New York: Dramatists Play Service, 1949.

TCG   Clifford Odets, *The Country Girl*. New York: Viking Press, 1951.

TFP   Clifford Odets, *The Flowering Peach*. New York: Dramatists Play Service, 1954.

TFY   Harold Clurman, *The Fervent Years*. New York: Da Capo Press, 1983.

TIR   Clifford Odets, *The Time Is Ripe: The 1940 Journal of Clifford Odets*. New York : Grove, 1988.

Introduction

Throughout his career, Clifford Odets (1906-1963) attempted to live with strange, persistent contradictions, caught between the acclaim he received in the 1930s as America's popular revolutionary playwright, and the subsequent criticism he received as a film writer, a studio "hack," in the 1940s and 1950s. In many ways, his is the same story he told in his work, the tale of the quick, sweet, fatal ride of the American Dream—the ride of Joe Bonaparte, the protagonist in Odets' *Golden Boy*. While limiting, the widely accepted notion of Odets as *the* playwright of the 1930s holds truth, for it is impossible to understand his work outside the context of the Group Theatre, the depression, the rise and fall of American leftism, or the development of an encompassing consumer culture. Indeed, his work parallels and participates in a radical questioning of the entire American ethos.

Odets certainly seemed to be the "Golden Boy" of the American theatre for at least a few years, beginning with his spectacular debut in 1935, when the first four of his plays were produced on Broadway: W*aiting for Lefty, Awake and Sing!, Till the Day I Die*, and *Paradise Lost*. Odets gained an instant reputation from these early plays. He was hailed by reviewers as a genuine talent, an heir to the legacy of Eugene O'Neill. Even after the box-office failure of *Paradise Lost*, Heywood Broun defended it—and its author—in the strongest terms possible in American drama: "I was present when the earliest work of Eugene O'Neill was first performed and I was no dope. I said that here was a new and glorious talent in the theater and that O'Neill would go far. Perhaps I am a little late in hurling myself, body and soul, on the Odets bandwagon. But I want to make no reservation in stating the opinion that this young man is a far greater figure than O'Neill ever was or will be" (B-G, 386). By 1938, Odets had appeared on the cover of *Time* as a leading spokesman for the new left with the title "Down with the General Fraud!" No wonder, then, that his frequent returns to Hollywood screenwriting forced many to call into question his ideals or his talent. Indeed,

Odets became for many the living embodiment of a struggle rooted deep within American culture: between idealism and materialism, between fervent hope and base practicality.

It need not be argued that the arc of Odets' career is of greater interest than his plays. However, his origins as a political playwright and his near-obsession with the idea of the marketplace—which deals in people as well as commodities—make his biography a necessary part of any study of his plays. Such an explanation seems so natural to his story and discussions of his work that critics have often commented on the virtual impossibility of separating Odets' life from his work, despite the risk of falling into a narrow biographical reading of the plays. Gerald Weales notes that Odets the "celebrity" cannot be separated from Odets the "playwright." Gabriel Miller agrees, suggesting that "because he himself was not immune to the success syndrome, the critical reception of his early work colored the critics', the audiences', and Odets' own attitude towards his subsequent efforts."[1]

Much of Odets' initial success was attributable to what the designer Mordecai Gorelik called "his amazing intuitive grasp of the American scene," his ability to dramatize large-scale cultural shifts: the loss of American idealism, the rise of consumer capitalism, the utopian hopes of American leftism and the development of popular culture as an expression of the common voice.[2] Perhaps more importantly, his plays and screenplays reveal the culture for which Odets' works were produced and the conditions under which they were written. Odets' close friend and biographer Margaret Brenman-Gibson notes: "Odets had scribbled, 'I will reveal America to itself by revealing myself to myself.'" (B-G, xiv).[3] An absolutely necessary step, then, in an examination of Odets' career, if we accept that the life and the work are part of the same conjunction of personal, historical, and artistic events, is an analysis of the economic conditions that prevailed in both the theatre and the film studios at the time he was working. An examination of the external pressures on a playwright working for a financially challenged theatre in the 1930's, as an independent playwright in the 1940s and 1950s, and as a screenwriter for the Hollywood studios from 1936 to the early 1960s provides insight into the plays and screenplays themselves.

In both the plays and the life, economics matter. It is absolutely central to an understanding of Odets' work that Sid and Florrie don't have a place to sit in *Waiting for Lefty*, that Ralph can't buy a pair of black and white shoes in *Awake and Sing!*, that Phil Cooper has to sell blood in *Rocket to the Moon*, that Charlie Castle is a film star who enjoys the Hollywood lifestyle while hating the films he works in. From *Waiting for Lefty* onwards, Odets' characters are caught up in the economic system, bullied by it; they try to beat it, sometimes work within it, but are conscious always of the ubiquitous power of the marketplace. Odets therefore tried to reconcile the utopian dreams of American life—abundance, opportunity, freedom—with the constraints placed upon those dreams by the mechanisms of the marketplace. He adopted ambivalent images that reflected both the promises and failures of American democracy. By dramatizing these struggles in the lives of ordinary people, Odets created a political theatre from the objects of everyday life.

NOTES

1.   Gerald Weales, *Clifford Odets, Playwright* (New York: Pegasus, 1971); Gabriel Miller, *Clifford Odets* (New York: Continuum, 1989) 117. The life and the career have been melded completely not only by Odets' use of the personal but even more so by the critical reception of his work. It is no accident that all six book-length works on Odets use his name as the title, sometimes followed by a descriptive phrase. In addition to the above, the books include R. Baird Shuman's *Clifford Odets* (1962), Edward Murray's *Clifford Odets: The Thirties and After* (1968), Michael J. Mendelsohn's *Clifford Odets: Humane Dramatist* (1969), and Harold Cantor's *Clifford Odets: Playwright-Poet* (1978). The descriptive phrases after Odets' name in each title represent not only a new take on the work but a new take on the life, a repositioning of the biographical as well as the artistic.

2.   Mordecai Gorelik, *New Theatres for Old* (New York: E. P. Dutton, 1962) 242.

3.   Brenman-Gibson's biography of Odets, *Clifford Odets, American Playwright*, covers the life and career of Odets from 1906 until the commercial failure of the last play produced by the Group, *Night Music*, in 1940. Brenman-Gibson's work is a psychoanalytical reading of the works within the larger context of the life. Not strictly the kind of correlation between work and life that Miller and Weales see, but rather the exploration of the private rather than the public Odets, her analysis is nevertheless extremely useful and detailed and indispensable for any student of Odets or the Group.

Chapter 1

Odets and America, 1906-1929

THE IMMIGRANT'S SON

Clifford Odets was born on July 18, 1906, in Philadelphia, the son of Eastern European Jewish immigrants. His mother, Pearl Geisinger, left her poor Romanian family to come to the United States with her sister Esther in 1896. Part of the third large wave of Jewish immigrants fleeing oppression in Europe, Pearl never quite adapted to her new country. On the other hand, Lou Odets, a sheet feeder in a Philadelphia printing business, was a Russian immigrant who had adopted his new country gleefully. He refused to acknowledge his birth name, Gorodetsky, or his European past, threatening family members who might reveal the secret. He also deliberately played down his Jewish heritage, refusing to speak Yiddish at home, taking only American papers, and becoming active in the Masons. Lou's actions were not unusual for immigrants of his generation, who faced enormous pressure to assimilate into American life. This process of assimilation was accelerated by the economic mobilization for World War I, which moved immigrant workers more rapidly into the workplace, and institutionalized in the postwar Americanization Act, requiring immigrants to take classes in language and American patriotism. In addition to outside pressures to either fit in or go home, even within the Eastern European Jewish circles the economic incentives to assimilate were irresistible; advancement seemed possible only if one played by the rules of the new country.[1]

The Odets family eschewed regular religious observance, though even Lou recognized the social benefit to maintaining the appearance of piety outside the home. Clifford never celebrated his *bar mitzvah*; though he briefly attended *cheder* to prepare for the ceremony in early 1919, he dropped out. Nevertheless, despite his immediate family's diffidence in matters of religion, Clifford was exposed to Jewish history and culture through other relatives and friends. For a time after Clifford's birth, Lou and Pearl lived with Esther and her husband, Israel Rossman, a would-be cantor who was forced to work as a fruit peddler to make ends meet, in a small flat in a Jewish neighborhood. Odets developed a great fondness for his aunt and uncle's home. In contrast to his own parents, his aunt and uncle spoke Yiddish and always had food ready for guests. Israel would spend pleasant hours entertaining guests with traditional songs in Hebrew and Yiddish. After his family moved away, Odets spent his Philadelphia visits in their home and would speak of them fondly throughout his life.

The Jewish working-class environment he found at the Rossmans' inspired much of Odets' work. When his second full-length play—an unproduced melodrama about a musical genius—was summarily rejected by Group Theatre director Harold Clurman in 1932, Odets began to reconsider his roots as source of inspiration: "I've begun to think abut the Greenbaum family play. I have much feeling for that sort of thing and could really do something with it. . . . the Greenbaum thing is much nearer to the truth of my own feeling and reality" (B-G, 236). The "Greenbaum play" would eventually become *Awake and Sing!*, Odets' first full-length success and in many respects his best play. Like his father, Odets rarely talked or wrote in his letters or journals about his heritage, and when he did, it was often to separate himself from it; his letters make occasional derogatory references to "low-class Jews." Yet when he wrote plays like *Awake and Sing!*, his sympathetic understanding of the problems of the Jewish-American immigrant earned him praise as the "lyric poet of American Jewry."

There is ample evidence throughout Odets' plays of Jewish influence. In addition to characters in *Awake and Sing!*, characters in his other plays are carefully drawn types of people he observed around him growing up, often second-generation immigrants (Joe Bonaparte in *Golden Boy*, Steve Takis in *Night Music*) trying to carve a place in the world. Odets' unique dialogue, too, is charged with Yiddish rhythms, phrasing, and vocabulary and salted with observations overheard in the Rossmans' kitchen and elsewhere. Harold Cantor notes that for Odets, the Yiddish rhythms (Bessie Berger's "I raise a family they should have respect" or Jacob's "give me for a cent a cigarette" in *Awake and Sing!*) not only captured the authenticity of Jewish-American speech but, even more, distilled the experiences of immigrant life into living language. The Bergers are a family in transition, from immigrants to assimilated: "Odets brought into play his sensitivity to the psychological implications of words and phrases for both the older generation and the younger."[2] Though his later plays moved away from specific concern with Jewish immigrants to the problems of American democracy, he nevertheless anchored those plays with Jewish characters as well: Siggie in *Golden Boy*, Rosenberger in *Night Music*, Prince in *Rocket to the Moon*. By 1946 Odets was so identified with Jewish-American characters that he was labeled the man who had made "by a considerable margin the most important achievement in the literature of the American Jews."[3] Odets' own ambivalence about his religion is the struggle of the immigrant in America who hopes to "melt" into the melting pot without losing a sense of personal individuality.

Life was difficult for the Odets family, as it was for most immigrants coming to America at the turn of the century. The conflicts they faced—between dreams of affluence and the harsh realities of immigrant life, between the desire for respectability and the shame inflicted upon foreigners in the strange land, between the freedom of opportunity in America and the responsibilities of family, religion, and society—reflect a new generation of American writers raised by these immigrants. Such writers, Odets included, were deeply marked by their experience; they express the need not only to fit in but to remake the New World so that all might fully participate. Alfred Kazin, a contemporary of Odets, talks about reliving through his family's stories the painful history of European Jews who had come to America to escape persecution. For Kazin, talk of *der heym* ("Home") was both painful and enchanting; it called up images of persecution and danger but at the same time confirmed the cultural unity of the Jewish people: "The most terrible word was *aleyn*, alone. . . . *Aleyn! Aleyn!* My father had been alone here in America as a boy. *His* father, whose name I bore, had died here at twenty-five of pneumonia caught on a garment workers' picket line, and his body flung in with thousands of other Jews who had perished those first years on the East Side."[4]

Kazin remarks that his Jewish identity and his leftist political beliefs had the same source—a vision of home: "Socialism would be one long Friday evening around the samovar and the cut-glass bowl laden with nuts and fruits."[5] While Odets' identification with Judaism as represented by his aunt and uncle's kitchen was never fully articulated, his own vision of America's promise was often expressed in images strikingly similar to Kazin's. Odets consistently returned to images of material plenty—fruit, for example, appears as a central metaphor throughout his work—as a symbol of the American promised land. These immigrants had seen a land where they could enjoy living conditions their ancestors never dreamed of, where high-quality consumer goods were widely available. Indeed, one of the ways in which new immigrants measured their assimilation was by the accumulation of material possessions; they gained a sense of fully belonging more as consumers—who could buy the same products as native-born Americans—than workers.[6] The work of writers like Kazin and Odets was born from the struggles of the immigrant experience filtered through the seemingly endless bounty offered by America. They chastened the promise of the new world with reminders that it was for many still unrealized.

During Odets' early childhood, his family moved around frequently in search of success. They left Philadelphia in 1908, but when Lou failed to find work in New York, the family moved back. But by 1912, Lou had found a job in New York, and the family remained in the Bronx for the rest of Odets' childhood. As Lou became successful, his marriage with Pearl was beset by increasing problems. Pearl was shy, sensitive, quiet, and chronically ill, probably with the tuberculosis that would eventually cause her death at age forty-seven. Lou was brash, overconfident, sociable, and concerned with keeping up appearances. The tension between his parents helped to forge a strong bond between Odets and his mother. A sensitive child, more at home with books than with physical activity, often alone, he sought constant affection from her. Her withdrawal from him worsened when Odets' sister, Genevieve (born in 1910; a second sister, Florence, was born in 1916), was disabled by infantile paralysis. Odets' biographer, Margaret Brenman-Gibson, argues that Pearl's withdrawal influenced Odets' relationships with women throughout his life. His anxiety about being abandoned by his mother developed into a form of misogyny that manifested itself in compulsive seductions and abandonments of scores of women over the course of his life.

Brenman-Gibson exhaustively details the manifestations of Odets' misogyny. A charming and handsome man, he was a compulsive womanizer and carried on elaborate correspondence with potential or actual lovers that was playful and tender, yet also aggressive and accusatory. Odets would berate correspondents who did not respond quickly enough and constantly sought the attention of women, especially those whom he perceived as soft and motherly. Yet at the same time he evinced a hostility toward them that proceeded from a fear that they, like his mother, would withdraw their affections; at times, Odets withdrew completely from female companionship, working feverishly in isolation. He married three times: the first, a secret marriage made in 1928, when Odets was twenty-one, ended apparently in a murder-suicide in July 1929, when his wife killed their infant daughter, then shot herself. Odets never publicly spoke about this marriage, and even the exhaustive biographical information compiled by Brenman-Gibson can turn up only a few fleeting references to it. The other two marriages, to actresses Luise Rainer and Bette Grayson, were tempestuous, ending in divorce. Odets also had countless affairs with actresses and other famous women of his day, including Fay Wray, Ruth Gordon, Frances Farmer, and others. The complex relationship with women may help to better understand Odets' persistent commodification of the female body in his plays. His female characters are often seen as sexual objects, but at the same time are often as witty, powerful, and emotionally complex as his male characters.

Odets' relationship with his father was equally difficult. He admired his father's ambition, hard work, and determination to become a success yet at the same time was unable to reconcile himself with the personal costs of such ambition. At times throughout his childhood, Odets felt completely isolated by his lack of connection to either parent. On several occasions, he referred to himself as an "orphan," and some of his early attempts at writing, such as a melodramatic story titled "The Boy Who Ran Away," underscored both his need for human connection and his need for recognition. Indeed, anxiety about "making it big" would recur throughout his mature work. In Odets' plays, characters such as Ralph Berger and Moe Axelrod in *Awake and Sing!*, Joe Bonaparte in *Golden Boy*, Kewpie and Ben Gordon in *Paradise Lost*, Edna and Florrie in *Waiting for Lefty*, Charlie Castle in *The Big Knife* are both fascinated and frightened by the power of the marketplace, driven to create a sense of home in a world that seems hostile or indifferent. Never feeling fully at home himself, this conflict between sympathy and success would serve as a cornerstone for both his work and his life.

ODETS' AMERICA IN THE 1920s

Odets spent his childhood and adolescence in New York, attending Public School 52 in the Bronx and hanging out with the "Beck Street Boys," a loose aggregation of schoolmates and neighborhood friends. Meanwhile, the world was changing rapidly; the tense European political situation exploded into world war in 1914, and though Woodrow Wilson honored for a while the isolationist feelings of most Americans, a sense of inexorable change both at home and abroad was in the air. The Socialist candidate for president, Eugene V. Debs, had garnered almost a million votes in 1912, suggesting that an increasing number of the immigrants and workers facing poverty and squalid conditions in the burgeoning cities sought significant changes in the social order. Arriving in America at the rate of about 1 million per year, many of the new immigrants, including Italians and Eastern European Jews, had joined ranks, officially or unofficially, with the Socialists and the labor unions, fighting for social justice.

The years leading up to and including World War I had been a period of moderate social reform in the United States. Though reform was often slow and tinged with moral righteousness in the first part of the century—child labor or minimum wage laws faced fiercer opposition than temperance legislation—significant changes had already been made by 1917. Progressive municipal governments, settlement houses such as Jane Addams' Hull House in Chicago, the muckraking journalism of Upton Sinclair and others, and the establishment of labor unions after violent strikes in textile mills in Paterson, New Jersey, and Lawrence, Massachusetts, in the 1910s marked a new spirit of reform combating the ravages of uncontrolled greed and monopoly capitalism. Allied against big business and the "trusts," these reformers also attempted to fight the alienation brought about by modern technology, rapid population growth, and the increasingly impersonal city.[7]

Despite advances, such struggles indicated a growing gap between rich and poor, between the political left and the political right, between nativists and foreigners. Elected to his second term in 1916 partly on the claim that "he kept us out of the war," Wilson's liberalism had lured many voters away from the Socialist Party following the 1912 election. But when the United States entered the war, many felt he had betrayed his ideals to protect American economic interests. After the initial fear of involvement, war fever soon ran high; a jingoistic patriotism swept the country. Congress hurried the Espionage Act into law in 1917, adding to it a Sedition Act in 1918, which made it a crime to openly criticize the American form of government or the Constitution. These laws gave the government broad powers to punish outspoken opposition to the war, powers used not only to fight legitimate threats to national security, but also to punish dissenters, or to coerce into silent cooperation those who questioned America's motives. Rose Pastor Stokes, a noted feminist and Socialist, was given a ten-year prison sentence for declaring, "I am for the people and the government is for the profiteers."[8] Debs himself was imprisoned for his opposition to the war in 1917, and leftist organizations such as the International Workers of the World (the "Wobblies") were persecuted.

Odets was still too young to have a clearly defined politics in place, but he was sensitive to the talk that swirled around his immigrant Jewish and Irish neighborhood during the war. Already, he was drawn to the idea of fighting the establishment. As he later said, at this time he began to understand that "in a capitalist society, criminals, artists and revolutionists are brothers under the skin. For related reasons they are all men of opposition" (B-G, 44). Odets' political beliefs, coupled with his own personal sense of being on the outside, would take the fertile soil of the depression and the Group Theatre to develop fully, but it is fair to say that World War I was a powerful influence on his development. Discussions of war recur throughout his work: in his plays *Waiting for Lefty*, *Awake and Sing!*, *Rocket to the Moon, Night Music,* and *Clash by Night* and his screenplay for *None but the Lonely Heart.* In the 1930s, on the eve of another war, Odets and his leftist contemporaries would remember the last, cautioning his audience about the dangers of blind obedience to authority.

The beginning of Odets' personal transformation paralleled powerful changes taking place in American politics and social life. As the postwar adjustment began, America had become overnight the leading world economic and military power, a creditor nation, and a strong, if reluctant, force on the world stage. Yet there was in the aftermath of the war a violent reaction against involvement in world politics, a calculated effort to return America to its prewar cocoon. First, there was the scuttling of Wilson's proposal for American participation in the League of Nations by the Senate. Henry Cabot Lodge, who led the opposition to the treaty, voiced fears common to many that European entanglements would prevent America from acting in its own best interests. Second, the Russian Revolution of 1917 had precipitated a fear of similar rebellion in the United States, which culminated in the "Red Scare" of 1919-1920. New immigration laws had made membership in the Communist Party a criminal offense, and Wilson's attorney general, A. Mitchell Palmer, executed raids in which 10,000 suspected "reds" were arrested and many of them deported.

The fear of foreign radicals combined the separate fears of leftist politics and immigration. Members of leftist groups and unions were lumped together as "bolsheviks" or "reds." One of the outgrowths of the Palmer paranoia was one of the most famous cases of the 1920s: the arrest and trial of two Italian anarchists, Nicola Sacco and Bartolomeo Vanzetti, for a payroll robbery and murder in Massachusetts. After a trial of dubious legitimacy, they were convicted in 1921 and eventually executed in 1927.[9] The Sacco-Vanzetti trial became a rallying point for leftists during the 1920s, a symbol of the political battle lines of postwar America. Maxwell Anderson, one of the leading American playwrights of the 1920s and 1930s, would find the events surrounding the case so important that he would make it the subject of two full-length plays, *Gods of the Lightning* (1927) and *Winterset* (1935), and composer Marc Blitzstein—who would find fame in the 1930s with his Federal Theatre Project musical *The Cradle Will Rock*—worked his entire life to find a way to express the events surrounding the trial in musical form. Odets himself was impressed enough with the trial to specify that a picture of the two men be visible to the audience in his play *Awake and Sing!* (SP, 40). Sacco and Vanzetti became a sort of shorthand, as the theatrical left began to merge art and politics more overtly—and more successfully. In the same way, trials and labor conflicts in the 1930s would galvanize the literary left; artists and writers used their work to openly support a particular political goal.

The anxiety driving the Sacco-Vanzetti trial and the Palmer raids would manifest itself in the passage of increasingly isolationist laws. The Immigration Act of 1917 had prevented illiterate immigrants from entering the country, and for the first time in 1921-1922 immigration quotas were set—at 35 percent of the projected immigration for that year. Thousands of immigrants, most from Southern and Eastern Europe, were stranded at Ellis Island or returned to their homelands. Congress also passed a series of strong tariffs on foreign goods, protecting the homegrown products of American industry against invasion. On the domestic front, the Ku Klux Klan was revived in the South and Midwest in 1915, tapping into a deeply rooted American xenophobia and racism. Membership in the Klan skyrocketed, from 2,000 members in 1920 to almost 4 million by 1924 (though membership would decline precipitously, falling to 200,000 by 1929, partly as a result of highly publicized scandals). Floggings and lynchings occurred all across the South, and violent disturbances flared in the North as well.[10]

The Klan's rise, like the Palmer raids and the new immigration legislation, evinced a growing fear of "radical" European influence and a nostalgia for a pioneer Americanism that eschewed "foreign" influences. Indeed, the plight of African-Americans in the South had been growing steadily worse since the end of Reconstruction. The imposition of restrictive Jim Crow legislation prevented most from voting, and violence was common against those who tried to assert their rights. As a reaction, African-Americans began to move North in enormous numbers—over half a million in the years 1916-1920—looking to industrialized cities in the Midwest and Northeast for employment and new opportunities. These men and women settled in places like Chicago's South Side and New York's Harlem, creating new areas composed entirely of black Americans. These communities soon developed a rich, vibrant culture and economy, manifested most significantly in the flowering of the Harlem Renaissance. Nevertheless, race relations throughout the country were tense: Wilson had segregated federal offices during his administration, race riots occurred in Chicago, Texas, Arkansas, and elsewhere in 1919, and an antilynching law was defeated by a filibuster led by southern senators in 1922.

Changes were also taking place in the American workplace. With virtually full employment because of the war effort, labor unions had prospered during the war. The American Federation of Labor more than doubled its membership between 1916 and 1921. In addition, workers went on strike with greater frequency than ever before: more than 3,000 strikes involving 4 million workers were called in 1919 alone. Many of the strikes failed, however, and by 1921, unions began to lose many of the gains they had made during the war. One sign of coming economic trouble was that membership in unions declined steadily throughout the 1920s, an unusual trend in times of prosperity.[11] Coupled with the decline in industrial production in the years immediately after the war—business profits fell from $8 billion in 1919 to $1 billion in 1920—antiworker sentiment accelerated inflation and unemployment so that $5.00 in 1914 wages was worth only $2.40 in 1919.[12] Even more importantly, unions, weakened by the shutting down of governmental war supports, became increasingly desperate. Strikes grew more violent and were more violently suppressed. Also, throughout the 1920s, judges issued restraining orders against labor, and Congress and the Supreme Court marshaled legislation effectively curtailing union activity. In 1919, Massachusetts governor Calvin Coolidge earned a national reputation by firing the striking Boston police force, backing his decision with the power of the state guard. Coolidge's action was supported even by Wilson, who admired the "man who had defied Bolshevism and won."[13]

Despite labor unrest throughout the decade, the 1920s were marked by an unprecedented economic boom, largely fueled by an aggressive consumer capitalism. Productivity rose sharply throughout the decade; in fact, production increased an astonishing 63 percent in the years 1920-1929, while there was an actual 7 percent decrease in the number of person-hours worked. Wages rose as well, though not as quickly, largely because continued capital re-investment of the huge profits that large companies made in the 1920s increased productivity still more and created a growing abyss between rich and poor: "Between 1920 and 1929, per capita disposable income for all Americans rose by 9 percent, but the top 1 percent of income recipients enjoyed a whopping *75 percent* increase in disposable income."[14]

Thus, despite the low inflation and the overall increased earning power of American workers that drove the economic boom between 1922 and 1929, there were signs of trouble. For example, many workers in unskilled factory jobs barely earned enough to survive. Even more importantly, the boom was in part built upon a farm recession that kept commodity prices low throughout the 1920s. Farmers who had been encouraged to mortgage their farms and cultivate more land during the war found themselves with huge, virtually worthless surpluses of grain at its conclusion. Wheat, corn and wool prices dropped 60-75 percent when wartime purchasing plans were abandoned in 1920; farmers struggled to unload their crops. Though prices rebounded somewhat in the mid-1920s, the crisis on smaller farms continued into the depression, when the plight of farmers became truly desperate. Because the basic problem of the small farmer stemmed from overproduction during the war, it was exacerbated by increased productivity as better seed, pesticides, fertilizer, and the gasoline-powered tractor became widely available. Though legislative attempts were made to alleviate the crisis, farm unrest grew throughout the decade.

The cracks that had appeared in the facade of wealth weren't visible enough to deter most Americans. The country was generally wealthy; the wartime prosperity of the country in general was shared by the Odets family. Indeed, Lou Odets had made enough money during the war boom to buy his own printing business and had moved the family to a bigger place on Longwood Avenue, one of the nicest apartment buildings in the Bronx. They would move a number of times over the course of a few years, each time to a bigger place; Lou advertised his elevated economic status by improving the family's material conditions. Thus, in a relatively short time, the Odets family had risen from a working-class immigrant family to enjoy membership in the middle class, capable of participating in the material abundance that America offered. Odets' father bought a pianola, which served as much as a symbol of success as a musical instrument.[15]

Looking back later, Odets would question the purpose of such aggressive socioeconomic climbing, seeing in his own disjointed childhood experience a crystallization of the American myth of success. In notes filed in a folder titled "783 Beck Street" he examined his own family's relationship to the dream: "The American and dehumanizing myth of the steadily expanding economy. To move into this house was thought a terminal, a mission accomplished. But it became a mere wayside stop on the line and one moved to something higher and bigger. Where does America stop? When does it begin to make homes and sink nourishing roots? . . . Oh, the waste of it all" (B-G, 38). Odets formulated an idea to write a play tracing the history of a house, a play that would reflect what he called "social ideals" in the people of the play, that would effectively transmute his personal experience into an examination of American life and culture.

As the war ended, the family was living in the building at 783 Beck Street, where Clifford had his own room for the first time. He read voraciously, performed in small school plays, and wrote outlines for stories and sketches. It was in school that he first encountered the work of Victor Hugo, whose *Les Miserables* he later called "the most profound art experience I have ever had . . . Hugo inspired me, made me aspire; I wanted to be a good and noble man, longed to do heroic deeds with my bare hands, thirsted to be kind to people, particularly the weak and humble and oppressed" (TIR, 334). Hugo's sympathies for the dispossessed helped to define Odets' feelings of dissatisfaction with the status quo and offered him a clearer object for his compassion. A Hugoesque sympathy for the weak and downtrodden became a defining characteristic of Odets' later work; the same romantic longing for connection and usefulness would be later enkindled by others, including the Communist Party and the Group Theatre. Odets' reaction against oppression and degradation was romantic at base rather than political. His politics developed not as conscious leftism, but as an instinctive reaction against the poverty and isolation he saw around him, as well as a personal reaction against the crassness of his own father's social climbing. As he was to later tell the House Un-American Activities Committee in 1952, "When I wrote, sir, it was out of central, personal things. I did not learn my hatred of poverty, sir, out of Communism."[16]

The 1920s were much as F. Scott Fitzgerald had chronicled, a giddy return to prosperity, wild and nervous. The Republican candidate for president in 1920, Warren G. Harding, was elected by a wide margin on the promise that he would give the country a political and economic stability that it longed for. Harding's administration, while far more probusiness than Wilson's, continued with a course of cautiously progressive legislation. But the return to "normalcy" was ultimately a political retrenchment to the conventional values of middle America—before he entered public office, Harding had been a conservative newspaper editor in the small town of Marion, Ohio. Though Harding's tenure in office was cut short by a heart attack, his administration left at least one lasting legacy. The appointment of four conservative Supreme Court justices, including former president William Howard Taft, shifted the balance of judicial power to the right and ushered in a period of inordinately probusiness, antilabor legislation that would feed the boom of the 1920s and, later, would hinder the early years of Roosevelt's New Deal.

There are indications, though, that the widespread poverty of the 1930s had begun during the 1920s. Rick Szostak argues, for example, that the 1920s can really be seen as a boom only in relation to the Depression of the 1930s: technology in the 1920s did not develop quickly enough to allow for sustained economic growth.[17] America had moved to the right as much as a result of the perception of unequaled prosperity as actual fact. As Odets' family had prospered, so did many members of the middle class. Radio, the automobile, and electric appliances all became commonplace items, available for purchase by almost anyone on the installment plan. Contentment reigned; the elimination of poverty seemed to many a realizable goal. There were flashes of reform from the left, especially Robert La Follette's campaign for president in 1924. Running as a third-party candidate for the Committee

for Progressive Political Action—a loose affiliation of leftist groups including paci-
fists, labor unions, feminists, and farmers and endorsed by the Farmer-Labor Party,
the Socialist Party, and the American Federation of Labor—the Wisconsin senator
earned 4.8 million votes. In fact, La Follette and his running mate, Burton K.
Wheeler of Montana, defeated the Democratic party in eleven states, contributing to
the Democratic movement toward the left during the early Franklin Roosevelt
years.[18] Nevertheless, the Republican hands-off approach to the economy, coupled
with America's standing as the leading economic power in the world, gave big
business the freedom to increase production without restraint, betting—wrongly—
that the supply would create its own market.

Even under the banner of "normalcy," different visions of America were in
conflict: radicals and reformers against the old guard, minorities and immigrants
against traditional visions of Americanism, internationalists against isolationists.
Added to this mix was an upheaval in the arts no less powerful. Since the 19th century, American writers had attempted to create a unique culture that would stand
independently of European models. Yet despite limited success during the literary
renaissance of the mid-19th century, the United States had never been able to match
its political democracy with a similar progressivism in the arts, nor had it ever escaped the literary shadow of England. In the early years of the 20th century, however, inspired by revolutionary ideas imported from European thinkers and writers—Marx and Lenin, Freud, Nietzsche, Zola, Dostoevsky, and others—and horrified by the pointless destruction of the war, American writers began to experiment,
looking to fuse new artistic forms with political leftism. Many American writers—
the "Lost Generation" of Ernest Hemingway, Gertrude Stein, H. D., Ezra Pound,
and others—would go abroad in search of new forms, escaping the increasing
commercialization, narrowness, and pettiness of American life. Others felt that the
real struggle for the American arts, especially theatre, was in the United States;
artists such as novelist Sinclair Lewis and composer Aaron Copland, among many
others, challenged the growing "Babbitry" of American life with satire, experimentation, and fierce energy.

Some of the first outgrowths of this movement before the war were new literary journals such as *the seven arts*, founded by Van Wyck Brooks and Waldo
Frank, and *The Masses*, founded by Max Eastman. These new journals sought to
bring about a connection between the developing American arts and a more consciously radical politics, though "while they advocated socialism . . . their leftism
was generally more lyrical than practical. A Socialist America represented to them
the fulfillment of their aesthetic theory."[19] While these writers were forging new
paths in search of a genuine American literature and drama, Odets, young and politically naive, was building an aesthetic that would dovetail with the new movement. He was introduced to modern European drama at age fourteen through silent
film versions of Ibsen's *A Doll's House* and Wilde's *Salome*. Odets became so excited by the productions that he ran to the library to read the plays. Struck by the
power of performed drama, Odets even briefly entertained an idea that his father
might allow him to attend drama school. Failing to see how drama could lead to
business success, his father refused; Odets reluctantly entered Morris High School
in September 1921 at the age of fifteen.

During high school, Odets began to resist more openly the idea of success promulgated by his father. Lou had already determined that Clifford would work as a copywriter in the advertising agency he was planning to start and so pushed his son to take practical courses toward that end. Trapped, Odets became an increasingly unhappy student, escaping to his room at home to bury himself in his own reading and writing. He failed a number of subjects and barely managed to pass others. One of the few highlights of Odets' abbreviated high school career was earning the declamation medal for his recitation of the narrative poems of Robert Service. He was proud of his voice and nurtured it as a talent that could give him a career in the theatre, first as an performer in vaudeville amateur nights, then as an actor in stock companies, as an actor in professional Broadway theatres, and eventually as a playwright.

Odets' only other involvement in the high school was his participation in the Junior Dramatic Club, into which he threw himself with great enthusiasm, skipping other classes to watch lessons. Though he started as an actor, he immediately began to think about directing and writing plays as well. He wanted to learn everything he could about theatre and would often watch rehearsals silently for hours, recording snatches of the conversations taking place around him. Acquaintances were often astonished to hear something they had said reappear years later in one of Odets' plays. But despite these small successes, by November 1923, Odets left high school. He couldn't reconcile his dreams with the tedium of school, partly because he knew that going to college was never a real possibility. Under his father's domination, he felt condemned to the life of a middle-class Jewish businessman, a life thoroughly at odds with the loftier pretensions revealed by his self-consciously literary letters and journals. He started to read the literary and dramatic columns in the newspapers, act in local amateur productions, and when he could, attend the theatre either in the Bronx or downtown.

THE NEW AMERICAN THEATRE: PROVINCETOWN AND THE THEATRE GUILD

The American theatre had started to blossom in the first part of the 20th century. Though American drama had made great strides in "pictorial" realism through advances in theatre technology and the work of playwright-directors such as David Belasco and Augustin Daly in the late 19th and early 20th centuries, the drama in the first part of the new century relied heavily on melodramatic plots and sensational staging. However, in the years just before the war, a number of "little" theatres had sprung up, taking as their model neither commercial Broadway houses nor the local stock companies, but progressive theatres such as André Antoine's Theatre Libre in Paris, the Abbey Theatre of Dublin, and the Moscow Art Theatre. These European theatres staged plays in a way that broke away from facile acting and pictorial realism to show deeper meaning in a new drama. Equally important was the "new stagecraft" influenced by the theories and practice of European designers such as Edward Gordon Craig and Adolph Appia and the new drama pioneered by playwrights such as Strindberg, Shaw, Ibsen, Chekhov, and Maeterlinck.

Fighting to make theatre a vehicle for social engagement, they reacted against the tradition-bound practices of the 19th century theatre, bringing social content–plays about politics, disease, poverty, social institutions–and more consciously artistic methods of acting and directing to the fore.

In the United States, the first little theatres were established in 1912: in Chicago, the Chicago Little Theatre; in Boston, the Toy Theatre; in Fargo, North Dakota, the Little Country Theatre; and in San Francisco, the Player's Club. *Theatre Arts Magazine*, founded in 1916 by Sheldon Cheney, became one of the main connections between American practitioners and the ongoing experiments of European theatre. From these pioneers, the movement boomed in the 1910s: over sixty such theatres were founded in large cities and small towns. Amateur theatres with limited budgets, the little theatres nevertheless embraced experimentation in playwriting, direction, and performance that opened the door to larger and more lasting experiments in the 1920s and 1930s. Mark Fearnow has argued that these theatres were an aesthetic counterpart to the progressivist movement in politics that had cleaned up city governments and attempted "trust busting."[20] Indeed, the little theatres had at base a similar main goal: to establish an alternative to commercial theatre that would embrace the newest developments in European drama. Some also encouraged the development of a stronger tradition of American drama.

From the little theatre movement, two important groups emerged that would permanently change the direction of American theatre: the Provincetown Players and the Washington Square Players (later the Theatre Guild). These two groups helped to develop a repertory of American drama and a tradition of theatrical production that could rival Europe's. Even more, they marked the beginning of a professional theatre in America not in thrall to the star system or to the commercial pressures of Broadway, mingling art with commerce for the first time. In essence, the little theatre movement allowed a truly political drama to develop in the United States, for it fused the aesthetic experimentation of European drama with American political leftism characterized by Socialism, progressivism, and an opposition to 1920s Republican normalcy.

Initially, most of the little theatres depended upon European models for staging and playwriting. American playwrights were overlooked, probably because America had not yet produced a critical mass of quality plays. But the Provincetown Players—founded in the summer of 1915 by a group of Greenwich Village writers and radicals vacationing in Provincetown—had different goals. The group was organized by George Cram ("Jig") Cook, a tireless experimenter who had theatrical connections in Chicago's Little Theatre. The Provincetown group also included Susan Glaspell, Eugene O'Neill, John Reed, Robert Edmund Jones, Harry Kemp, and others. Provincetown took inspiration from European political and aesthetic spirits of revolt, but they wanted even more to establish an original and powerful American drama. By the second summer, the theatre had established itself as a collective dedicated to producing new work, and in 1916, moved their winter productions to a small theatre on Macdougal Street in New York, where they built a small, but important, audience.

As Provincetown developed from an insular group to a theatre specifically dedicated to aid playwrights who might not otherwise see their plays produced, they began to articulate their mission more clearly. A 1917 circular outlining the upcoming season also defined their goals for a "Playwright's Theatre" in language fired by zealotry:

We mean to go on giving artists of the theatre—playwrights, actors, coaches, designers of set and costume–a chance to work out their ideas in freedom . . . We are still not afraid to fail in things worth trying. This season too shall be an adventure. We will let this theatre die before we let it become another voice of mediocrity. If any writers in this country—already of our group or still to be attracted to it—are capable of bringing down fire from heaven to the stage, we are here to receive and help.[21]

By all standards (except perhaps financial) they were successful. Provincetown was the first company dedicated to plays written by American authors; by 1925, they had produced ninety-three new plays by forty-seven different playwrights, including the first productions of O'Neill's one-act sea plays, as well as Glaspell's *Trifles* and *Inheritors*. In 1920, they had their first great success with an experimental production of *The Emperor Jones*, by O'Neill—who gave the theatre even greater legitimacy by winning the Pulitzer Prize the same year for *Beyond the Horizon*. *The Emperor Jones*, a critical and commercial hit, was the first Broadway crossover of a play produced by a little theatre and helped to fix O'Neill's reputation and Provincetown's position at the forefront of the new American theatre.

If Provincetown established itself as a home for American writers and offered O'Neill the chance to produce his epoch-making drama (he continued to stage experimental work with them even after he had become successful on Broadway), another New York group was founded in 1914-1915 that would develop American theatre in another direction. The Washington Square Players were also inspired by European developments in theatre, but unlike Provincetown, they depended almost entirely upon European dramatists for their repertory. Like Provincetown, the Washington Square Players had begun as an amateur group, but unlike Provincetown, which was restlessly experimental and never comfortable with the idea of success, the Washington Square Players developed into a successful, organized professional company. After a halting start as an amateur theatre, the initial group was forced to disband partly because of complications caused by American participation in the war. But the group was reconstituted on a more permanent basis in 1919, taking on a new name, the Theatre Guild, and organizing themselves under a board of directors who would oversee all theatre operations.

As their adoption of the term "guild" suggests, the Theatre Guild was founded as a craft association by a group of professional theatre people, among them director Phillip Moeller, executive director Theresa Helburn, and designer Lee Simonson. They wanted to establish a permanent company that would over a period of years build a tradition of progressive theatre in the United States. Furthermore, by becoming professional, the Guild hoped to free itself from the taint of amateurism that plagued the Little Theatre movement. But perhaps the most important goal of the Guild directors was to establish a theatre as free as possible from the hit-or-miss pressures of the Broadway marketplace. The theatre was structured on a subscription basis in part because they believed that only a self-supporting theatre would be forced to maintain contact with its public.

The Guild began on shaky financial ground, but eventually the professional productions of good, noncommercial plays helped to establish them as one of the most important theatres of the period. By 1925, they were successful enough to build their own theatre on West 52nd Street, raising over $600,000 for the project through the sale of public bonds. However, the responsibilities of a permanent building added to their reliance upon a subscription audience. The Guild was increasingly driven to reflect the tastes of a large audience whose subscriptions allowed the Guild to continue, a shift not always in keeping with their original goals. Indeed, the decision to move early successful Guild productions to Broadway brought forth acrimonious debate among the board of directors. The questions raised were ones that Provincetown, by remaining resolutely experimental and amateur, had not really faced: how could a company produce artistically viable theatre if it were forced to operate on the Broadway principle of reaching as large an audience as possible? How it could afford to survive if it didn't? How could a politically progressive theatre reach a large enough audience to survive?

While other professional theatres enjoyed scattered success—for example, the independent producer Arthur Hopkins produced a successful *Hamlet* with John Barrymore in 1922, and the New Playwrights Company in the late 1920s offered experimental plays outside the confines of the Broadway box—they didn't have the staying power of the Guild. The Guild was successful because they managed to tread a middle ground between creativity and the marketplace, to meld progressive (never radical) politics with professional theatre. In many ways the flagship American theatre of the 1920s, the Guild's particular problems raised questions about the relationship between art and commerce that would resonate in American theatre for years, particularly in Odets' plays with the Group Theatre. The pressure to produce a hit that would keep the theatre afloat remained in conflict with the desire to produce socially progressive theatre. To reach the people, theatres had to produce drama of a certain quality and scale; to move them, they had to be able to understand and express their beliefs and desires.[22]

Provincetown and the Guild, therefore, were created as art theatres in an era that saw America consolidating its economic strength abroad, defending its political hegemony at home, and attempting to establish a literary tradition equal to Europe's. But even though the plays produced by the new theatres were aesthetically progressive, and though many of the individual members of the theatres (especially Provincetown) were outspoken Socialists or Communists, neither the Guild nor Provincetown were particularly political in terms of the plays they produced—though some, such as Glaspell's *Inheritors*, were overtly concerned with issues of social justice. Even those of O'Neill's plays that dealt with class differences tended to focus on metaphysical rather than political conflicts, what he called "the hidden conflicts of the mind." For the most part, both theatres tried to bring American theatre forward through a development of form more than specific political content. The Guild's means of expression were quite different from Provincetown's, though both were influenced by a bohemian-aesthetic view of theatre. For example, the mandate of the Washington Square Players, implicitly adopted by the Guild, asserted, "We have only one policy in regard to the plays we produce—they must have artistic merit. Preference will be given to American plays. . . . Though not organized for purposes of profit, we are not endowed. Money alone has never produced an artistic theatre. . . . Believing in democracy in the theatre, we have fixed the charge of admission at 50 cents."[23]

The Guild's democratic impulses were an outgrowth of a desire for self-expression more than a desire for political expression; they wanted to be able to work as freely as possible from the economic constraints of Broadway. The founders were dissatisfied with the American commercial theatre; they saw an opportunity to create new work and elevate tastes rather than reform the political structure of America. In fact, the Guild—whose espoused preference for American plays did not materialize until they had built a solid financial base with European plays—believed that there was something inherently progressive about doing the newest and best drama, regardless of social message or country of origin; in essence, they were, as one contemporary commentator said, "more conspicuously bohemian than revolutionary."[24] Of course, in addition to important productions of nonpolitical plays, the Guild did produce politically-oriented plays from both sides of the Atlantic, including Elmer Rice's *The Adding Machine* in 1923, and premieres of a number of Shaw's plays.[25] Nevertheless, their primary focus was the creation of high-quality drama that would elevate as much as express the tastes of its audience, that would expose them to a great tradition of European drama that might, in time, call forth an American equivalent. In essence, the Guild's policies were structured much like the dominant conception of political democracy current in the 1920s, with its deep-rooted distrust of radical leftism and its striving for a truly American culture based upon, but not beholden to, European models.

FINDING A ROLE: ODETS IN THE NEW THEATRE

European influence on American theatrical practice increased during the 1910s and 1920s when prominent companies visited the United States. Among the visiting troupes were the Abbey Theatre, in 1911 and 1915, Jacques Copeau's company, in 1917 and 1919, the Moscow Art Theatre, in 1923-1925, and German director Max Reinhardt. Reinhardt brought his celebrated production of *The Miracle* to New York in 1924, where it was hailed as one of the season's highlights. In his limited theatrical experience, Odets had never encountered anything like the new theatre in live performance. He was so moved by Reinhardt's production that he saw it dozens of times, taking a job as an cloakroom attendant in exchange for free tickets. Months afterward he still wrote journal entries about the production.

After leaving high school, Odets had been seriously contemplating a career in the theatre, though pressure from his father had driven him into a series of menial jobs in various businesses: an apprentice copywriter in his father's firm, a bookkeeper and general office help, even an abortive stint as a door-to-door Fuller Brush salesman. However, his aspirations for a theatrical career were sharpened by the Reinhardt production. In late 1924, for example, he contemplated auditioning for the Neighborhood Playhouse, one of the more influential little theatres in New York. Nevertheless, the extent of Odets stage experience at this time was his work as a "ringer" elocutionist for the Moss vaudeville circuit. He recited poetry for a small fee at amateur nights at theatres around the city, winning additional prizes by bringing his friends along to cheer loudly for him. Eventually, he began to perform in productions in small Greenwich Village theatres.

Odets finally moved to the Village in 1925 and later recalled the atmosphere of experimentation there:

At the time I got to Greenwich Village, around 1925, most of the so-called great ones had gone. Floyd Dell had moved; George Cram Cook was dead. I knew his daughter, Nilla Cram Cook. . . . And O'Neill was part of this wonderful, glamorous world that a youth enters. . . . He was gone, but it was as if his fragrance, or the awesome sense of this man still lingered around the dirty alleys and streets. Macdougal Street meant the Provincetown Playhouse and Eugene O'Neill. In that sense I was influenced by Eugene O'Neill. (B-G, 84)

By 1925, O'Neill had already won two Pulitzer Prizes and had recently astounded audiences with his groundbreaking *Desire under the Elms*. Though Odets would continue throughout his life to deny direct influence from O'Neill as a playwright—he liked *Desire under the Elms* but was unimpressed by *The Great God Brown* when he saw it in 1926—he was always inspired by O'Neill's honesty and his desire to become a "big American playwright."

In the Village, the eighteen-year-old Odets joined Harry Kemp's Poet's Theatre. Kemp, known as the "Tramp Poet," was a former member of the Provincetown Players who wrote poetic dramas and directed his own and other poetic plays at St. Mark's-in-the-Bowerie. The connection to Provincetown was important to Odets; it made him feel as if he were part of the vanguard of American theatre. At the same time, he continued his work with the Drawing Room Players, one of the amateur theatres he had joined uptown. Odets remained with Kemp for two years, playing leading parts, until he was fired in one of the many disputes between the two egocentric and temperamental men.

After leaving the Poet's Theatre, Odets remained in the Village. He would live hand-to mouth as a struggling performer for the next few years, working only intermittently in the theatre. One of his regular sources of income was a series of summer jobs at various children's camps, where he moved from washing linens in his first summer to directing children's drama programs in succeeding years. Despite his increasing loneliness and frustration—he contemplated suicide on more than one occasion—Odets still considered himself an actor. He had business cards secretly printed on his father's press, billing himself as an actor, elocutionist, and drama critic, and wrote blurbs advertising himself as the "Rover Reciter," which were published by a friendly columnist in the *New York Evening World*. Through these advertisements of his elocution skills, Odets was able to land as many as ten jobs a week—mostly unpaid—performing live on the radio.

Radio was a very young industry, and Odets broke into it on the ground floor. Part of the boom that harnessed war technology for commercial ends, radio had begun to show signs of what would soon become ubiquitous presence. In 1920, the first station, KDKA, was licensed in Pittsburgh; by 1922, there were 576 licensed stations in the United States and over 3 million homes with radios (the Odets family, in keeping with Lou's need to demonstrate status, was the first in their building to own a radio set). Sales of radios increased faster than for any other product in history, from $1 million in 1920 to over $400 million in 1925. By 1927, the new medium was so popular that the National Broadcasting Company and the Columbia Broadcasting System had been formed, as had a governmental regulatory body charged with reining in the potential chaos such quick growth had brought with it.[26]

As the number of stations multiplied, performers, writers, and advertisers were needed to fill expanding airtime. During the rest of his time downtown, Odets worked on and off in radio, taking a regular job at WBNY in New York, where he debuted as what he would later call "America's first real disc jockey," compiling entire programs of classical or contemporary music and improvising patter to fill dead space. Rather than a regular salary, he would often get paid in trade by the merchants who advertised on the station. In addition to providing him an outlet for his need to perform, Odets' willingness to try the new technologies indicated a fascination with the possibilities of mass media to reach a large audience that would last through his career. Partly driven by the Hugoesque impulse to reach out to people and partly driven by his father's impulse to be a "big" man, Odets would repeatedly seek opportunities to reach as many people as possible with his words.

The radio work pushed Odets to write more as well; he finished two one-act radio plays, *Dawn* and *At the Water-Line*. *At the Water-Line*, a sea melodrama that steals some of its plot and virtually all of its setting from O'Neill's *The Hairy Ape*, premiered at WFBH in January 1926 and later played on other stations in New York and Philadelphia. Odets himself took the part of the hero, Garfield Grimes, a stoker on a ship who is reunited with a society woman whom he had loved and lost years before. He also played parts in other radio plays, notably Simon Legree in a production of *Uncle Tom's Cabin*, and still performed occasionally as the Rover Reciter. However, Odets was beginning to grow tired of his recitations and longed to work as an actor in legitimate theatre. He would occasionally receive bit parts in stock company productions in New Jersey, but little else.

One of the benefits of working for the radio station, Odets found, was that he could see plays and films for free as a critic (his status as a reviewer was confirmed when columnist Walter Winchell called Odets New York's "youngest critic"). During the last few months of 1926, he took full advantage of the opportunity, attending as many plays and films as possible: on Broadway, in stock theatres throughout the area, even at small neighborhood theatres. Odets' diary from this period records an increasing study of theatrical technique. He took extensive notes on the playwrights and actors whose work he had seen, dissecting the techniques of the stars of Broadway: Alfred Lunt and Lynn Fontanne (the cornerstones of the Guild's ensemble), Pauline Lord, the Barrymores, and others. At the same time, he would test his acting theories in stock productions of popular plays like Maxwell Anderson and Gene Stalling's *What Price Glory* or Sidney Howard's *They Knew What They Wanted*. Of the plays he saw that year, Sean O'Casey's *Juno and the Paycock* was Odets' favorite. He especially admired O'Casey's interplay of humor and pathos, a combination that he would attempt to capture in his own plays about the immigrant middle class: *Awake and Sing!*, *Waiting for Lefty*, *Paradise Lost*, and *The Flowering Peach*.

One other event of 1926 would alter the course of Odets' career, though it did not seem significant at the time. He began to watch rehearsals of the Chrystie Street

Players, an amateur group directed by a young Guild actor, Lee Strasberg, who had been influenced by the Moscow Art Theatre (MAT) and the actor training pioneered by Konstantin Stanislavsky. Strasberg had taken classes from two former MAT members, Richard Boleslavsky and Maria Ouspenskaya, who had remained in the United States to found the American Laboratory Theatre. He was attempting to adapt Stanislavsky's methods to his actors. As Harold Clurman, a friend of Strasberg's, remarked, the focus on acting was more scientific and precise than anything Clurman had seen in his work with the Guild or elsewhere, in part because Strasberg believed that "the manner in which a play is done is in itself a content" (TFY, 11). Odets, too, watched rehearsals intently, recognizing that what Strasberg was doing with his actors was far different from the training Odets was getting from the theatrical elocution espoused by old-time stock players in Hoboken and Union City.

In October of 1926, Odets landed his first acting job of note, a one-week stint with the Rialto Stock company in Hoboken. But when that job ended, he was forced to return to his parent's house in Philadelphia, where they had moved after L. J. lost his business less than a year before. In Philadelphia, Odets was accepted into the Mae Desmond stock company as an assistant stage manager who would also take on small acting parts as necessary. Though the pay was abysmal—most of the money he made was spent for food and lodging—Odets watched rehearsals and performances as carefully as he always had, taking detailed notes about the dramatic structure of the plays and the acting of his fellow company members. He stayed with the company for two years, gradually growing into larger parts. It is during this time with Desmond that Odets probably met and married Roberta, his first wife, in Chester, Pennsylvania. Though they had a child together, the couple never lived together, and Roberta killed the child and herself in July 1929. No record remains of the marriage or the deaths, though Brenman-Gibson argues that "Clurman's account and Odets' later references . . . widely spaced in time, have a coherence which point to a genuine event, not a fantasy" (137).

Though it would be years before Odets would turn to writing full-time, the real significance of his work in stock companies was on his writing rather than his acting. Over the course of his time with the company, he learned how theatrical effect could be created and maintained. As he remarked in a letter to a friend written during this period, "I can't kick when I look back on the last year and see how much vital knowledge of the stage and its mechanics I have gained" (B-G, 113). Even more significantly, Odets was beginning to exhibit self-confidence, even to see himself as a "man of the theatre" whose apprenticeship in the stock companies was only a stepping-stone to better things. After another camp summer in 1928, he planned a return to New York to visit Broadway producers. Though he had written nothing for performance since the radio plays, he had begun work on a long novel and several short stories and poems. Indeed, Odets felt torn between writing and acting even at this juncture, though he was always deterred from pursuing writing full-time by his father's disdain. Living at home between trips with the company, Odets fought violently with his family; during one such altercation, L. J. destroyed the typewriter Odets carried with him everywhere.

Odets' only real pleasure outside of work lay in the other cultural interests he cultivated during his stay in Philadelphia. Odets' ongoing interest in classical music became almost an obsession. He spent hours listening to records or the radio and attended the symphony faithfully, a habit that would continue throughout his life. Though he never trained as a musician, Odets often fantasized that he should have been a composer rather than a writer; throughout his career he satisfied this longing by utilizing musicians and musical metaphors in his plays—Jacob's Caruso records in *Awake and Sing!*, Pearl's piano in *Paradise Lost*, Joe's violin in *Golden Boy*, Steve's saxophone in *Night Music*—or discussing his plays in terms of their "musical" structure. Whenever Odets found work as an actor, he celebrated by buying records and playing them at full volume. For Odets, music was a more powerful means of expression than words could ever be; during times of great stress or great joy he buried himself in notes. He also became an admirer of visual art, spending time in museums whenever he could. Later, he would collect art, amassing at one point one of the largest collections of Klees in the world. Odets' voracious appetite for culture—music, theatre, art—often served as a way for him to feel at home, to express his sympathy and commonality with others. It served as his refuge as well as his means of expression.

By the fall of 1928, Odets was back in New York. He picked up more stock roles with the Rialto company, including a small part in *Desire under the Elms*, but the work was neither artistically satisfying nor lucrative. He returned to Philadelphia in January 1929, frustrated and ashamed of his inability to get regular work. However, on one trip back to New York, he finally got a break. He won a small part on Broadway as a prohibition agent and the understudy to Spencer Tracy in Vincent Lawrence's *Conflict*. Though the play closed quickly, Odets' hopes were briefly revived. Still, by the late spring of 1929, he was already beginning to think acting was a chore rather than an art and vowed to himself that he would leave the profession entirely if he didn't get a role in the fall. In the fall, however, Odets' connection with the art theatre was finally made; he landed small roles with a Theatre Guild touring company taking three plays—Carl Capek's *R.U.R.*, O'Neill's *Marco Millions*, and Ben Jonson's *Volpone*—through the Midwest. By this time, the Guild had established itself as a major force in American theatre. Odets' place in the company, however small, was a significant break in his career. Even more important was his connection with Cheryl Crawford, who served as the Guild's casting director. Through Crawford, Odets became more intimately acquainted with the current developments in the theatre. Always eager to learn, Odets wrote Crawford often from the road, sending her news and gossip and asking for news of the theatre back in New York. At this point, Odets was still an apprentice, still unsure of himself both as an actor and as an artist. His ongoing infatuation with Sylvia Field, one of the lead actresses on the tour highlights his need for human connection, his desire for status, his immaturity, and his self-conscious desire to express himself, to be listened to: he wrote her constant letters, followed her, dreamed of her. In one self-dramatizing letter after she rebuffed his advances, he crystallizes the tension he feels between human (usually, but not always, female) acceptance and his calling: "With a stern code of life, with a realization of artistic creation, necessary creation within me, I have become hardened, have lost the urge to sing to every woman who attracted my eyes and other things, such as a need for feminine warmth and sympathy" (B-G, 146).

While Odets was on the road with the Guild company, the stock market crashed on October 29, 1929. At first, no one seemed to have a real sense of how long and how serious the fallout from Black Tuesday would be. The company played to full houses, and the financial problems of the rich—for so the crash seemed to many—seemed unimportant. The giddy fervor of the 1920s, both artistic and financial, was hard to relinquish. Still, within a year, signs of deep and permanent change would be seen both in the streets and in the theatres; as the depression took hold, the theatre spiraled slowly into its own depression: theatres closed, actors were thrown out of work, producers went bankrupt. Odets would find in these events the impetus for his playwriting career.

NOTES

1.   A number of excellent books examine the experience of Eastern European Jewish immigrants in the early 20th century. Susan A. Glenn's *Daughters of the Shtetl: Life and Labor in the Immigrant Generation* (Ithaca: Cornell UP, 1990) focuses on the roles of women in the new land, arguing that much of the burden of assimilation was placed on women who had to participate in the marketplace in ways they hadn't anticipated. Andrew R. Heinze's *Adapting to Abundance: Jewish Immigrants, Mass Consumption, and the Search for American Identity* (New York: Columbia UP, 1990), details how material goods were used as a means of assimilation into the new culture.

2.   Harold Cantor, *Clifford Odets: Playwright-Poet* (Metuchen, N. J.: Scarecrow Press, 1978) 154. Cantor notes that Alfred Kazin recognized in Odets' depiction of the Berger family "a lyric uplifting of blunt Jewish speech, boiling over and explosive. . . . Everybody on that stage was furious, kicking, alive—the words, always real but never flat, brilliantly authentic like no other theatre speech on Broadway" (150).

3.   Quoted in Stephen J. Whitfield, *In Search of American Jewish Culture* (Boston: Brandeis UP, 1999) 117.

4.   Alfred Kazin, *A Walker in the City* (New York: MJF Books, 1951) 60-61.

5.   Kazin, 61.

6.   Heinze, 42. Talking about the ability of material goods to supersede even language as a marker of assimilation, he notes, "New clothes, foods, and furnishings were as tangible as syntax was abstract and as obtainable as idioms were elusive."

7.   Gilman M. Ostrander, *American Civilization in the First Machine Age, 1890-1940.* (New York: Harper, 1970) 111-117.

8.   Geoffrey Perrett, *America in the Twenties: A History* (New York: Simon and Schuster, 1982) 51.

9.   Perrett, 59-62.

10.   Michael E Parrish. *Anxious Decades: America in Prosperity and Depression, 1920-1941* (New York: Norton, 1992) 111; Perrett, 73-75, 192-193.

11.   Stephen J. Baskerville and Ralph Willett remark that there was a steady decline in membership from a high of about 5 million in 1920 to a low of 2.9 million in 1933. Unions did not regain their 1920 strength until 1937, when the newly formed Congress of Industrial Organizations (CIO) boosted union membership to 7.2 million ("Introduction," In *Nothing*

Else to Fear: New Perspectives on America in the Thirties [Manchester: Manchester UP, 1985] 1-12).

12.   Perrett, 31, 49.

13.   Parrish, 7.

14.   Robert S. McElvaine, *The Great Depression: America, 1929-1941* (New York: Times Books, 1984) 22, 38.

15.   Brenman-Gibson notes that the increasing sense of dispossession and injustice that Odets felt in his teenage years—manifested in thefts of money and small objects from stores and classmates—came from a sense of personal rebellion rooted in a feeling of not belonging rather than any real material deprivation (B-G, 40-41).

16.   Eric Bentley, *Thirty Years of Treason* (New York: Viking, 1971) 520.

17.   Rick Szostak, *Technological Innovation and the Great Depression* (Boulder, CO: Westview, 1995) 13.

18.   Parrish, 68-70.

19.   Ira Levine, *Left Wing Dramatic Theory in the American Theatre* (Ann Arbor: UMI Research Press, 1985) 13. Levine's book encapsulates of the development of radical theories of theatre in the United States. He argues that the search for a genuine American art led to the development of left-wing theories of artistic expression—applied to the particular problems of America. While Brooks and Frank advocated a radical approach to the arts and believed that aesthetic rejuvenation would lead to social and political rejuvenation as well, their early theories were often romanticized visions that saw Socialism as an outgrowth of artistic theories rather than a specific method political change. In the theatre, this romanticization led to a dramatic theory largely dissociated from theatrical practice.

20.   Mark Fearnow, "Theatre Groups and Their Playwrights," in Don B. Wilmeth and Christopher Bigsby, eds, *The Cambridge History of American Theatre, Volume II: 1870-1945* (Cambridge: Cambridge UP, 1999) 348-349.

21.   Robert Károly Sarlós, *Jig Cook and the Provincetown Players* (Amherst: U of Massachusetts P, 1982) 86-87.

22.   The establishment of American art theatres outside the boundaries of traditional commercial theatre continued the search that Brooks and Frank had started in *the seven arts* to create an American literature that would accurately reflect the important developments in American culture. Generally applauding the creative spirit exhibited by the new theatre, Frank questioned the Guild's commitment to American ideals. Frank argued that theatre was the *best* way to show the problems of society and urged Americans to put the theatre to its best use. One of the questions raised was that of dependence on European authors; the political and social ramifications of a largely European repertory seemed antithetical to the creation of an important American drama. The founders of the Group, following Frank's lead, believed that American drama needed to reflect American feelings and problems in order to be truly progressive.

23.   Walter Prichard Eaton, *The Theatre Guild: The First Ten Years* (New York: Brentano's, 1929) 21. Eaton also suggests that perhaps the gesture toward democracy was hollow, as the founders of the Players never expected that anyone would be willing to pay more than fifty cents to see one of their productions.

24.   Joseph Wood Krutch, *The American Drama Since 1918* (New York: Random House, 1939) 228.

25.   A list of the plays from the Guild's first few seasons gives an indication of their emphasis on European authors but also indicates how far from the commercial fare normally offered on Broadway their plays were. In their first season, 1919-1920, for example, they produced Jacinto Bentavente's *Bonds of Interest*, St. John Ervine's *John Ferguson* (their first big success) and *Jane Clegg*, John Masefield's *The Faithful*, an

adaptation of William Dean Howells' *The Rise of Silas Lapham*, Tolstoy's *Power of Darkness*, and Strindberg's *Dance of Death*. Later seasons included productions of Shaw's *Heartbreak House*, *Back to Methuselah*, *Devil's Disciple*, and *St. Joan*, A. A. Milne's *Mr. Pym Passes By*, Ferenc Molnar's *Liliom*, Leonid Andreyev's *He Who Gets Slapped*, Kaiser's *From Morn to Midnight*, Capek's *R.U.R.*, and Ibsen's *Peer Gynt*. Important production of American plays included Elmer Rice's *The Adding Machine*, which premiered in 1923, and Sidney Howard's *They Knew What They Wanted*, which won the Pulitzer Prize for 1924. By the late 1920s, though the Guild still emphasized European authors, especially Shaw, they had become the producing organization for a number of O'Neill's plays, including *Marco Millions* and *Strange Interlude* in 1928 and *Dynamo* in 1929.

26. Parrish, 33; Perrett, 230-231.

Chapter 2

Art and Politics in the Marketplace: Odets, the Group, and America, 1929-1940

ODETS' GROUP: REFLECTING AMERICA FROM THE STAGE

Despite the relative success he enjoyed on tour with the Guild, by the spring of 1930 Odets was again struggling financially. He won a small part in two Guild productions in the fall—*Roar, China* and *Midnight*—but both shows closed quickly. Still, he was making inroads into the New York theatre scene. As a result of his work on the second play, Odets struck up a strong friendship with Phillip Moeller, one of the Guild's founders. In his effusive letters to the older Moeller, Odets chronicled his thoughts about the theatre and music and his desire to create something of artistic importance. Moeller responded by discussing, among other things, his difficulties in preparing the new O'Neill play, *Mourning Becomes Electra*, for the stage. Odets' strange, short-lived, mentor–apprentice friendship with Moeller allowed him extensive contact with a giant of the American theatre and allowed him to test ideas on a sympathetic ear.

More important than his friendship with Moeller was his connection with a group of young theatre idealists. After a matinee of *Midnight*, Harold Clurman, who worked as a play reader for the Guild, came backstage to invite Odets to a series of meetings that he and Cheryl Crawford were holding with young actors and writers on Friday nights. The meetings were geared toward finding a way to create a new, deeper American theatre. Clurman, like many of his contemporaries following the war, had traveled, steeping himself in European culture and traditions. He took a degree in French drama at the Sorbonne and studied in Paris with Jacques Copeau, becoming increasingly interested in the new European drama. But even amid the avant-garde theatres of Europe, Clurman felt something missing. He was extremely dissatisfied with the theatre as it then existed in America; despite the great talent and energy, "nothing tie[d] the fast-moving forces together, no governing principle, no aim, no deep and final simplicity" (TFY, 29). With Strasberg and Crawford, he planned a new theatre, not of commerce but of the true collective. Even more significantly, the theatre would be resolutely American, reflecting the anxiety and triumphs of his own country. Odets respected both Clurman and Crawford and felt flattered to be asked. He didn't know that Clurman never saw much potential in Odets' acting, though Clurman had secretly told Strasberg that "something will develop from that man" (B-G, 170).

Clurman was generally apolitical, but he shared much with those openly dissatisfied with American political life. The stock market collapse and its aftermath had shifted the political climate; dissatisfaction with the status quo, formerly a province of the left, became increasingly mainstream. As economic conditions worsened, identification with the "forgotten man"—a phrase from a 1932 Roosevelt campaign speech—became the guiding principle for many who hoped to forge a new nation from the crisis. For these idealists, the capitalist system seemed destined to fail because it was a self-contradictory system: based upon broad private ownership of property, it worked to concentrate the vast majority of that property in the hands of a few. No wonder, then, that it had stalled: the mass of people didn't have enough money to purchase the array of products offered to them.

The Group Theatre was formed in a climate of social and economic crisis as a countering force to the demoralization of the depression. The economy—indeed, the promise of American life—seemed to be disintegrating before the eyes of a disbelieving public. By concentrating economic power in urban areas, industry had eroded the rural and semirural sense of community that had characterized much of America until the late 19th century. The impersonal city, with its pollution and poverty, became one of the most powerful symbols of modern society's indifference. The alienation of modern industrial life, metaphorized in the impersonality of Henry Ford's assembly line—Ford was, after all, the man who claimed that "Machinery is the new Messiah"—had given people a real fear of the tyranny of mass production. Efficiency seemed to be its own reward, production its own end. The seemingly endless multiplication of goods was a common fear, satirized tellingly in Chaplin's *Modern Times* (1936), in which the great factory machinery literally swallows the main character.

Added to a growing mistrust of technology was the continuing devastation of American farm life. Farmers had suffered from low prices and high mortgages since the end of World War I; the advent of the depression, exacerbated by a severe drought, made their situation desperate. The entire system upon which America imagined itself to be based, the Jeffersonian notion of small landowners and businessmen, was speeding out of existence. Many reform movements of the late 1920s and early 1930s, therefore, were attempts to find new ways to reconstitute a new sense of community, to find the village in the city.[1] Just as tentative steps toward American forms of art had been taken in the 1920s, theatre artists of the 1930s would respond to the crisis of the depression by establishing a social and political theatre that could accurately and powerfully reflect the times.

Clurman notes in his history of the Group, *The Fervent Years*, that the theatre was rooted in the idea of a communal bond with its audience. Begun as an attempt "to establish a theatre in which our philosophy of life might be translated into a philosophy of theatre" (32), the Group hoped to create a permanent company that could develop the skills of its members over a period of several years. The ultimate goal of this joint venture was the establishment of a community with its audience, whose lives and sympathetic understanding, rather than some "abstract standard of artistic or literary excellence," were the only real basis for judgment. Thus, the Group deliberately set itself against the Guild—with which the three directors of the Group had all worked at one time or another and under whose auspices their initial efforts were conducted. Clurman believed that while no other American theatre had produced as many good plays, the Guild had "no blood relationship" with their playwrights, no real social investment in the plays they chose (24). The Guild was not a true theatre, but rather a respectable collection of individual artists that depended on a middle-class subscription audience. Its directors were "admirers rather than makers. They were imitators rather than initiators, buyers and distributors rather than first settlers or pioneers" (23).

Because both Group and Guild were committed to high-quality drama professionally produced, the difference between the two theatres is most evident in Clurman's idea of community. The Group was founded upon a significantly different concept of democracy than the Guild, as suggested by the names. The Guild, with its associations of a small aggregation of talented craftspeople producing something for others, is in striking contrast to the Group, which suggests a conscious effort at collectivity. Also, in contrast to the Guild's emphasis on European writers, the Group was also unabashedly American. All of the plays produced by the Group in its ten-year history, save one—Erwin Piscator's adaptation of Theodore Dreiser's *An American Tragedy*—were written by Americans.

Clurman zealously proselytized the theatre people who came to the Friday meetings, preaching that a new kind of theatre, like American innovations in music, dance, and the visual arts, could give artist and audience "a feeling of true personal significance" and could bring freshness to an otherwise commercial institution (5). Odets was at first baffled by Clurman's fierce vision. Though he had worked with the Guild, Odets had never considered theatre as more than a business; as an actor, he dreamed of little more than a steady income. Still, after a few weeks Clurman's ideas began to resonate with Odets; Clurman's insistence on theatre as a deep human experience combined Odets' desire for conventional success with a deeper purpose. For Odets, Clurman's ideals, ultimately, were more compelling than Moeller's.

Recognition of the Group's importance is essential to any discussion of Odets' life and work; at the heart of his writing—both with the Group and afterward—is an overarching sense of communal work toward a common goal, a struggle against alienation. Furthermore, the difficulties that the Group faced, most notably the problem of being a progressive theatre in a capitalistic society, underscore the questions faced by political playwrights and theatres of the period: how to reconcile the economic freedom of American democracy with the social and economic constrictions of the depression, how to create socially useful work while maintaining artistic integrity. The flowering of political drama during the depression—from the productions of small radical theatres like the Worker's Laboratory Theatre and the Proletbühne, proletarian theatres modeled on German agitprop groups, to the Living Newspapers of the Federal Theatre Project to Broadway plays like Odets' *Awake and Sing!* and *Paradise Lost*, Robert E. Sherwood's plays, Irwin Shaw's *Bury the*

Dead, the Mercury Theatre's "Fascist" *Julius Caesar* and *The Cradle Will Rock*—reflected an increasing sense of urgency to change the world. In one sense, then, Odets' own work was not so much experimental as intuitively expressive; his plays articulated the tensions and hopes of an entire generation.

The Group goal of an audience of like-minded people would remain with Odets. Throughout his career, he attempted to reach as wide an audience as possible, turning to popular plays, films, and even, at the end of his career, television. Odets' desire to understand and express the needs of the forgotten man, which had remained inchoate until his association with the Group helped him to articulate it, remained with him long after the Group had disbanded. For example, in a speech he gave to the Cultural and Scientific Conference on World Peace in 1949, we can still hear echoes of the Group concern with society and the social integration of the artist: "The world that pushes the artist to a solitary view is a sick world. Then it is the first task of the artist. . . . to reach out to the healthy world of the people and there find his problems mirrored" (LCA, 3-4). Even more importantly, an understanding of his relationship with the Group helps place into a larger context the "individual" protest against the system that we see in his plays.

The Friday night meetings also inspired Odets to write more. Throughout the fall of 1930 and into the spring of 1931, Odets worked on his first full-length play, *910 Eden Street*. The play was never produced—Clurman, reading it later that year, remarked, "I hardly thought of it as a play, or of its author as a potential playwright" (TFY, 67). Despite Strasberg and Clurman's misgivings about his writing and acting, Odets was nevertheless chosen as one of the thirty or so members who would rehearse the Group's first production, Paul Green's *The House of Connelly*, during the summer of 1931. Odets was thrilled to be one of the chosen, and wrote about his conversion in the Group's public diary in strikingly religious terms:

I am done! done with chasing my febrile self down the nights and days. From the ashes of the phoenix! The clamoring hatred of Life has been hushed to less than a whisper. On the pivotal point of a quarter of a century of living . . . I have begun to eat the flesh and blood of *The Group*. I partake of these consecrated wafers with a clean heart and brain; and I believe—as I have wanted to believe for almost ten years—in some person, idea, thing outside myself. . . . I am passionate about this thing!!! (B-G, 194)

Odets' joy at having found a home and a purpose was echoed by other members as the Group worked toward a revolution in American drama.

The Group spent the summer focusing on developing a common method of acting based on Strasberg's version of the system first used by Stanislavsky at the Moscow Art Theatre. Outsiders watched with interest. For example, Waldo Frank (whose *Rediscovery of America* had inspired the company's name) urged the members to recognize the political ramifications of their work, to see it as a way to revitalize not only the theatre but American life itself. The Group, despite internal conflicts, was driven by a common purpose and a sense of righteousness; they expected that individual members would compromise for the good of the whole. For actors, such compromises included questions of salary and exclusive commitment to the Group's productions. The Group wanted all actors to be paid year-round on a scale that reflected overall worth to the company, regardless of how large their part was in a particular production. Odets, though he had only one line in the Green play, was paid his salary for the whole season. Still, the Group required sacrifice: most of the actors were earning less than they might make in other Broadway productions.

Perhaps more importantly, the Group placed pressure on playwrights—first Green, and later John Howard Lawson, Maxwell Anderson, and Odets—to revise their work. Clurman notes Green's reluctance to change the original ending of *The House of Connelly*, in which the tenant farmer Patsy is strangled by the two servant women. Arguing that Patsy was a symbol of the old South overcoming its past, the Group found the original ending, in Clurman's words, "historically and humanly untrue. . . . Our own sense of the perfectibility of man, or at least, the inevitability of the struggle against evil, not only made us impatient with the play's violent ending but roused Paul's own verve and decision in our direction" (TFY, 48). While Clurman's analysis of the victory is questionable—in a later production elsewhere, Green reverted to the original ending—the Group's power to force compromise would become an important factor in their staging of Odets' plays.

The Group's production of *The House of Connelly* opened on September 23, 1931. It was an immediate success, Strasberg's acting ensemble praised in the highest terms. But other successes did not follow so easily, and the Guild, who had financed the first production, refused further funding without guaranteed control. The Group refused and were cut adrift in February 1932. The rancor between the two theatres would persist for years afterward, the Group accusing the Guild of pandering to middle-class tastes, the Guild mocking the Group's upstart pretensions.

Once separated from the financial support of the Theatre Guild, the Group struggled to finance their productions. Maxwell Anderson's *Night over Taos*, produced in early 1932, was financed piecemeal with contributions by Anderson, Group actor Franchot Tone, and the father of another Group actor. This was the start of an ongoing practice of looking to individuals with a personal stake in the theatre as the main source of funding. The play failed quickly, however, forcing Clurman and Crawford once more into a desperate search for money. Clurman relates a significant story in *The Fervent Years* about his visit, with Crawford, to the philanthropist Otto Kahn:

He had seen our last two productions and was impressed by them, We had ideals, he said, and the ability to realize them. What did we want? Not money, I said, and went on to explain the Group's problems generally. He interrupted me: "But you are talking of nothing but money!" No matter how it was put, the economic problem was closely related to all the others. (75-76)

Discussions of money appear as often as discussions of plays in *The Fervent Years*; the Group story is a history of scrambling for cash.

As Clurman admits, the economic instability of the Group was probably the most important factor in its dissolution, as the pressures to avoid financial ruin drove wedges between members of the collective: "A play poorly directed might prove the massacre of our material hopes for the season, a faulty performance by one or two individuals might spell penury for all of us" (284). The panic over finances was directly related to artistic concerns. Frequent arguments arose about play selection; should they look for a "hit" that would fill the coffers, or should they gamble on something more artistic but perhaps less commercial? Certainly, the actors and directors of the Group made repeated financial sacrifices in the name of art. For example, for Dawn Powell's *Big Night*, only the stagehands and scenic designers were paid for the production, despite the fact the actors and directors had worked on it for weeks. Additionally, a number of shows they felt artistically worthwhile were kept running because Group members agreed to forgo some or all of their salaries.

Clurman's own history of the Group undercuts his desire that they would—or could—somehow be free of the marketplace. Even with considerable sacrifices in the name of idealism, concessions to the marketplace became necessary. Funding came from Hollywood for a number of Group plays, and a number of the actors went periodically to work in films—as did Clurman and Odets. The Group also produced and performed plays such as Sidney Kingsley's *Men in White* in 1933 for the simple reason that they believed a commercial success would fund more important works. Though Clurman and the actors were opposed to the script, they had no answer to Strasberg's rejoinder that there were no other scripts available and that continuous work was necessary for the health of the theatre; he believed "the entire enterprise was in danger of dissolution *without* the 'impurities' of plays sufficiently viable to keep the Group continuously active" (B-G, 276).

Looking back at the Group from the distance of a few years, Clurman suggests that "the basic defect in our activity was that while we tried to maintain a true theatre policy artistically, we proceeded economically on a show-business basis" (TFY, 281). Though artistically successful and influential, the theatre was always a Broadway organization. The members and especially its directors felt that "for all its faults, Broadway was the heart of the American theatre, and they wanted to be a part of it. . . . they wanted to change the mainstream, not abandon it" (RLD, 72). Throughout its history, then, the Group struggled to be autonomous and popular, both commercial and artistic. It offered seats to progressive drama at typical Broadway prices; it sought to build a base and reputation in the heart of the commercial theatre at a time when theatres and their audiences were burdened by the depression. Group designer Mordecai Gorelik's often-repeated semifacetious remark that most of the plays the Group chose to do dealt with the question "What shall it profit a man if he gain the whole world and lose his own soul?" underscores the paradoxical nature of the Group's goals.[2]

The tension between art and commerce was also tied up with the political movements of the day. Though the Group was organized as a Broadway organization, it was always seen as a leftist theatre, largely because of the personal affiliations of its individual members and its mandate to produce works of contemporary relevance. Certainly, the Group was progressive; its members were romantic, enthusiastic, and idealistic in their opposition to the forces of capitalism in general, though not necessarily rigorously analytical or aware of contradictions in their position.[3] Ultimately, then, Clurman's characterization of the Group's "show business" financial policies as a "defect" implies a desire to create a theatre less enmeshed in the marketplace.

Certainly, other leftist theatres founded in the 1930s answered the financial questions differently. Working outside the Broadway model, they were able to do more radical plays. On a practical level, however, these small leftist (often Communist) theatres such as the Proletbühne, the Theatre Collective, the Worker's Laboratory Theatre (WLT, later the Theatre of Action), and the Theatre Union, while successful in speaking to a small, committed, largely Marxist audience, never gained either a firm ideological or a financially powerful foothold in the American theatre.[4] They were rarely concerned with ensemble acting or dramatic subtlety; rather, all of these theatres took political action as their starting point. The plays they produced, either in traditional theatres (the Theatre Union) or as agitational street performance (the WLT and the Proletbühne often performed at strikes or labor actions) were aimed to provoke audiences to political change. Perhaps even more tellingly, they were constantly in need of money. Indeed, they often looked to other theatre organizations, including the Group, for support. Odets and other Group members contributed both money and time to the Theatre Union. He taught acting classes there starting in 1933; Group actors Art Smith, Elia Kazan, and John Garfield, among others, were involved in other left-wing theatres.

These radical theatres, unable to pay their costs from ticket sales, unwilling to compromise their ideals or the messages their plays espoused, folded quickly, usually within a few years. The argument that the Group would have been better able to survive as a less commercial theatre is simply not borne out by the experience of those theatres that tried. Had they been less tied to Broadway, perhaps they would have been even freer to experiment with their plays, even perhaps freer to take a more consciously leftist stance. But had they been freer from Broadway expectations and constraints, they would have also lost much of the audience which supported them. Perhaps the Group directors could have been better businesspeople, as the tales of monetary mismanagement suggest.[5] Nevertheless, to survive in the market economy, they had to participate.

In addition to its tightrope-walking commitment to a socially relevant commercial theatre, the Group was created during the most difficult financial times the theatre had ever seen. Broadway box office receipts in 1934 were less than half of what they had been in 1928 and total productions per year fell an astonishing 44 percent, from 264 to 145, in the same period.[6] There were three basic reasons for the decline of the theatres between the late 1920s and the mid-1930s. First, the sharp drop in income and employment in the early years of the depression made the theatre a luxury for most. The second reason for the initial decline in theatre attendance (and consequently, in the number of theatrical productions) was the spread of radio; the third—and most important—was the advent of sound film.

It was not necessarily the loss of audience to the radio or movies that most permanently affected the theatre but rather the demand for additional personnel who were lured away by the promise of secure work and higher wages. In 1934, Frank Gillmore, the president of Actor's Equity, estimated that a full 70 percent of actors working in Hollywood had come from the stage. The demand for personnel made the growing resentment of the mass media by people in the theatre understandable. Losing some of their most gifted people to film and radio, theatre workers began to see these new developments not as opportunities for greater expression but as powerful economic competitors with the potential to cause permanent damage. The quick decline of the vaudeville circuits after the proliferation of film in the early 1900s gives clear evidence of the economic power of the new technologies. The fact that the commercial theatre survived was as much because it was willing to make compromises with the film and radio industries as it was due to the power of live theatrical production.

One of the larger issues the experience of the Group raises—and a question with which Odets wrestled throughout his career—is the place of the artist in a commercial society. Because discussions of money and art invariably raise moral and political concerns, the possibility of a commercially viable art theatre questions the idea of artistic integrity in a market economy. It forces a reevaluation of the "sellout" when the society is constructed around the practices of buying and selling. That art doesn't pay (and its converse, that what pays is not art) has been a long-standing belief in American culture; ironically, it is an idea tacitly supported by Clurman's indictment of the Guild for pandering to a subscription audience. Never-theless, the Group's experience makes clear the cultural underpinning of the starv-ing artist cliché—artists exist on the fringes of the marketplace. After the financial failure of John Howard Lawson's *Success Story* in late 1932, a dozen Group mem-bers were forced to move in together to save money, sharing a damp brownstone with little food and less heat. While they made the best of a bad situation, Clurman notes the generally depressing attitude that financial straits had forced upon them. They were the marketplace whether or not they wished to be, the economic pres-sures on them real, persistent, and measurable in their effects.[7] Though art and commerce are often placed—by newspaper reviewers, by academics, by Clurman and other Group members, by Odets himself—in dichotomous opposition, the dif-ference between the two is not clearly defined. There *is* negotiation, and there is a blurring of categories; Odets' career is evidence of such negotiation in American political theatre of the period.

THE BIRTH OF A PLAYWRIGHT

As the Group struggled to find a foothold in the American theatre, Odets strug-gled to maintain his place in the Group. He was offered only small parts in the first season's shows, *The House of Connelly*, *1931—*, and *Night over Taos*, but even worse, was not offered any parts in either of the Group's second season shows. Odets' frustration mounted; his desire to be needed, to give his best, seemed to be stagnating. He determined to work harder, both as a writer and an actor, to reach out. While the Group rehearsed the new plays during the summer of 1932, Odets, who had been chosen to understudy Luther Adler in John Howard Lawson's *Suc-cess Story*, watched rehearsals with unusual interest. Odets was spurred by Law-son's idiomatic use of language—a combination of jazz rhythms, Yiddish syntax, the language of advertising, and moral righteousness—and by the internal struggle of Sol Ginsberg, a Jewish character caught between idealism and commercialism, between acceptance of his Jewish identity and pursuit of more assimilationist goals. A number of times in his journal that summer, Odets noted that Ginsberg's struggle was his own. Odets also wove themes from Lawson's play into a new play called *Victory*, about a musical genius who is forced to compromise his artistic goals of composing for the more financially remunerative goals of performing. The struggle of the artist against compromise in a commercial society, or more generally, the human being against the mechanisms of the marketplace, would be a theme to which Odets returned in his later plays, most specifically in his best-known play, *Golden Boy*.

As Odets went through his artistic awakening with the Group, he gradually came to recognize that his true gift lay in his intuitive ability to connect with people. Harold Clurman remarked that he liked Odets "for being so physical a person. He reacted to everything, not with words or articulate knowledge, but with his body. His senses were extraordinarily alive, though he was not professionally 'sensitive.' To be near him was like being near a stove on which a whole range of savory foods was standing ready to be served" (TFY, 119). Odets' need for love, which he had carried with him since childhood, expressed itself not just sexually (though he was by all accounts flirtatious, passionate, and demanding with both men and women, friends and lovers), but romantically in the broad sense. The love of humanity he recognized early in the novels of Hugo was transmuted into his own desire for connection. He wrote in his journal in mid-1931, "I never see a man or a women—when I am happy—that I don't want to kiss them or at least touch them with my hand. I want to be doing things for people all the time when I am happy and overspilling. When I am unhappy or dumped, then it becomes a different affair" (B-G, 225). Throughout his life, his need to be of use manifested itself in anxious self-doubt, passionate attentiveness to others, and later, in frustrated egotism as his work was rejected.

In New York, Odets busied himself by reading and teaching acting classes at Eva LeGallienne's Civic Repertory and by working on another play, called first *I Got the Blues* and later *Awake and Sing!* The Civic Repertory, founded in the mid-1920s to produce modern plays and classics, would soon fall victim to the depression. Still, Odets found his teaching experience there and at the Theatre Union important in the development of his playwriting technique. With material borrowed from Clurman and Strasberg, Odets became an effective teacher; some Theatre Union students even urged him to start his own theatre. Most importantly, through the two groups, Odets was for the first time in close contact with people who believed theatre could be a weapon in the class struggle. The Group, while it had a number of committed radicals among the actors, nevertheless didn't operate as a radical theatre, partly because the directors remained resolutely uncommitted and partly because their position on Broadway prevented them from moving too far left. Still, Odets was aware of a growing radicalism inside and outside the Group. As the Group's production of *1931*— (a play demonstrating the effects of the deepening depression) attested, even mainstream theatre was becoming a mirror of political and social turmoil.

While *Success Story* stayed on the boards until January 1933, it did not make enough money to give the Group breathing room. When the next play, Dawn Powell's *Big Night*, closed after only nine performances, the Group was forced to abandon the season. Some of the actors latched onto other productions, including Odets, who landed a small role in a production of *They All Come to Moscow*. When it closed, Odets was out of work. Things looked bleak everywhere; the depression was strengthening its grip on the country. Clurman recounts the trips he and Odets took past the long bread lines on Times Square, to ratty burlesque halls and run-down movie houses, and to Stewart's Cafeteria in the Village, where a new "lost" generation had gathered. Though they were both depressed, Clurman noted that Odets' innate sympathy for the downtrodden inspired him as well: "Odets seemed to share a peculiar sense of gloomy fatality, one might almost say an appetite for the broken and rundown, together with a bursting love for the beauty immanent in people, a burning belief in the day when this beauty would actually shape the external world. These two apparently contradictory impulses kept him in a perpetual boil" (TFY, 117).

Their experience reflected the growing sense of desperation running through the country. Roosevelt had been resoundingly elected the previous November largely because Hoover's laissez-faire economic policy, modified only slightly from that of his predecessors, depended on a fierce individualism and the free market system. Roosevelt, on the other hand, had campaigned on an idea of cooperation rather than competition; his first inaugural address, given in March 1933, when economic conditions were near their nadir, was filled with the language of collective effort: "We cannot take but must give as well. . . . if we are to go forward, we must move as a trained and loyal army willing to sacrifice for the good of a common discipline."[8] Roosevelt's legislation geared toward common action for the common good was a direct repudiation of Hoover's preference for volunteerism, his economic reforms a direct renunciation of the previous administration's high tariffs and probusiness policies.

Following his inauguration, Roosevelt began an ambitious project of economic reform that seemed to conservatives almost criminal in its willingness to uproot traditional economic practices. Indeed, the administration was assaulted from the left as well as the right. Many Socialists and Communists—including Odets in his first and most radical play, *Waiting for Lefty*—complained that New Deal compromises with big business left capitalist structures unchanged. Roosevelt's plan was to accelerate economic growth by promoting consumption, a relatively new economic theory developed most fully by British economist John Maynard Keynes. Keynes opposed conventional supply-side economics, which assumed that increased supply would increase demand. He theorized, rather, that increased purchasing power would stimulate production again; demand would call forth its own supply.

Most economists agree that one of the major causes of the Crash was a serious underconsumption of what was produced. Keynes himself in 1932 said pointedly that "this is not a crisis of poverty . . . but a crisis of abundance."[9] In fact, though the gross national product stood in the early years of the depression at only a fraction of its precrash levels, the standard of living rose somewhat because prices stayed low and durable goods were readily available through the installment plan. There was a surplus of goods; people who had money would buy. Accordingly, Roosevelt made public works programs the backbone of his plan for economic recovery; he wanted to make workers—and consumers—of the unemployed. Despite its limited success, Roosevelt's emphasis on spending into recovery emphasized the way America had begun to view its economy. The depression era, in fact, has been defined by Warren Susman as a time of shifting emphasis in American history, a movement from a "culture of production" to a "culture of abundance."[10] The move toward an emphasis on consumption also can be seen as part of a utopian vision geared toward a better distribution and consumption of goods. As Roosevelt noted in his first inaugural address, "Plenty is at our doorstep, but a generous use of it languishes in the very sight of the supply."[11]

While some argue that the drift toward a consumer society took place much earlier, certainly by the time Odets started writing there was a significant culture of consumption in the United States, cemented in place by Roosevelt's national policy and fueled by increasing sophistication in advertising.[12] Production had become so efficient and advertising so ubiquitous that sociologists Robert and Helen Lynd characterized the culture as "hypnotized by the gorged stream of new things to buy. . . . a culture in which private business tempts the population in its every waking minute with adroitly phrased invitations."[13] The son of an advertising man himself, Odets would examine the effects of this shift toward consumerism in the lives of his characters. Like the Lynds' hypnotized Middletowners, Odets' forgotten man characters are both tantalized and paralyzed by the material abundance surrounding them. The disparity between American industrial productivity and widespread poverty—over 12 million were unemployed and over 32 million lived below the poverty line by 1933—fed a growing national desperation. "The new radicalism" of the 1930s was born "from the plain man's instinctive resentment of poverty surrounded by shops bursting with food and farms smothered under their own production surplus."[14] Such a powerful paradox did not escape Odets' critique; virtually all of his early plays, especially *Awake and Sing!*, *Waiting for Lefty*, and *Paradise Lost*, as well as later ones such as *The Big Knife* (1949), examine in detail the ideals and failures of this "culture of abundance."

As the summer of 1933 began and Roosevelt instituted the striking reforms of his first few months in office—bank holidays; the de facto repeal of Prohibition; emergency relief for farmers, industrial workers, and homeowners; the Social Security Act and the Securities Act—the Group readied for another summer. They were contracted as performers at an adult camp in upstate New York; in return for room, board, and rehearsal space, they would provide a series of performances for the guests. The Group immediately put into rehearsal Sidney Kingsley's *Men in White*, a melodrama about interns in a hospital. Even more importantly for Odets, who had been given only a small role in the Kingsley play, the Group agreed to do two performances of the second act of Odets' *I Got the Blues*. Clurman remained doubtful of the play's merits, but Odets felt vindicated by the enthusiastic reaction of the Green Mansions audience. He failed, however, to convince the Group to produce it as part of their regular season; Strasberg hated it, objecting to its limited horizon of experience, and Clurman disliked the messy vulgarity of the first and third acts, though he was encouraging enough to recommend the play to an agent.

At the end of the summer, the Group returned to New York, where *Men in White* opened in September 1933. It was the Group's first resounding financial success. The production—Strasberg's direction, the ensemble acting, the set by Mordecai Gorelik—was universally praised. The actors and designers had researched the hospital environment all summer, consulting surgeons, visiting hospitals, purchasing authentic surgical equipment as props. The climactic scene, an operation scene performed without dialogue, had been meticulously choreographed. Brooks

Atkinson saw it as a confirmation of the Group's goals: "After two years of real hardship, the Group Theatre is not only still in existence but still determined to keep the theatre in its high estate" (NYT, September 27, 1933). Even more, their success had given them the financial freedom to plan another season.

At the time the Group was making box-office hay with *Men in White*, many Group actors agitated for political plays like those done at the Theatre Union. The upstart Theatre Union, with actors trained in part by Odets and other Group performers, had produced *Peace on Earth* and *Stevedore* during the *Men in White* run. The first play, an antiwar drama written by Paul Sklar and Albert Maltz, found enthusiastic audiences, as did the second, a play dealing with racial tensions and labor issues among dockworkers. *Stevedore* called for racial solidarity among the working classes, backing its message by defying Broadway's de facto segregation in the audiences who saw it. Most importantly, the Theatre Union's successes signaled a change in the way Americans saw leftist theatre; as Atkinson said in his glowing review, the Theatre Union was beginning to establish itself "not only as a labor group but a vigorous producing organization" (NYT, April 19, 1934). Leftist theatre had begun to reach outside its small circle of the converted, drawing praise from uptown. The mainstream audience was more willing to embrace socially progressive drama. Even the more conservative Theatre Guild had gone forth in February with a Moeller-directed production of John Wexley's *They Shall Not Die*, a stirring defense of nine African-American youths wrongly convicted of rape in Scottsboro, Arkansas.

Odets, who had been revising all fall, brought another draft of *I Got the Blues* to the Group directors, threatening to take it elsewhere if they turned it down. He did not tell them that the play had already been rejected by Moeller as incompatible with the Guild's vision. When Clurman and Strasberg refused the play again, Odets optioned it to Bess Eitingon, an independent producer associated with agent Frank Merlin. But almost immediately Eitingon noted that there were problems with casting: "Although she did not realize it had been written by him specifically for the ensemble company of the Group theatre, finely trained by Strasberg to work as a unit, she found herself imagining each of eight Group actors in his appropriate role" (B-G, 280). Ultimately, she decided not to produce the play because it was too closely connected with the Group.

The story of Odets' first successful full-length play gives an indication of how deeply ingrained in him the Group ideal of ensemble acting had become. He had written much of the play during the dark winter of 1932 and had envisioned his Group friends playing the roles as he wrote them. In fact, though he sold the rights to Eitingon, Odets really identified himself as a playwright only when the Group finally produced *Awake and Sing!* in early 1935. Before that, though he told Clurman that he was leaving the Group a number of times, he confessed that "I was leading him on a bit because I wouldn't have known where to go. Where else could you go? All I really ever wanted was to have the Group theatre do my plays" (B-G, 297). Odets implied that the offer from Eitingon (and belated interest shown by the Guild), while perhaps allowing *Awake and Sing!* to be produced, would not have satisfied him as a playwright. His need to be connected, to use his gifts in the service of a communal good, made the Group his ideal producing organization.

Odets began writing another play to answer Strasberg's objections to *Awake and Sing!*. The new play, *The Fruit Is Ripe* (eventually renamed *Paradise Lost*), consciously attempted to de-emphasize the "small horizon" Jewishness of the earlier play, to make it more sweepingly American. At the same time, Odets again tried to fit the roles to the Group actors he already knew. In his first drafts of characters, for example, Odets penciled in the names of the Group performers who he thought should take the roles: Morris Carnovsky as Leo Gordon, Stella Adler as Clara Gordon, Sanford Meisner as Julie Gordon, and so on. Odets, like Eitingon, had difficulty imagining another company performing his work. Throughout 1934, Odets wove into this new script headlines reflecting growing tensions both at home and abroad. In addition to the ongoing debate about solutions to the depression—many of Roosevelt's early reforms were opposed by business and struck down by the Supreme Court—Hitler's rise to power in Germany augured danger in Europe. At home, increasing labor unrest, racial tensions, and the political demagoguery of Louisiana senator Huey Long and radio priest Father Charles Coughlin highlighted growing class antagonism. As Leo Gordon would say in *Paradise Lost*, the world was suffering from a "profound dislocation" (SP, 161).

After another summer of rehearsals in which *Paradise Lost* was encouraged by Clurman and rejected by Strasberg, the Group tried out their next production, *Gold Eagle Guy* by Melvin Levy, in Boston. It was doomed from the beginning, a weak script in which neither the actors nor the directors had real confidence. When it failed in New York, the Group, without a viable script, was faced with the possibility of shutting down for the rest of the season. Odets once again offered *Awake and Sing!* to the company. Strasberg violently objected: "You don't seem to understand, Cliff. We don't *like* your play. We don't *want* to do your play" (B-G, 311). The actors felt differently, however, and in November 1934, the Group decided to put the play into rehearsal over Strasberg's objections. Clurman was chosen to direct, and Odets worked feverishly on rewrites of the third act. After years of drifting with the Group as an actor, Odets had finally found a home as a playwright.

As *Awake and Sing!* readied for a February production, Odets put the final touches on a one-act play he had written during *Gold Eagle Guy* rehearsals. *Waiting for Lefty* was a strike play, a direct attempt to encapsulate the social and political upheaval of the 1930s and rouse the audience to action. It was agitational in the tradition of the plays done by the workers' theatres. *Awake and Sing!* was topical, but it was also more traditional. It had a conventional three-act structure and fully developed characters and, perhaps most importantly, had deep roots in Odets' Jewish experience; *Waiting for Lefty* was fueled by current events seen through a Marxist lens. Odets had seen the work of the Theatre Union and the other leftist theatres and became convinced that political theatre was a powerful means of change. Certainly, his membership in the Communist Party—he joined for eight months starting in 1934, leaving when he found the constrictions of walking the party line inimical to his artistic goals—helped to shape *Waiting for Lefty*. But however familiar with Marxist thought, Odets was never committed to revolution. He justified his party membership at this time in romantic terms harking back to his love for Hugo and Emerson; he told Clurman he wanted to be part of "the largest possible group of humble, struggling men prepared to make a common effort to build a better world" (B-G, 302).

Waiting for Lefty arose primarily from Odets' instinctive reaction to the struggles of the forgotten man, his characters enacting on their small stage the theories
leftist intellectuals wrote about: "No one gave himself to radical thought stemming
from Marxist dialectics as wholeheartedly in the theatre as did Odets, just as no one
succeeded in investing cold theory with so much palpitating and tormented flesh."[15]
Odets was one of many who looked to Communism as a harbinger of change. In the
1932 elections, the Communist Party had tallied five times as many votes as they
had in 1928, and the Socialist Party gathered another 800,000, three times as many
as in 1928. Certainly leftist thought and theatre had become more mainstream by
1935. The Group's *1931—* had been condemned for its shrill tone and radical politics, but four years later the times had sufficiently changed that *Waiting for Lefty*
captivated both critics and audiences.

The play, directed by Odets and Meisner and with Group actors in the roles,
premiered while *Awake and Sing!* was still in rehearsals, on January 6, 1935, at a
benefit for *New Theatre* magazine. No one expected the riotous reception it received. The first performance of *Waiting for Lefty* became, as Clurman describes it,
a defining moment of the times as well as a landmark performance in the history of
American theatre:

The first scene of *Lefty* had not played two minutes when a shock of delighted recognition
struck the audience. Deep laughter, hot assent, a kind of joyous fervor seemed to sweep the
audience toward the stage. The actors no longer performed; they were being carried along as
if by an exultancy of communication such as I had never witnessed in the theatre before.
Audience and actors had become one. . . . It was the birth cry of the thirties. Our youth had
found its voice. (TFY, 138-139)

If Clurman can be indicted for overstatement, it was clear to everyone who witnessed the production that something unprecedented had happened. By the next
day, dozens of people had requested rights to produce the play; in a short time, over
300 groups had sent money for advance royalties.

The play accomplished what the Group had tried to do from the beginning; it
had established a real communion between performer and audience. More than one
account—including Odets' own—of the opening night of *Waiting for Lefty* dis-
cusses the union of actors and audience, the disappearance of the proscenium arch.
Indeed, all the early reviews of *Waiting for Lefty* remark on its compelling theatrical power, the absolute hold it took over its audience. John Mason Brown, review-
ing *Waiting for Lefty* and *Till the Day I Die* (written to accompany *Waiting for
Lefty* when it moved uptown), remarked, "They have the rare virtue of so occupying your attention at the moment they are being played, that at the time, they—and
they alone—seem to exist."[16] Odets was rough and undeveloped, more promise
than polish, but he had captured the mood and language of his times more perfectly
than any other contemporary playwright. Brooks Atkinson of the *New York Times*
went further, noting that *Lefty* was "one of the most dynamic dramas of the year in
any department of our theatre." Atkinson openly urged his readers to see the play:
"People who want to understand the times through which they are living can
scarcely afford to ignore it" (March 27, 1935).

The form Odets used was not new—worker's theatres had presented agitprop plays since the early 1930s—but the style and its effect were particularly powerful. With *Waiting for Lefty*, Odets demonstrated an uncannily accurate sense of the trends of the day, an ability to define in vibrant language the frustration felt by millions of Americans. The conflict between the cabbies' lives and the union leader Fatt's lies echoed a struggle that repeated itself daily outside the theatre. In 1934 alone, almost 2,000 strikes had broken out across the country, including violent conflicts in Toledo, Minneapolis, Harlan County, Kentucky, and San Francisco. Odets' play, therefore, captured the mood of a country filled with strikes, bread lines, apple vendors, and young men traveling the country in search of work. Its message struck home with those audiences who heard in Edna's desperate plea— "God, Joe, the world is supposed to be for all of us!"—a moving articulation of their own frustrations and in Keller's culminating call to action a bold statement of their own hopes for change: "When we die they'll know what we did to make a new world! Christ, cut us up to little pieces. We'll die for what is right! put fruit trees where our ashes are!" (SP, 31). In one sense, then, Clurman, was mistaken; *Waiting for Lefty* was not the "birth cry of the 1930s," because the pleas Odets so forcefully presented had been part of the left for some time.[17] But in another sense, Clurman was correct, for when he asserted that "our youth had found its voice," he recognized that Odets' play articulated a current of thought that had worked its way into the national consciousness.

THE GROUP'S "MOST CONGENIAL" PLAYWRIGHT

The success of *Waiting for Lefty* made Odets an overnight celebrity. By the time *Awake and Sing!* opened in February, its advertising flyers described it— ironically, as *Awake and Sing!* was written first—as the "new play by the author of *Waiting for Lefty*." The new play, more measured and mature, reassured critics of Odets' real talent. Brooks Atkinson noted presciently that the Group had discovered its "most congenial playwright" among its members (NYT, February 20, 1935). Indeed, it is difficult to overestimate the importance of the Group to Odets' work, or of his plays to their reputation. Their collaboration over ten years and seven plays was an artistic symbiosis that provided an impetus for Odets' work and a focus for the Group's. Early plays like *Awake and Sing!* and *Paradise Lost* were fashioned with the ensemble technique developed by Strasberg in mind: there are six or seven roles of relatively equal importance. On the other side, the Group began to depend on Odets, a dependence that later took a double edge: they needed his plays to be both artistically progressive and financially viable.

With *Awake and Sing!* running (though not profitably) on Broadway, *Waiting for Lefty* was moved uptown with *Till the Day I Die* to the Longacre theatre, opening on March 26. The show was recast to allow actors not in *Awake and Sing!* to take roles in the two one-act plays; Odets himself played the last role of his career, as Dr. Benjamin in the Broadway version of *Waiting for Lefty*. *Till the Day I Die*, about Communist resistance to Fascism in Germany, was based on a letter he read in the *New Masses*. Written under pressure in five days, its roughness and clearly demarcated lines of good and evil make it little more than a melodrama.

Still, the play serves to point out two characteristics of Odets' development within the Group. First of all, he was willing to write under pressure if the Group needed him. Looking back years later, Stella Adler would remark that "where there was a need, he would always meet it. If you needed a part, a rewrite, a sketch, a monologue, you'd never be stranded" (B-G, 328). The second thing revealed by *Till the Day I Die* was how little Odets knew about the day-to-day operations of either Fascism or Communism; his political understanding was tied to a romantic vision of a brotherhood of men. In many respects, the characters in the play are generalizations, the idealistic Communist Ernst pitted against the sadistic German officer Schlegel. Yet if Odets was enamored with Communism as an idea rather than a political practice, certainly he was not alone. Especially during the Popular Front period of 1935-1939, the entire left community enjoyed a sort of honeymoon with Communism. Officially tolerated by Communist Party policy, leftists of all stripes—liberal democrats, Socialists, and others of varying degrees of commitment to world revolution—joined the fight against Fascism abroad and narrow conservatism at home.

Odets' new acclaim drew him into stints as a spokesperson for left-wing causes. In July 1935, he was chosen to join a delegation to Cuba to investigate charges that Cuban president Carlos Medieta was oppressing students and intellectuals. Though the mission abruptly ended when the delegates were arrested and deported (a result that the Communist organizers anticipated but that surprised Odets), Odets' articles in the *New York Post* about the debacle ensured that he maintained a high profile throughout the summer. Similarly, when Luigi Pirandello came to New York in July, Odets, who with John Howard Lawson, Elmer Rice, and others had condemned the playwright for remaining silent about Italy's invasion of Ethiopia, met with Pirandello to discuss not playwriting but rather the political situation. Odets was testing the limits of his political power as a playwright-celebrity.

His mother, long ill with tuberculosis, had died in May. He struggled throughout the summer to reconcile his personal grief and his public success, but the stress often forced him into tense relations with his friends. In midsummer, for example, he blew up at the Group, shouting that they had become complacent. Odets' belief that the Group actors were better equipped to handle his plays than other actors began to erode as he became disenchanted with Clurman's artistic direction. In one blowup in 1937, Odets exploded that he was "tired" with the Group actors and would prefer to write a play for Jimmy Cagney. But even then, he admitted to them, "I can't write plays in a void. I must write because you need my plays. If you don't need my plays I would never have written them" (B-G, 570).

Apart from the contribution of Odets, the Group lacked successful scripts almost as much as they lacked money. Perhaps, as Malcolm Goldstein claims, the Group lacked the ability to evaluate scripts.[18] Certainly, apart from Odets' plays, the list of shows produced by the Group in its ten-year existence contains few recognizable names. Many of the plays closed quickly: Nellise Child's *Weep for the Virgins*, Anderson's *Night over Taos*, and Levy's *Gold Eagle Guy*, the play that prompted Group actor Luther Adler to remark in rehearsal "Boys, I think we're working on a stiff." The Group, in fact, turned down two plays, Anderson's *Winter-*

set in 1935 and William Saroyan's *The Time of Your Life* in 1940 that not only became critical successes for the Guild but also would have provided the Group with
some much-needed income had they decided to produce them.

Many of the internal conflicts lurking beneath the surface of the company came
to light during the process of play selection. After *Waiting for Lefty*'s success, the
progressive actors urged their fellows to move the theatre to the left, to produce not
only plays of "social significance" but plays with an identifiably Marxist or Socialist bent. However, Clurman, Strasberg, and Crawford tried to steer the theatre toward plays with a wider, less politicized appeal. Following the closing of Odets'
Paradise Lost, Clurman even issued a public statement declaring that the Group did
not necessarily share the political views of its playwrights. In it, he claimed,

The impression has arisen that the Group Theatre is primarily interested in the production of
so-called 'propaganda' plays. This is false. The Group is essentially interested in plays that
make for exciting and intelligent theatre. . . any of the following types of plays would have
been considered by us as possible Group material: *Journey's End, First Lady, Russet Mantle,
Winterset, The Petrified Forest, The Road to Rome, Pride and Prejudice, The Children's
Hour, The Jest, Dinner at Eight.*" (RLD, 250-251)

The bulk of these plays (save *Winterset*, which the Group had turned down already,
and *The Children's Hour*) were relatively traditional dramas, certainly not politically charged; the rift between what the actors wanted and what the directors felt
they could successfully produce was widening rather than narrowing. Ironically, the
failure of the Group to find enough viable scripts underscores the collaborative nature of the theatre. The Group depended on community: a playwright without a
theatre was a contradiction, a theatre without an audience an impossibility.

No longer a member of the acting ensemble, Odets began to feel increasingly
responsible for the Group's success. In the beginning, Odets was proud to be
needed. For example, when the Group needed a popular play to help its sagging
finances in 1937, Odets provided *Golden Boy*, which became one of the most profitable and popular shows the Group ever produced. Yet as he wrote the script, he
was almost paralyzed by the Group's dependence on him for a hit and had trouble
finishing the third act. Nor was Odets free from pressure to rewrite. He had promised to rewrite the third act of *Awake and Sing!* even before the Group agreed to
produce it and worked with Clurman up to opening night on the script. Of course,
the rapport between Odets and the Group made such compromises less bitter than
they could have been—at least in the beginning—but the significance lies not in
Odets' willingness to do rewrites but in the power of the Group to force them. Nor
were the changes always in keeping with the socially progressive goals of the theatre; financial considerations were also involved. As production costs increased
throughout the 1930s and as the theatre industry faced stronger competition from
films and radio, the pressure to produce a hit increased; longer runs became necessary just to break even. With the Group verging on financial collapse, the pressures
on Odets became financial and moral as well as artistic.

THE RAVENOUS MAW OF THE MARKETPLACE: ODETS, THE GROUP, AND HOLLYWOOD

At first, the fervor surrounding Odets' initial efforts showed little sign of slowing. *Waiting for Lefty* and *Till the Day I Die* ran well into the summer; *Awake and Sing!* toured the Midwest. Odets continued to speak out publicly in support of left-wing causes, helped to organize a symposium for the benefit of *New Theatre* magazine, and continued to write for left-wing benefits.[19] By the end of October, however, Odets' attention was refocused on rewrites of *Paradise Lost*, which the Group had put into rehearsal earlier in the month. Despite minor misgivings, *Paradise Lost* was a play of which Odets was genuinely proud, an examination of American idealism in the depression across a wide spectrum of characters and events. In fact, Odets described the play later as his "favorite" (SP, ix); when it was greeted coldly by the critics, his disappointment was profound.

Reviews of the play were almost uniformly negative. Only Heywood Broun of the *World-Telegram* phrased his support in the strongest terms possible: "There is in my opinion no play in New York at present which is as alive and vital and stirring as *Paradise Lost*. Clifford Odets has more to say and he says it better than any living dramatist in this country" (December 18, 1935). Virtually all of the Communist Party critics condemned the play for failing to make the move from diagnosing the ills of American society to proposing a Marxist solution. The Group tried a public relations campaign to keep the play running, but the play struggled along through the early months of 1936, never really finding an audience beyond the enthusiastic balcony crowd.

Odets was frustrated and discouraged with the Group and Broadway. In addition, he was financially insecure, most of the money he made in 1935 already spent or given to relatives. Suddenly, the offers that he had previously turned down from Hollywood studios seemed more attractive. With the money, he thought, he could help to prop up *Paradise Lost* until it found the audience it deserved, reinforce the Group financially, and guarantee future time for writing. In film, he could even reach a ready-made audience. All of these reasons—especially the last—are ones to which Odets would return repeatedly in his discussions of Hollywood's promise. The quickly expanding sound film industry offered seemingly unlimited potential for artistic expression. Films were popular culture, but for Odets and many others, their appeal lay precisely in popularity.

If Odets was the voice of his generation, the possible silencing of that voice in Hollywood seemed ominous to many, a symbol of something deeply flawed in American culture. The trend of leading theatre writers working in film was already well established, however; many American and European writers of note went to Hollywood (with varying degrees of enthusiasm and success), including successful playwrights such as Elmer Rice, Philip Barry, Irwin Shaw, S. N. Behrman, Bertolt Brecht, Lillian Hellman and, later, Arthur Miller and Tennessee Williams. The only prominent name missing from the list of American theatre writers in film is O'Neill, who, despite winning the 1936 Nobel Prize, had virtually disappeared from

Broadway by the mid-1930s. Odets himself was ambivalent about the movies in early 1936, when he left to work for Paramount Studios, or so it seemed as he looked back from the perspective of the 1960s: "I thought going to Hollywood was the most immoral thing I could do, and yet who wouldn't want to go to Hollywood? When I finally went it was with a sense of disgrace, almost" (HPT, 70).

The "almost" that qualifies Odets' statement underscores the mixed feelings he would continue to hold about the movie studios (and, less vehemently, about Broadway). The motion picture industry was a financial boon, even if it offered him less substantial artistic rewards than the stage. Still, Odets' willingness to stay for long periods of time "somewhat muddies the classic picture of Odets as the young talent raped by success: he was willing, even eager."[20] In fact, critics looked at Odets' time in the film industry as evidence of a sellout. For example, Malcolm Goldstein remarks that in *Golden Boy*, "Odets' intellectual battle left its impress on the play. This battle he had lost: he had gone to Hollywood." Like Odets' use of "almost" to qualify his shame, Goldstein's description of the battle as "lost" gives Odets' choice moral, political, and ideological overtones. The comparison to Joe Bonaparte—in Joe's brother Frank's words, a "waste," the very same word Odets' Group friend Elia Kazan would use to describe Odets after his death—implies a moral failure as much as an unwise career choice.

Odets' contemporaries used similar arguments. Clurman delineated the dangers of financial success facing the playwright in the commercial theatre, using Odets as his example:

Had Odets been a poet, a painter, a composer, even a novelist, the step to Hollywood would not appear so inevitable. . . . The theatre is in the very heart of the market-place, where a feverish and fabulous exchange of goods seems the essential drama. The playwright cannot but be affected by it. If he has had some success, why not more? If he has had little success, and greater rewards for his efforts are open to him in Hollywood, why not take advantage of the situation? (TFY, 169)

Part of Clurman's impetus for warning Odets against Hollywood was a fear felt by many theatre people in the 1930s. The rapid development of sound films in the late 1920s had an instantaneous, measurable effect on both film and theatre attendance. Motion picture box office receipts nearly doubled in New York City from 1927 to 1931, while those of the musical theatre plummeted by more than two-thirds. To combat falling attendance, Broadway producers raised ticket prices an average of 21 percent over the same period.[21] Far from being insulated from the market by their artistic purpose, the Broadway theatres were fighting for their lives.

As Hollywood drained talent from the stage, those who chose to go west, even for a time, were seen as traitors. The defense against the film became moral as well as aesthetic. For example, a 1929 *New York Times* article spoke for many when it lamented that "the American theatre is on its last legs. We are being mechanized out of the theatre by the talkies, the radio, and the people who prefer convenience to beauty."[22] This problem was worsened by increasing dependence of theatrical producers upon the sale of screen rights. The average payment for film rights to a Broadway show was between $30,000 and $35,000 in the years 1928-1935. Furthermore, by 1935-1936, 25 percent of Broadway shows had been financed with

Hollywood money. Such financial considerations had aesthetic effects: "regardless of the degree to which plays were produced or written under the influence of a possible movie sale, the fact remains that the revenue accruing from this source was largely responsible for allowing the commercial theatre to operate at the level of activity it did."[23] The Group, while trying to shield individual members from Hollywood's predations, willingly accepted studio money to fund a number of their productions, including *Men in White, Gentlewoman, Golden Boy*, and *Night Music*. In fact, MGM had given $17,000 to help finance the production of *Paradise Lost*, the only way the Group would have been able to produce it. Film studios were interested in backing such plays not only because it was cheaper than buying scripts after successful productions but also because "play backing afforded Hollywood the opportunity to become more deeply involved in trends developing in the drama and to be more aware of the talent emerging."[24] By the time Odets went to Hollywood, then, Broadway and the film industry were already in uneasy alliance.

Odets' first assignment at Paramount was *The General Died at Dawn*, a film about a corrupt Chinese warlord directed by Lewis Milestone and starring Gary Cooper and Madeline Carroll. Milestone later recalled that Odets was "of all playwrights, the least cynical toward film-making. . . . He approached the prospect with interest, but in tremendous fear" (B-G, 398). At the same time, Odets worked on two plays for the Group, *The Silent Partner*, a labor play about a strike in a bakery, and *The Law of Flight*, a play about a dictator loosely drawn from his experience with the Communist Cuban delegation in the summer of 1935. Odets, busy with work and somewhat at sea without the Group, didn't really acclimate to the Hollywood lifestyle, but at one of his few social outings, he met Luise Rainer, a twenty-year-old European actress who had won an Academy Award in *The Great Ziegfeld* the previous year and would soon win another for *The Good Earth*. Rainer had come to America in 1935 from a distinguished stage career with Max Reinhardt and saw herself as a theatre person. She, too, felt somewhat bewildered by the excesses of Hollywood and formed a bond with Odets as much from aversion to the Hollywood limelight as from their shared theatre backgrounds.

Odets quickly grew frustrated in Hollywood. His film, which he hoped would bring a new leftist consciousness to Hollywood, ended up a conventional melodrama in which the heroic O'Hara (Cooper) triumphs over the warlord despite being betrayed by Carroll's character. Despite some flashes of the kind of dialogue that had excited audiences on Broadway, the film operated well within the Hollywood framework; as he would say later, "On a set of clichés we made some good birthday decorations" (B-G, 408). The reviews of the film were mixed, a number of critics pointing out that the revolutionary playwright's screenplay was much like any other in Hollywood. Odets himself joined in the criticism; the first interview he gave condemning the fraudulence of the film industry was part of the publicity campaign for *The General Died at Dawn*.[25]

Despite such pronouncements, however, Odets moved only on the periphery of Hollywood radicalism in his ten-week stay. If Hollywood films remained mainstream, many in the industry worked behind the scenes for leftist causes, organizing meetings to combat Fascism and support labor unions. Indeed, the radicalism was so widespread that it drew the investigative attention of Congressman Martin Dies of Texas, who was determined to stamp out subversive activity in Hollywood. Supported by the studio heads who wanted to protect their profitable industry from political ideology, Dies' investigations would eventually turn in the late 1940s and early 1950s into a full-scale investigation, interrogation, and blacklisting of suspected Communists.

The leftism of the screenwriters had a personal outlet as well. They had struggled for the first half of the decade to form a union to combat the worst abuses of the studio system: the absence of a fair screen credit system, lack of artistic control, and unfair pressures placed on them to support particular political candidates. Among the Hollywood screenwriters in the early 1930s there were two warring factions: the Screen Writers Guild, made up largely of leftists and moderates, and the Screen Playwrights, which was for all practical purposes a company union. Facing strong resistance from the studios, the writers persisted in their demands. After a long court battle, the National Labor Relations Board (NLRB) ruled that the movie producers were financially dependent on the work of the writers but that the writers had no control of the final products of their labor.[26] Paradoxically, the writers were allowed to gain more control over their work only by admitting—even legalizing—their lack of control over it. Odets would soon face an analogous situation within the Group, where his work as a writer was increasingly viewed as a commodity, a means to the Group's solvency.

The Group ideal was also becoming increasingly compromised by the "enemy's" money. In early 1936, its directors were caught between the attempts of the Dramatist's Guild to get more control over sales of their scripts to the movies and the loss of Hollywood funding that would follow the Group's support of the union. The actors wanted to side with the Dramatist's Guild, but the directors hesitated: they had, in essence, "betrayed their principles and ignored the wishes of the members in favor of financial considerations" (RLD, 252). Ironically, the movie studios withdrew their funding anyway. The directors' wavering had gained them nothing and had precipitated a confrontation with the actors that led to the Group's reorganization.

THE SILENT PARTNER: POLITICAL CRISIS IN THE GROUP

Odets spent much of the summer of 1936 working on rewrites of *The Silent Partner*, which Clurman wanted for a fall production. The Group, financially struggling and stung by the failure of *The Case of Clyde Griffith*—Erwin Piscator's adaptation of Dreiser's *An American Tragedy*—had undergone internal changes. Following the crisis concerning the Dramatist's Guild, Clurman had presented a proposal for reorganizing the Group that would place him in charge as managing director, with advisement from an actor's committee. The actors reluctantly adopted Clurman's proposal and the Group now waited for Odets' script as well as plays from John Howard Lawson and Paul Green. Green's *Johnny Johnson*, an antiwar musical written with Kurt Weill, was scheduled to open the season. In 1936, civil war had broken out in Spain, pitting the Fascist forces of General Franco against Loyalists supported by communists and the Popular Front, so the choice of an antiwar play seemed prescient. The civil war in Spain served to heighten the tensions in

American politics as well. A few leftists joined the Lincoln Brigade fighting for the loyalist cause, and others offered vocal support, but many were wary of involvement in another war. At the same time, right-wingers increased their attacks on radicals and Communists at home.

The idealism that had characterized the early Roosevelt years was tempered not only by reports leaking out of Russia of political purges but even more by American isolationist attitudes. Some of the most important plays of 1936, including Irwin Shaw's *Bury the Dead* and Robert E. Sherwood's *Idiot's Delight*, examine such attitudes toward impending war. Shaw's play, set in *"the second year of the war that is to begin tomorrow,"* concerns a group of soldiers who refuse burial, bringing the war machine to a grinding halt. Sherwood's play, produced by the Theatre Guild, is set in a northern Italian resort where a group of international travelers—a British couple, a German scientist, a French radical, an American vaudeville troupe, a mysterious war profiteer, and a "Russian" countess—are trapped by the beginning of another pointless war.

The anxieties surrounding the Spanish civil war and the threat of another world war hovered over American playwriting through the second half of the 1930s. Even mainstream playwrights chose sides, deliberately examining—or deliberately avoiding—idealism, war, politics, and America's place in the world picture. For example, S.N. Behrman's brittle comic piece *No Time for Comedy* (1939) deals with a writer of comedies who wants to do something more worthwhile with his life. He begins by writing a "political" play, at which he fails; he then considers rushing off to Spain to fight for the Loyalist cause. At the end, he is finally persuaded that his talents are best put to use at home. His wife, the voice of reason, argues that if he leaves, "You're leaving the *only* country left in the world where one may still live with a little decency—but paralyzed by fear. Stay here, while and where it is still possible to live."[27] Behrman's play aptly captures the mood of late 1930s America: paralyzed by the fear another war, but driven by idealism to fight for freedom.

Other mainstream writers, including George Kaufman, Edna Ferber, and Thornton Wilder, maintained an even more ironic isolationist stance about both world and domestic political events. Kaufman followed the success of his 1933 satirical political musical *Of Thee I Sing* (written with Morrie Ryskind and the Gershwins) with a less successful sequel, *Let Them Eat Cake*. He then turned away from politics altogether in his wild 1936 farce (written with Moss Hart), *You Can't Take It with You*, in which the main characters, the Vanderhof family, deliberately shut themselves off from the outside world. *Stage Door* (1936), written by Kaufman and Ferber, contains a parody of a leftist playwright, Keith Burgess, clearly modeled on Odets. Sharing many of Odets' particular habits such as writing at night and obsession with music, Burgess also speaks in wild leftist exclamations—"Who cares whether a play makes money! All that matters is its message!" and "I write about the worker! The masses!" Ultimately, he is seduced by the money of Broadway and then Hollywood, though, like Odets, he says, "I'm going to use Hollywood. It's not going to use me."[28] When he returns from Hollywood in act 3, he has been thoroughly compromised by the film industry, so that the "masses" he refers to now are the millions of movie viewers who saw his last picture. Kaufman and

Ferber's parodic warning to Odets underscores the attitude many writers—and audiences—held about the limits of political drama and the possibilities of progressive content in Hollywood films.

Some scholars have argued that political drama's significance has been overemphasized. Certainly some of the most successful shows of the 1930s, including *Tobacco Road* and *Life with Father*, hardly qualify as social drama. Even within the artistically oriented commercial theatre, most of the plays produced were only tangentially political. Thornton Wilder's *Our Town* (1938), for example, deliberately downplays political issues, placing contemporary life in the context of millennia of history. Wilder's view of life, strongly seasoned by a sense of political detachment, stands as a deliberate counterpart to the kind of direct political engagement suggested by the plays of Odets and his leftist contemporaries. Nevertheless, the critical and commercial success of overtly political plays, including the Federal Theatre Project's simultaneous production of Sinclair Lewis' anti-Fascist *It Can't Happen Here* in seventeen cities in October 1936, indicates an interest in political drama far surpassing anything seen before on the American stage. Within 1930s American theatre there was a range of political engagement—Odets and the Group stood further left than most.

The Group's production of *Johnny Johnson* failed miserably at the box office, despite positive reviews. After it closed, Clurman was desperate enough to put *The Silent Partner* into rehearsal over the objections of Crawford and Strasberg, hoping that Odets could once again salvage the Group's season. Clurman thought Odets' play showed great promise. Set during a labor conflict in a small city, its title was lifted from a statement by Andrew Carnegie asserting that "where the wealth of a nation is honorably accrued, the people are always the silent partner." Odets had turned this axiom on its head so that became an assertion of violent oppression. In many respects, it is among Odets' most ambitious plays. It has a wide and variegated scope, largely because he conceived it as an allegory of American life. Some of its scenes, including the opening one, a strike meeting set in a graveyard, are sharp and powerful. But Clurman soon decided that the Group couldn't afford to produce it:

After *The Silent Partner* was in rehearsal for three or four days Clurman said to me, "Look, we'll produce any play you write. But you know this will be a very heavy and expensive production. We budgeted it for $40,000." So I said, "Why are you telling me all of this?" and he said "Well, the play will fail. We'll be out all that money and the actors will be out of work. But if you want us to do the play we will. (HPT, 73)

Odets acquiesced, but he felt abandoned by his own company, his script an unwanted orphan. The pressure to finish rewrites of *The Silent Partner* placed Odets in the curious position of having to work for his own company without compensation and without promise of a production or any other rewards. Even in his own theatre, Odets was a worker, with as little determination over the final use of the products of his labor, almost, as the screenwriters in Hollywood.

Frustrated with Clurman's bungling and the directors' insistence on a moneymaker, the actors forced the resignation of all three Group directors in early 1937 with the intention of reforming the Group upon a different basis. Talks failed to produce a workable plan, however, and by mid-1937 the company was on the verge of dissolution. Crawford and Strasberg left the Group permanently, Crawford confessing that "the inner situation seems to me incapable of solution at this time."[29] Odets had returned to California in January 1937, where he married Luise Rainer (Odets' second marriage, her first) and settled into screenwriting again. With the Group in indefinite hiatus, other Group members, including Clurman, followed Odets to Hollywood. Odets helped to find many of them jobs on the new picture he was writing for Milestone about the Spanish civil war, *The River Is Blue*—shelved but later rewritten by Lawson into the controversial film *Blockade*.

Odets was busy in Hollywood. In addition to the Milestone screenplay, a new screenplay, *Gettysburg* (never produced), and rewrites of *The Silent Partner*, Odets had begun working on another play, *Golden Boy*, the idea for which he had gotten from a prizefight he attended. His need for constant work and the public pressure surrounding his marriage to a movie star had begun to cause marital strain, causing Rainer to leave Odets for an extended New York trip a month into the marriage. In fact, for much of their marriage, the two would live apart, trading alternately endearing and angry letters, telegrams, and phone calls. But for Odets, work was most important, especially when it was compounded by pressure to make something that would be of immediate use to the Group. After *The River Is Blue* was shelved, Group members in Hollywood made tentative plans for reconstituting the theatre, with Odets' new play as its first production.

By now it was clear that the Group wouldn't produce *The Silent Partner* without complete revisions. Instead, Odets returned east during the summer of 1937 to finish *Golden Boy*, which showed greater commercial promise. Odets would draw upon his Hollywood experience in this play about a young violinist who gives up his art for the more tangible rewards of the prizefight, a conflict that critics often see as connected to Odets' own ambivalence about Hollywood. It is not surprising that Odets' play deals with issues of selling out and artistic integrity, given his anomalous position within the Group. The pressures on Odets influenced not only the content of his work but also the way in which he wrote and the audience he sought. As Lucien Goldmann has commented, the broad structures of the marketplace shape the day-to-day behavior of those within it: "any individual in a market society finds himself at certain moments of the day aiming at qualitative use values that he can obtain only through the mediation of exchange values."[30]

The Group was counting on Odets; they forced him to work on rewrites of *Golden Boy* without distraction; Elia Kazan even shielded Odets from Rainer when she visited New York. Similarly, the letters of encouragement that he received from Kazan and John Garfield while writing the play continually mentioned how important a commercial success would be for the Group. Odets' anxiety rose as opening approached: "Awareness that it was essentially his responsibility to 'bring in a hit' for the economic survival of the Group all but stopped him in his creative tracks" (B-G 480). In addition, with the third act of the play still unfinished, the Group was forced to put it into rehearsal without having secured the financial backing they needed to produce it. Throughout the fall, Odets spent the time he wasn't writing searching for financing for the play; he and Rainer eventually contributed about $5,000 each. After a hectic final month, *Golden Boy* opened on November 4, 1937.

It was the commercial and artistic success the Group had hoped for. In fact, it ended up being one of the most profitable shows the Group ever produced; the money raised (including the sale of its movie rights) would be enough to support the Group for two more seasons. Perhaps more importantly, Odets had redeemed himself in the eyes of many critics who feared the dissolution of his talent in Hollywood.

DEMOCRATIC VISTAS: *GOLDEN BOY* AND THE POPULAR AUDIENCE

Golden Boy's success reconfirmed Odets' status as one of America's leading playwrights, though many critics derided the similarities between the play and Hollywood films. Responding to criticism that the play was tainted by his Hollywood experience, Odets wrote an article in the *New York Times* two weeks after the play opened called "Democratic Vistas in Drama." In it, he calls for theatre practitioners to recognize that *Golden Boy* borrowed themes from film because "the movies are now the folk theatre of America":

They have spoken to this people. The movies have explored the common man in all of his manifestations—out of the Kentucky mountains, out of the Montana ranch house, out of the machine shop, from the docks and alleys of the great cities, from the farm, out of the hospitals, airplanes and taxicabs. (NYT, November 21, 1937)

Odets believed that film's power lay its ability to reach the common man by fostering a direct connection between artist and audience. The Broadway theatre, on the other hand, often existed in a symbolic—and authoritarian—relation to audiences, as a mark of high culture. During rehearsals for *Golden Boy*, Odets remarked to the *Daily Worker* that "social theatre isn't dying. It never really lived. . . . I don't think the left theatre belongs on Broadway. . . . it belongs all over the country in the Federal Theatre, in union halls, in the hinterland. What's the sense in writing plays for a few bourgeois intellectuals on Broadway at $3.30 a head?" (B-G, 482).

The Group had brought Odets to believe in a particular kind of theatre, one rooted in the life of his time and aimed at social action; his ideal was a socially committed theatre such as the Group or the Federal Theatre Project (FTP). The FTP, begun in 1935 as part of Roosevelt's recovery plan, had established itself as a progressive, innovative theatre on a scale never before seen in America. In its four-year history (it was eliminated in 1939 by an increasingly conservative Congress) the FTP presented thousands of plays of all kinds: classics, musicals, melodramas, children's shows, religious dramas, premieres, vaudeville, and dance shows. Some of the more famous productions—a swing version of Gilbert and Sullivan's *Mikado*, an Orson Welles-directed version of *Macbeth* set in Haiti, the Living Newspapers, which tackled contemporary issues in a documentary style—were hailed as some of the most powerful productions of the decade. Even more significantly, FTP shows were performed all over the country, often for poorer audiences who paid little or nothing for admission.

Odets admired the FTP; he had always relished the idea of his work being produced on a large scale. In fact, Odets was preoccupied throughout 1938 with a plan to have the FTP mount simultaneous productions of *The Silent Partner* all over the

country as they had with Sinclair Lewis' *It Can't Happen Here* in 1936. Odets'
primary goal was to bring a meaningful work of art to a great number of people. In
a telling example, Brenman-Gibson relates a conversation Odets had in 1938 with
actress Helen Hayes and her husband, playwright Charles MacArthur, detailing his
ideas for a "Charlie Theatre":

When Miss Hayes asked what he meant by a "Charlie Theatre," Odets replied, "Well, you're
an actress married to a man named Charlie. I'm a playwright and I have a brother-in-law
named Charlie. So-and-so is a director and he has a son named Charlie. Suddenly the government passes a law everybody named Charlie is going to be electrocuted at midnight, New
Year's. So you and I, so-and-so the director, all of us who have Charlies threatened, get together and we write, direct, stage, and act a play, and the audience comes and everybody in
the audience has some Charlie whom he's trying to save and then you get something going
on between the people on stage and the people in the audience that I call a Charlie Theatre,
and that's what we need. (B-G, 491-492)

This strange vision of a progressive, popular theatre is characteristic of Odets. Artistic, democratic, and political, it aims to systematically re-create the effect
achieved on the opening night of *Waiting for Lefty*, where the struggles of the depression were crystallized onstage in a form instantly and joyously recognizable to
the audience.

     Still, Odets remained wary of Hollywood's constraints. He acknowledged in
"Democratic Vistas" that though Hollywood adeptly captured social conditions, the
economics of the industry prevented progressive uses of that ability. Like many
other critics of popular culture during the late 1930s, Odets believed that films had
a deleterious influence on audiences: "Hollywood has set our citizens examples of
conduct and behavior patterns fit only for the lower animals." Still, Odets kept a
belief that film structures could be harnessed for socially productive ends:

The movie producer in this country, it seems, is cleverer than the playwright. He goes
"where the masses are" for his material—it is his business to do so. Why not make that the
business of the playwright, too? Why should the phrase "movie theme" be tossed around so
scornfully by the critic? The playwright would be wise to look at movies as "documentation."

 In Odets' curious adaptation of the language of capitalism, the playwright's "business" is to reflect society, and the "profit" is moral rather than financial—though he
implies that financial rewards are possible, as the success of *Golden Boy* indicated.
Furthermore, Odets suggests that because the film industry exists solely to earn
profit, it is natural for producers to find themes that reflect the desires of the largest
share of the people. Odets craved a similar audience without claiming to seek similar financial rewards. In essence, like Clurman's characterization of the Group on
Broadway, he wanted to be in the world but not of it, to use the audience created by
the financial structures of Hollywood toward a more socially useful end.

VEAL CHOPS ON THE TABLE: *ROCKET TO THE MOON* AND *NIGHT MUSIC*

In early 1938, *Golden Boy* was still running in New York and had made a successful debut in London, where Odets was hailed as the "white hope of English dramatic letters" (B-G, 509). Nevertheless, things were not as golden as they seemed. Immediately before Odets left for London, Luise Rainer had filed for divorce; he was given the news on the voyage over. They would reconcile briefly but split for good in 1939. The Group also continued to pressure him for another play for the 1938 season, *Rocket to the Moon*. Less overtly concerned with social and economic themes than his earlier work, the play deals with a mild-mannered dentist, Ben Stark, who hopes to break out of a midlife rut by having an affair with his secretary. Nevertheless, political tensions—Hitler's anschluss of Czechoslovakia in September 1938, the growing antileftist tide at home—interested him more than his "dentist" play: as he wrote *Rocket to the Moon*, Odets also took notes for a full-length anti-Nazi play and worked on revisions to *The Silent Partner* and *The Law of Flight*. By October, however, he had finished two strong acts of *Rocket to the Moon* and had written a draft of the third, though he would continue to tinker with the unsatisfactory ending until opening night.

Odets' move from politics toward psychology in his new play mirrored a shift away from the radical left throughout the United States. Roosevelt's resounding triumph in the 1936 elections had helped to cement his mandate for progressive reform. During his second term, his policies began to withstand the legal challenges that had hampered the first administration, allowing him to institute and sustain more striking reforms. He was, in fact, so successful in co-opting leftist programs that neither the Communists nor the Socialists had garnered much support in 1936. Odets himself wrote a letter of "verbal admiration" to Roosevelt in 1939, offering his services as a speechwriter if Roosevelt chose to run for a third term. Like the more successful playwright Robert E. Sherwood, who would indeed work as a writer for the president, Odets was by the late 1930s able to reconcile his zeal for reform with the government's policies. Part of this shift was Odets' own, but part reflected a general American slide toward a more moderate leftism. A 1937 recession brought a conservative wave into Congress in 1938, furthering the shift to the right.

In mid-1938, Clurman wrote Odets a letter summing up Odets' strengths as a playwright, urging him to consider the Group's—and America's—need for his plays:

Of all people *you* Clifford Odets are the nearest to understand or *feel* this American reality . . . the reality only half-experienced but nevertheless present for most Americans like us—of whom there are many millions. . . . Write—write—write—because we need it so much. "We" is not the Group alone, not the American theater (pfui! on the American theatre) but our folks, we Americans, we guys who live on University Place, Hester St., Fifth Ave., Central Park West, Santa Monica Blvd., Oshkosh, and Kalamazoo. . . . for the love of your brothers—*give out!!* (B-G, 496)

Clurman's insistence that Odets was the voice of his generation, that he had more to offer than other writers, was a calculated move to make Odets feel needed. But it also served to underscore the importance Odets' plays had for the Group as a whole, a pressure that would come to a crisis with Odets' final two Group plays.

Rehearsals for *Rocket to the Moon* in the fall of 1938 were tense. The play was strong in many aspects but seemed destined for financial failure. When it opened on November 24, reviews were mixed. Virtually everyone praised the first act, the humor, the sharp, incisive dialogue. Others welcomed the shift away from overtly political writing. However, many took exception to the third act, finding it unconvincingly resolved. The leftist press was especially virulent, accusing Odets of ignoring history and politics in favor of psychology. Later, his friend and mentor John Howard Lawson—who had become increasingly committed to Communism throughout the 1930s—publicly attacked him for abdicating social responsibility with the play.

Odets was disappointed that he had become so alienated from the far left, though he didn't necessarily disagree with evaluations of the plays' weaknesses. He saw the problems as lying in the Group's often frantic process of production rather than in the play itself:

He (Clurman) finally got to think that I was kind of like a cow who dropped a calf, didn't know anything about it. Because this is what happened in the Group Theatre and I was very resentful of it. I dropped this calf and some people would rush up and grab it, wipe it off and take it away, and I would be left there bellowing. . . . They had to have those veal chops on the table. For the next week, or everybody would go hungry. So in a certain way this gifted calf that I'm talking about, that I dropped, was also veal chops for everybody to eat. (B-G, 515)

Odets' bitter comments make it clear that the economic pressures within the Group deeply affected the way he worked. But perhaps more importantly, they mark the alienation he felt—even as a Group member—from the final disposition of his labor. Finally, because it is a particular habit of Odets to couch his discussion of the marketplace in food images, the characterization of his own play as "veal chops" shows how much he was able to view it as a commodity.

Indeed, the use here of the same images of food and consumption that fill his plays tie his own feelings of exploitation to the idea of the marketplace. As it had been for many immigrant families, food in Odets' plays, from *Waiting for Lefty* through *The Big Knife* and *The Flowering Peach*, is both the utopian symbol of a good consumer society and an indication of the degradation one is forced to undergo in order to participate in such a society. The "fruit trees" that Agate Keller asks the audience of *Waiting for Lefty* to plant over his grave are a fundamental symbol of new world plenty. Nevertheless, as Keller acknowledges, in order to feed, one first has to be taken into the market and consumed. Taking up one of his most familiar image patterns to define his writing for the Group, Odets identified his position in the marketplace and at the same time demonstrated the ambivalence he held toward it.

Rocket to the Moon struggled at the box office; Odets offered $19,000 of his own money, keeping it alive for 131 performances. Shortly afterward, he left New

York to work on *The Silent Partner* in Florida and Mexico. He also began work on two new (unproduced) plays, *Night on Steel Mountain*, about a coal miner's strike, and a "quartet" play, about a musical quartet who are forced to reevaluate their commitments when individual needs conflict with those of the group. Clearly, he was rethinking his commitment to Clurman and the Group Theatre. In a long letter to Clurman, he talked about the "unsatisfactory relationship": "I am in the anomalous position of being the Group's main dynamo and at the same time as far out of the texture of the Group as I was eight years ago" (B-G, 553). He was annoyed, too, that without asking him, the Group had decided to remount *Awake and Sing!*, running it in repertory with *Rocket to the Moon*. Ironically, *Awake and Sing!* was lauded in the highest terms by most of the New York critics; Richard Watts, Jr. called it "a classic of the modern theatre."

The summer of 1939 was a summer of turmoil, both in world politics and in the Group. The American left was in decline, it was increasingly clear that Franco's fascist troops would win the Spanish Civil War, and news about Soviet purges became impossible to ignore. The Group spent the summer working toward another season, though many noted that the mood inside the Group had changed along with the darkening political climate. Members, tired of constant struggles about money and the relationship of individual aspiration to the Group's goals, fought all summer. Odets continued to work on *The Silent Partner*, but Clurman rejected it again, partly for financial reasons: the play had a large cast and a number of settings. Odets continued to complain about the actors' complacency, monetary mismanagement and Clurman's unwillingness to take a risk on the labor play. For his part, Clurman was desperate enough to consider asking Lee Strasberg to return as a director for the Group.

Odets wanted to prove that he had not lost his ability to write socially meaningful plays. In the preface to his *Six Plays*, published that summer, he had noted that *The Silent Partner* was more of a piece with the other five than *Rocket to the Moon* had been, attributing its absence to "theatre exigencies." He recognized that he had shifted from his original goals, though he nevertheless believed strongly enough in the social uses of art that he could assert that "we live in an age when new art works should shoot bullets" (ix). By August, however, it was clear that Clurman wouldn't produce *The Silent Partner* under any conditions: Instead, the Group would plan to open with a new adaptation of Chekhov's *Three Sisters*, followed by another Odets play, *Night Music*.

Night Music, like *Rocket to the Moon*, was a departure from the overtly political plays of Odets' first period. He conceived of it as variations on a theme—homelessness and the search for meaning—set against the backdrop of the coming war. Odets' turn away from leftist politics in the play was deliberate, though he maintained a personal commitment to the left. In a 1940 journal entry, he comments:

My personal feeling about social change is this. I have one opinion as a private citizen. But in the world of the theatre, in relation to my plays and audiences for them, Leftism as understood by the communists is impossible. Any excessive partisanship in a play defeats the very purpose of the play itself. To be socially useful in the theatre, one cannot be more left than, for instance, La Guardia. (TIR, 15)

Odets had perhaps sensed a shifting American mood. The FTP had been shut down in 1939, apolitical plays began to reassert themselves on the Broadway stage in the late 1930s, and the film industry had come no closer to realizing its "folk theatre" promise in the two years since Odets had written "Democratic Vistas in Drama."

Odets' new political strategy took a new dramatic form in *Night Music*. Unlike earlier anti-fascist or anti-war plays that directly or allegorically attacked political questions in sharp language and clear statements, *Night Music* is a romantic comedy that seems almost whimsical; it hints rather than shoots bullets. Still, a cloud hangs over the play, reflecting the darkening world situation. As Odets worked on the play, Europe was engulfed in war. The first crushing blow to the American left was the Stalin-Hitler non-aggression pact signed in late August. In a stunning betrayal of all the anti-Fascist Popular Front had worked for since 1935, Stalin agreed not to attack Germany, thereby opening the door for the German invasion of Poland on September 1. For most, the pact tolled a death knell for American radicalism.

Against this gloom, the Group was desperately trying to put together another season, and Odets was attempting to salvage his personal life. When Luise Rainer returned from a long European trip in October, Odets quickly and cruelly abandoned his mistress Frances Farmer (who had played Lorna Moon in *Golden Boy*) for a final, abortive attempt at reconciliation.[31] A scheduled production of *Three Sisters* fell through, and the Group quickly put into rehearsal a play called *Thunder Rock* by Robert Ardrey. The play, dealing thoughtfully with questions of how far to participate in violence, was a clear reflection of America's own ambivalent position during the "phony war." Despite winning a special award from the Playwright's Company—a commercial organization formed by playwrights Robert E. Sherwood, Elmer Rice, Maxwell Anderson, S. N. Behrman, and Sidney Howard to produce their own plays—*Thunder Rock* closed after twenty-three performances, leading Odets to assert again that there was no place for noncommercial work in the professional theatre.

Odets' own noncommercial play—his last for the Group—was having trouble finding backers. He finally realized that the only way the play would be produced was with Hollywood money. Accordingly, Odets contracted to write the screenplay for *Night Music* in exchange for a $20,000 advance to open the show. Odets' desperation is indicated by the fact that this was the only screenplay he wrote based upon one of his own plays (though a number of his plays were made into successful movies by other writers). Indeed, at the time he was writing *Night Music*, Odets was so insecure about his position that he sent a pseudonymous letter of application to an agency for a position as an "ad-man."

In many ways, *Night Music* was a fitting play to close Odets' Group career, for it deals with the question of finding a home in a world where everything is in upheaval. The Group continued to suffer from internal conflict. For example, as rehearsals progressed, Odets became more and more anxious about Clurman's direction, feeling the staging was too heavy for the lightness of the script. But where Clurman thought the play would work best in a small, intimate theatre, Odets wanted to open in a more impressive Broadway house. Tensions mounted during the tryouts in Boston: Odets found fault with everything, especially Kazan's "oafish" performance as Steve. The Boston reviews were tepidly unsupportive, often focusing more on Odets' radical politics than the play itself—the non-aggression pact had made Communists fair game for the mainstream press again.

Night Music opened in New York on February 22, 1940; the cast gave, by Odets' account, an excellent performance. But the critics were unimpressed with Odets' new direction, and the reviews saw the play as meaningless or rambling. Even Brooks Atkinson dismissed the play with the barb, "Now that Odets writes like Saroyan, Doomsday is near." Clurman and Odets were stung deeply, feeling the reviewers had missed the way the play captured the tentative mood of the country during the phony war. Frustrated by the Group's inability to counteract the negative reviews, Odets felt even more isolated: "My one desire is to get out and away from this painful treading on water" (TIR, 52). Odets and the Group were on hold, frustrated, as rootlessly homeless as the characters in the play. The political and social conditions that had helped to create the company had shifted; the personal sacrifices that had allowed the theatre to survive were intolerable. Odets summed up his feelings about the Group and the theatre in terms that violently undercut the images of hopeful abundance woven through his plays: "I sit here, believe it or not, like a juicy melon, and they all keep coming at me with a spoon or a fork or both! I am enraged by all sides, the critics and theatre conditions below, the Group personalities above" (TIR, 69). Odets' sense of outrage, though achingly personal, was also that of his generation on the eve of the war. Despite their best intentions, despite the New Deal, despite sacrifices and work and idealism, nothing had changed.

NOTES

1.   Reuel Denney has noted that the perception of the city as a self-contained culture was a recent shift in attitude; he argues that it was not until the art of the Ashcan School in the 1910's that the city began to think of itself as a cultural as well as an economic entity, that popular art began to emerge distinctively from high culture and almost immediately be blended back into it.

2.   Malcolm Goldstein remarks that this theme embodied the Group's "general admonition against moral compromise" in *The Political Stage: American Drama and Theater of the Great Depression* (New York: Oxford UP, 1974) 75 but notes that "most of the Group's playwrights were content to stop with the admonition rather than preach the Marxist doctrine that under capitalism the 'sellout' is inevitable; with the exception of Odets, the Group's few plays offering that variation on the theme were failures" (82).

3.   John Gassner, Introduction, in Morgan Himelstein, *Drama Was a Weapon: The Left Wing Theatre in New York, 1929-1941* (New Brunswick, NJ: Rutgers UP, 1963).

4.   Gassner, Introduction. While admittedly virulent in its hatred of Communism, Himelstein's book remains the best source of information about the small, radical leftist theatres of the 1930s, as Goldstein's *The Political Stage* is about leftist theatre in general. Himelstein argues that the sole purpose of these theatres was to "indoctrinate a new audience" and asserts that the importance of the social drama in American theatre has been seriously overestimated. Significantly, Himelstein points to the Guild as an example of a theatre that retained "a healthy skepticism toward the theatre of the left" (125). According to Himelstein, the Guild "understood that entertainment was as important as didacticism, even in an

unsteady decade, and also that the theatre was supposed to teach an understanding of the human heart as well as the social mood" (152).

5. Clurman, Wendy Smith, and Odets all relate the same story in which Strasberg, approached by Bess Eitingon with a gift of $50,000 for the Group, simply stared at the would-be donor in disbelief, so that she finally withdrew her gift. Odets recalled his saying at the time, "I honestly couldn't think what we could use 50,000 dollars for." Similarly, in late 1938, the Group discovered that the theatre manager of the Windsor and Belasco theatres had misappropriated $17,000 of Group money. Kermit Bloomgarten, the Group's business manager, was too busy with his outside work for Herman Shumlin to notice, and the other office workers were too inexperienced to realize what was happening until it was too late.

6. Thomas Gale Moore, *The Economics of the American Theatre* (Durham, NC: Duke UP, 1968) 14, 147.

7. While many commodities can be mass-produced by machine, theatre cannot. Economists Bruno Frey and Ward Pommerehne note that in terms of simple economics, art cannot be set apart from the market, because, like commodities, it is subject to the economic principle of scarcity. That is, when labor and capital are used for theatre, they are unavailable at the same time for other purposes, and so by its very existence, theatre becomes a commodity in competition with other commodities for limited resources. Likewise, within the arts themselves, resources are scarce; the same writer or actor cannot be doing two things at once, and competition arises for the services of those workers.

8. Kenneth S. Davis, FDR. A History. Volume 1: The New York Years, 1928-1933 (New York: Random House, 1985) 31.

9. Arthur Schlesinger, Jr., The Age of Roosevelt. Volume 1: The Crisis of the Old Order, 1919-1933 (Cambridge, MA: Riverside, 1957) 188.

10. Warren Susman, Culture as History: The Transformation of American Society in the Twentieth Century (New York: Pantheon, 1984) xx.

11. Schlesinger, 7.

12. Daniel Horowitz dates the consumer culture from the late 19th century in America (earlier in England), though he notes that even in the late 1920s it was not complete (*The Morality of Spending: Attitudes Toward the Consumer Society in America, 1875-1940*. Baltimore: Johns Hopkins UP, 1985). T. J. Jackson Lears places the rise of consumer culture earlier than Susman as well, arguing that the culture of abundance was a very old concept, but that the developments of the Industrial Revolution shifted the emphasis on production from women to men, from hearth to factory, and the emphasis on consumption shifted the other way, from men to women (*Fables of Abundance: A Cultural History of Advertising in America.* New York: Basic Books, 1994) 1-36.

13. Robert S Lynd and Helen Merrell Lynd, *Middletown in Transition: A Study in Cultural Conflicts* (New York: Harcourt Brace, 1937) 46. Rita Barnard, in *The Great Depression and the Culture of Abundance* (Cambridge UP, 1995) notes that this characterization is "hardly devoid of hyperbole: the continued sluggishness of the economy well into the next decade indicates that the transition to a culture of abundance remained in the 1930s more a matter of commercial ideology rather than of actual practice" (23-24).

14. Bernard Karsh and Phillips K. Garman, "The Impact of the Political Left," in *Labor and the New Deal*, Milton Derber and Edwin Young, eds. (Madison, WI: U of Wisconsin P, 1957) 84.

15. John Gassner, "The American Galaxy," in *Masters of the Drama* (New York: Random House, 1940) 689.

16. John Mason Brown, *Two on the Aisle* (New York: W. W. Norton, 1938) 216.

17. Malcolm Cowley notes that Clurman was wrong for another reason, namely, that no other similar dramas followed *Waiting for Lefty*: "The mood of the left wing writ-

ers had begun to change. Already their dream of uniting with the workers to fight for a new society on American soil was giving way to fears of a new world war that Hitler might win." "While They Waited for Lefty," *Saturday Review* (June 6, 1944) 61.

18. Malcolm Goldstein, "Clifford Odets and the Found Generation," in *American Drama and its Critics*, Alan S. Downer, ed. (Toronto: U of Toronto P, 1965) 137.

19. He wrote a monologue, "I Can't Sleep," for Morris Carnovsky to perform at a union benefit. In it, tapping into both the anxiety of mid-depression America and the communal spirit of leftist political movements, Odets created the character of a middle class man who pours out his guilt for having forgotten those less fortunate: "The blood of the mother and brother is breaking open my head. I hear them crying, 'You forgot, you forgot!'" (B-G, 335). Odets also wrote a short play called *Remember* for a Negro People's Theatre benefit in October. It was never produced again, and no copy of it has survived.

20. Gerald Weales, *Clifford Odets, Playwright* (New York: Pegasus, 1971) 11.

21. Moore, 14-15. Moore cites the Census of Manufactures to show the astonishingly rapid replacement of the silent film with the "talkie." Of the 1,347 films produced in 1927, the year the first sound motion picture, *The Jazz Singer*, was made, only a few were "talkies." Two years later, a full 78 percent of the 1,204 films produced were pictures with sound (13).

22. Robert McLaughlin, Broadway and Hollywood: A History of Economic Interaction (New York: Arno, 1974) 93.

23. McLaughlin, 122. There is strong evidence that many producers became increasingly leery in the 1930s of scripts that did not have the potential for sales to Hollywood. Robert McLaughlin notes that the Dramatist's Guild was wary of Hollywood's investment in production, arguing that too great a dependence on film money would, as Guild president Sidney Howard, put it, mean "the virtual elimination of all plays which do not, on the face of things, offer promising picture material" (152).

24. McLaughlin, 124.

25. Weales, 110.

26. Nancy Lynn Schwartz, *The Hollywood Writers Wars* (New York: Knopf, 1982) 123.

27. S. N. Behrman, *No Time for Comedy* (New York: Samuel French) 106.

28. Edna Ferber and George S. Kaufman, *Stage Door*, in *Twenty Best Plays of the Modern American Theatre*, John Gassner, ed. (New York: Crown, 1939) 833, 852.

29. Cheryl Crawford, *One Naked Individual: My Fifty Years in the Theatre* (Indianapolis: Bobbs-Merrill, 1977) 100.

30. Lucien Goldmann, "Problems of a Sociology of the Novel," in *Readings in Marxist Sociology*, Tom Bottomore and Patrick Goode, eds. (Oxford: Clarendon, 1983) 179.

31. Many Group members, shocked at Odets' cruelty, date Farmer's spiral downward into drug addiction, alcoholism, and mental illness to this break. Farmer herself saw it as part of a number of factors that ended her acting career and institutionalized her for seven years in her thirties. Odets kept a file on Farmer his entire life, planning to write an "Actress" play loosely based on her story.

Chapter 3

"Life Printed on Dollar Bills": The Marketplace in Odets' Group Plays

EXPECTATIONS OF ABUNDANCE MARKETING THE AMERICAN EDEN

Because the Group was always an American theatre, it is not surprising that Odets' Group plays reflect the deepest American concerns of the period: war, economic failure, class struggle, and most importantly, the collapse of American idealism. Clurman suggests that *Paradise Lost* was an incisive examination of the psychic state of mid-1930s America:

Wherever I went it seemed to me I observed an inner chaos. People hankered for things they didn't need or really want, belied their own best impulses, became miserable over trivialities, were ambitious to achieve ends they didn't respect, struggled over mirages, wandered about in a maze where nothing was altogether real for them. *Paradise Lost* seemed to me to reflect this almost dreamlike unreality and, in a measure, to explain it. (TFY, 156)

By the time of Roosevelt's second inauguration in March 1936, one-third of the country was "ill-housed, ill-clad, ill-nourished": the American Dream of abundance had become a nightmare of scarcity. Like the Gordon family of *Paradise Lost*, the entire country had been thrown out of Eden, wandering with no sense of direction and only a vague cognizance of what had been lost. It was clear, however, that something certainly *had* been lost.

Prior to the 1929 crash, the American ideal of individual success had been propped up by two interlocking mythologies. First, the Puritan belief that hard work necessarily merited moral and financial rewards was given its most fantastic manifestations by the rags-to-riches novels of Horatio Alger and the only slightly less incredible stories of people like Andrew Carnegie.[1] Even in the Eisenhower years, C. Wright Mills could argue that "as an ideological figment and a political force, [the Algeresque hero] has persisted as if he inhabited an entire continent. He has become the man through whom the ideology of utopia is still attractively presented to many of our contemporaries."[2] In the 1920s and 1930s, however, the rags-to-riches ideal was under steady attack from the left. Plays such as John Howard Lawson's *Roger Bloomer* and *Success Story,* Elmer Rice's *The Adding Machine,* O'Neill's *The Hairy Ape,* as well as the novels of Fitzgerald, Dreiser, Dos Passos, and Nathanael West suggest that the Gospel of Wealth was a myth challenged and ironized from the very moment of its formulation.

Odets added his voice to the criticism in his examination—and condemnation—of the Alger myth. Odets was most concerned about the effect such ideologies had on the daily lives of people, the concretization of the myth in American life. *Waiting for Lefty, Paradise Lost,* and *Awake and Sing!,* especially, but in fact *all* of Odets' plays chronicle his characters' attempts to make sense of a culture predicated upon economic success. In *Awake and Sing!,* Myron responds to Ralph's complaints with the Puritan answer, "Never mind son, merit never goes unrewarded. Teddy Roosevelt used to say—," but his daughter Hennie answers his platitudes with mockery: "It rewarded you—thirty years a haberdashery clerk!" (SP, 41). Similarly, Morty is another part of Odets' response to the Alger myth. A self-made man, Morty is wealthy and even generous, yet "something sinister comes out of the fact that the lives of others seldom touch him deeply. He holds to his own line of life" (SP, 39).

The idea of "success" appears over and over in Odets' plays, most often as an indication of something twisted or petty. Thus Jacob in *Awake and Sing!* can mock Morty and Myron's platitudes with the sardonic "Don't live, just make success!" (66) and "A boy don't turn around without having shoved in him he should make success" (71). In *Golden Boy,* Mr. Bonaparte pleads with Lorna to "[h]elp Joe find truthful success" (269). But by the end of the play, the idea of a truthful success has been completely submerged in the violence of the marketplace: Roxy remarks to Joe's father, after Joe has killed another fighter, "You see how a boy can make success nowadays?" (317). The idea of success is always related to social expectations; it moves outward from the individual to the marketplace, finding value only as a commodity to be purchased by others. Success means selling, in Joe's case, the selling of his talent his ideals, for a socially determined notion of what is admired.

Odets' plays are more than a repeated diatribe against the development of consumer capitalism, however. Certainly, his plays express outrage at the lack of opportunities for his characters; he condemns outright the systematic denigration of the poor and outcast. But he also delineates the deep utopian visions that drove left-wing politics during the 1930s, the promises—including material abundance—that a truly democratic land offered. As immigrants to the new "promised land" understood, there is a deep connection between material abundance and political equality. In spite of his condemnation of heartless capitalists like Morty, Odets possessed an undeniable, egalitarian optimism that mirrors the hopes expressed by the Alger myth. His deep awareness that life was "printed on dollar bills" is modified by the equally fervent belief that it would be possible someday to have a life not printed there. Odets both identifies with and distances himself from consumer culture, the daily marketplace in which his characters participate, creating dramatic tension from the gap between a utopian vision of plenty and the historical fact of depression-era poverty and want. He is extremely sensitive—largely because of his own position as the son of an immigrant, a leftist, and an artist in the theatrical market-place—to the paradoxes of a culture that drives people to expect abundance but never leaves them satisfied.

Concomitant with a belief in financial success as the necessary reward of hard work was an exultation in the natural bounty of the land, its magnitude, its rich soil, its mineral and timber reserves, its rivers and lakes. Historian Frederick Jackson Turner's address in 1893 titled "The Significance of the Frontier in American History" articulated a "frontier" mythology—suggesting that this land had made Americans, among other things, self-reliant, work-oriented, progressive, and democratic—which would take root in the American imagination. In addition to forming the American character, Turner's thesis suggested, "the frontier *naturally*, if too rapidly, gives way to industrial society."[3] In the early 1900s, others expanded upon these implicit ideas of rapid change and expansion. American business turned to the new frontiers of technology and engineering to better control the natural world; the future was planned with an eye toward the qualities that the frontier experience had supposedly already imbued in the American people.[4] In short, the Turner thesis was thus adopted and fine-tuned by various groups—business, science, religion—for their own purposes.

Of course, economic expansion also had a dark side, for by persistently seeking the frontier, expansion had necessarily destroyed it. There was from the beginning, then, an ambivalence about unchecked progress in American thought, what Christopher Lasch calls a "curious conjunction of 'improvement' and regret."[5] Perhaps in reaction against this uneasiness, the quest for new frontiers in technology and business took on greater political as well as economic meaning; expansion was increasingly viewed as a democratic use of the land, and "the idea of democracy came to be associated more and more with the prospect of universal abundance. America came to be seen as a nation not of citizens but of consumers."[6] The vast expanses of untouched frontier, long looked upon in the popular and literary imaginations as the modern Garden, had virtually disappeared. They had been brought under control by the telegraph, the factory, the combine and thresher, the railroad, and eventually the radio, telephone, and automobile. The goal of modern American society was now simple and industrial: to ensure production—and consumption—enough for all. It was without irony that President Hoover, an engineer by profession and a firm believer in the beneficial power of technology, said in 1928, "We in America today are nearer to the final triumph over poverty than ever before in the history of any land." Even progressives like Lewis Mumford noted that the apparent triumph of technology over the natural world manifested itself in the paradisiacal ideal of abundance.[7] In short, the development of industrial technologies became the promise of admittance to a new Eden, an efficient, progressive, democratic, productive Garden.

At the time Odets was writing, the frontier ideal, still a powerful force in American thought, was being transformed into a scramble for consumers. Most historians agree that the rise of the department store in the 1910s and 1920s, the birth of the supermarket in the late 1920s, the quick acceptance of electric refrigeration, the standardization of automobile production, and the popularization of radio as a means of mass communication helped to secure the place of American consumer society. T. J. Jackson Lears, among others, has traced the rise of modern advertising in the 20th century as evidence of this development, though as he notes, the association of products with personal transformation was only the institutionalization of a long-standing habit: "Advertisers' efforts to associate silverware with status or cars with sex were but a recent and well-organized example of a widespread cultural practice."[8]

In the frontier mythology, the subjugation of the land manifested itself in an industrial order separated from, but nevertheless dependent upon, the abundance of the natural world. Plenty was a Providential gift to be used, and early advertisers attempted to make the connections clear by awkwardly joining "traditional maternal imagery with an emergent effort to systematize bodily processes and sanctify physical symmetry."[9] As the industrial order began to dominate the natural order, the age-old notion of abundance symbolized by the natural world, especially the fecundity of women, was replaced by the efficient machine; by the early 20th century, the Madonna had become Mrs. Consumer.[10]

Despite the increasing depersonalization of the industrial economy—which the Group Theatre had been in part founded to combat—nostalgia for an Edenic, preindustrial productivity remained, reappearing in advertising and other cultural images during the lean years of the depression: "The reassuring vision of an organic, cohesive American Way of Life pervaded Works Progress Administration (WPA) murals and Popular Front posters as well as popular cultural artifacts from *Porgy and Bess* to the film version of *The Grapes of Wrath*, from *Oklahoma!* to *It's a Wonderful Life*."[11] Odets, too, recognized the cultural shifts taking place, the conjunction of natural and machine imagery, though he was unsure of their importance. In his 1932 journal, he remarked, "Certainly something is happening in America. Ads now feature halfnaked [*sic*] women; breasts pop out in ads for toothpaste, breakfast cereal and what not; women in ads are actually portrayed smoking cigarettes! these things would have been impossible only five years ago! . . . I can't go into what is responsible for such a change, but I think it may be for the best" (LCA, dated May 25, 1932). Odets' adoption of the new language—women's breasts figure as sources of nourishment in Odets' own iconography and plays as prominently as they do in the advertisements—indicates a growing fascination with the culture of abundance.

Conflicts between the facts of industrial progress and a nostalgic longing for Edenic abundance are central to Odets' work. The son of an advertising man himself and a man who had several times considered a career in advertising copywriting, Odets was both fascinated and repulsed by this shift from natural to industrial productivity and even more fascinated by the language and images used to convey it. His plays are a cornucopia of material objects, both of natural abundance—fruit is the most common—and of mass production. Thus, he is a playwright formed in the depression not only in his subject matter but in the language he adopts to speak of it. It is in the negotiations of the new marketplace that his conflicts are centered, where the gains of material culture are measured, often unfavorably, against the human costs necessary to attain them. Furthermore, for Odets, the family is the testing ground for this conflict, but not in any utopian way. Rather, his families, like the Bergers of *Awake and Sing!* and the Gordons in *Paradise Lost*, show tears in the fabric of an American way of life even as they attempt to wrap themselves in it.

Coupled with a shift from home to factory as the center of production was the shift from country to city as the center of consumption; by 1933, a majority of Americans lived less than a day's drive from a city of at least 100,000 residents.[12] Odets' plays, which are virtually all plays of and about the city, therefore absorb and reflect the increasing concern with consumption that urbanization implied. As he noted in a *New York Times* article in 1940, the intensity of New York was a result of the economic forces that shaped it: "We take it completely for granted that people ride jammed up in the subway. But this is a business made thing, not a human thing. This city hasn't grown up. It's never grown up in relation to the human needs of its people—always in relation to a business transaction" (NYT, March 31, 1940).

As Odets recognized, more people than ever were able to behave as urban dwellers with access to the same goods and services; the new city restructured relationships on an economic rather than social basis. Within these cities, consumer culture was gaining at the expense of traditional community associations. For example, the increasing importance of chain grocery stores eventually eroded neighborhood associations, which bound people together in a social matrix.[13] The development of brand names further standardized the process of consumption; working-class consumers became increasingly acculturated to the idea that buying these machine-made goods meant full participation in American culture. In *Waiting for Lefty*, Odets wove this shift into an exploration of the economic pressures on his characters. For example, Edna comments bitterly that Joe's claim that "conditions" are responsible for their poverty will do her no good at "the A & P," one of the national chain stores, most of which refused to offer credit to consumers. The "stack of grapefruit" Edna longs for is tantalizingly out of reach.

Just as the Alger-Carnegie myth perpetuated the idea that success was universally achievable, advertisers attempted to show that all commodities were universally available. It was up to the consumers to choose the products—or images—they preferred. Such desires took individual forms; each person would invest products with talismanic properties particular to his or her own hopes. Furthermore, the social context of consumption determined how products were received. In 1930s working class families, for example, access to brand-name products was a way to eradicate class differences. At the same time, the use of certain commodities fostered a sense of working-class solidarity across racial and ethnic lines:

These workers were also consuming the same kinds of standardized products from the same chain stores instead of buying from local ethnic grocers; listening to the same national, commercial network radio . . . and watching the same movies in theatres that were now owned by the Hollywood studio chains.[14]

Thus, while all may have access to the same products, the perception of those products can vary from individual to individual and from class to class. In Odets, for example, a simple piece of fruit, with its Edenic implications, means something quite different to Moe in *Awake and Sing!* from its meaning of bourgeois respectability to Bessie Berger.

To be sure, industrialization appeared to be working somewhat, making goods faster and more cheaply, allowing more farmland to be cultivated with less labor. In fact, even in the devastating early years of the depression, a greater number of people enjoyed a higher standard of living than at any previous time in history.[15] Indeed, the success of a consumer culture requires a connection of the marketplace to a democratic mode of thought: "Modern advertising requires a concept of 'consumer' which is at once general and specific, just as democracy requires a concept of equal and individual state citizens."[16] Paradoxically, advertisers claimed to give respite from the alienation and anonymity of modern life by offering commodities enmeshed in the mass production system that produced the initial alienation.

Odets was aware that consumer culture offered substantial rewards for its participants, both in the satisfaction of bodily—the sickness that Edna hopes to prevent with citrus in *Waiting for Lefty*, for example—and of psychological desires. He understood implicitly that advertisers used images to promote products only because there was a prior desire to be stimulated, that people "became consumers through their own active adjustment to both the material and spiritual conditions of life in advanced capitalist society."[17] Of course, the participation of the working-class families Odets depicts in *Waiting for Lefty* and *Awake and Sing!* in consumer culture was evidence of their adoption of a new worldview. To view oneself as a *consumer* meant to buy into the utopian vision upon which the marketplace was built—to see, as Moe does, "paradise" in the orange.

Advertisers also began to graft a therapeutic element onto the advertising image, suggesting how "the product would contribute to the buyer's physical, psychic, or social well-being" or how "his well-being would be undermined if he failed to buy it."[18] The guilt of Puritan self-denial, however, stood in the way of the ideal of therapeutic transformation seized upon by advertisers, so the new emphasis on consumption was yoked to the old emphasis on production to ensure an ever-growing market for the commodities produced.[19] One was *supposed* to consume, to help the economy. For example, instead of maintaining stable wages and increasing leisure time—despite phenomenal increases in productivity, the forty-hour work week had remained the standard since Ford instituted it in the early 1930s and Roosevelt made it law in 1938—workers were encouraged to buy more products.[20]

Linking guilt to consumerism, Pasi Falk has suggested that the Edenic myth is the archetypal story of luxury:

[There is] something deeply paradoxical in the Edenic situation: no *lack* in terms of *needs* but a fundamental lack in terms of *desire*. . . . So, there is simultaneously a desire for transgression (breaking the Law) and a transgressive desire (to acquire the perfecting supplement). . . . There is no solution to the problem. . . . the forbidden fruit will always be eaten and the Pandora's box opened—and that is what human culture in the last instance is all about.[21]

Similarly, Odets' protagonists—especially Joe in *Golden Boy*, Ben in *Paradise Lost*, and Charlie in the post-Group play *The Big Knife*—obtain what they desire but feel that in doing so, they have passed beyond the boundaries of what is permissible. They have obtained the forbidden fruit. Indeed, Odets' characters are filled, always, with desire for what they are not; Joe asks, "do you think I like this feeling of no possessions?" (SP, 252). The lack is not always lack of material goods, but the desire is for what is prohibited, either by law or by a moral code such as the one articulated by Joe's father: "What ever you got ina your nature to do isa not foolish" (250).

By the time Odets was writing his Group plays, the natural world and the marketplace had become intertwined under the apparent benevolence of a Providence much like Adam Smith's "Invisible Hand." The shift toward a culture of consumption offered the promise of a new paradise to its participants, a utopia of personal and societal transformation that would eliminate want, end poverty, and satisfy desires still only half expressed. In this context, the market crash and subsequent economic devastation were not simply financial disasters but spiritual disasters as well; the Great Crash became a second Fall. Likewise, the images Odets returned to again and again of a conflicted consumer culture caught between plenty and scarcity, consumption and production, the machine and the natural world, are his attempt to reflect the vicissitudes of American life from the stage.

HOW MANY GRAPEFRUITS DOES IT TAKE TO STARVE A FAMILY?: *WAITING FOR LEFTY*'S EDENIC MYTH

Much of Odets' work, especially his obsession with images of production and consumption, is an attempt to theologize the banishment from America's Eden. As R. Baird Shuman notes, "A full understanding of Odets' plays is dependent upon the willingness of the audience to realize that the author is very often writing allegorically."[22] While Shuman overstates the case—Odets' symbols work as objects as well as ideas, and his characters are more individuals than types—other critics have recognized that Odets uses significant, often-repeated images to carry the theoretical weight of his plays. For example, Harold Cantor identifies "the polarities of water and sleep images versus procreative and redemptive images; animal images; images of boats, cars, ships and planes," while Gabriel Miller remarks that "fruit is an important symbol in Odets' work, combining allusions to life, growth, sexuality, and nourishment."[23] Indeed, as Odets repeatedly examines the Edenic myth, food, the commodity most directly tied to human needs—the most basic symbol of production *and* consumption—helps to shape a body of work in which both processes are examined in the lives of his characters.

The centrality of fruit as a symbol in Odets' work is evident from a story told about the writing of *Golden Boy* (subtitled, significantly, "An American Allegory" in an early draft):

"You hung me up for weeks," [Odets] later told [Luther Adler] with that remark, "again fruit?" Adler, noting that Poppa Bonaparte was a fruit vendor, had asked Odets, to no avail, why he was so occupied with fruit trees and fruit. Odets did not know, but he was obsessed with it—and temporarily hung all his doubts about the play on this question." (B-G, 477)

Odets' use of fruit imagery was more deliberate than Brenman-Gibson suggests; always unsure about his third acts, he was sensitive to any criticism, especially about a metaphor so important to a play deeply connected with the American Dream.

Odets filters the immigrant's dream of Edenic plenty through the modern marketplace. The human is articulated by what is consumed; the alienation of his characters from their world is measured by their ability or inability to eat, metaphorically and literally, the fruits of their labor. The abundance and fecundity of the natural world are suggested by allusions to citrus; biblical associations are implied by apples. However, these are not simply the symbols of a paradise forever lost. Rather, consumer capitalism is formulated in terms that are profoundly utopian and offers real satisfactions to its participants: "We should at the very least . . . regard consumer society not as a universal rip-off in which the masses are mindless dupes, but as a bribe—a transaction that offers concrete benefits, including, for most Americans, a degree of comfort unparalleled in history."[24] Odets measures the utopian vision—and the real rewards—of a "culture of abundance" against the human price that must be paid for it, keeping sympathy and compassion for those characters whose lives are the testing ground for the new culture. Thus, in *Awake and Sing!*, Moe Axelrod's dreams of a paradisiacal place where fruit falls into his mouth is not deliberately ironic, nor is Leo Gordon's speech at the end of *Paradise Lost*, in which he announces that "no fruit tree wears a lock and key" (SP, 230).

Waiting for Lefty is a loosely structured one-act piece in which the theatre is set up as the scene of a taxi driver's meeting, the audience becoming both observers and participants. In formulating the play's structure, Odets used the agitprop dramas to which he had been exposed but also borrowed from the minstrel show tradition the idea of an "interlocutor," a constant onstage presence commenting on the action as it takes place. Harry Fatt, the corrupt union boss, and the strike committee remain onstage during a series of vignettes set in the drivers' own lives, commenting on the action as it takes place. As in all agitprop plays, the action of *Waiting for Lefty* is simple: the assembled members—including actors planted in the audience—await the arrival of Lefty Costello, a strike organizer for the union. As they wait, the members of the driver's committee reveal how situations in their own lives forced them to become drivers and forced them to the point of striking. At the same time, Fatt (who also stands in for other capitalist characters, including the industrialist Fayette and the Broadway producer, Grady) attempts to persuade the drivers not to strike. At the end of the play, the crowd is roused to action when someone rushes in announcing that Lefty has been killed, ending the play with a rousing call to strike.

Even in his simple agitprop play, Odets uses fruit as a central image, an organizing principle for the play. Fruit is held up as an ambiguous symbol of goodness, serving as an indication of plenty promised to the characters but also as a measure of their success or failure in achieving that promise. In this sense, it is both the Garden itself and the flaming sword signifying expulsion from it. When Edna, one of the committee member's wives, tries to persuade her husband to strike, she points at their inability to buy fruit as an indication of their failure to achieve the dream promised by consumer culture:

Sure, I see it in the papers, how good orange juice is for kids. But damnit our kids get colds one on top of the other. They look like little ghosts. Betty never saw a grapefruit. I took her to the store last week and she pointed to a stack of grapefruits. "What's that!" she said. My God, Joe, this world is supposed to be for all of us! (SP, 10)

We hear in Edna's words an echo of the modern consumerist creed: improved productivity will lead to a democratization of goods. But democracy has failed Joe and Edna. They peer through the bars of the Garden gates at the plenitude always promised but rarely delivered.

Nevertheless, the dream of paradise remains largely unchallenged. The problem is not primarily that paradise is bought and sold but rather that Joe and Edna cannot buy it—in Roosevelt's terms, a faulty distribution of goods. Indeed, the parallels between Edna's complaint and Roosevelt's attempts to stimulate the moribund economy point to the increasing expectations of consumers in a developing culture of abundance. The modified Keynesian economics of the first two Roosevelt administrations attempted (with moderate success) to eliminate bread lines by putting vast sums of government money into consumers' hands. At one point in 1933-1934, the government was giving money directly or indirectly to one-sixth of the nation, an estimated 26 million people. Furthermore, publicity generated about the projects emphasized that their task was to spend.[25] As Roosevelt and the papers promised, consumption had its rewards, not just for the individual but for the economy as a whole; it was politically therapeutic to spend.

As the New Deal attempted to alleviate the suffering of the impoverished, it found itself caught up in the problem of defining what was necessary to a healthy life, a difficulty that was exacerbated by growing consumer expectations. No longer were people satisfied with sufficiency; even the most minimal budget suggested by the government included the price of an occasional treat and even a movie once a month for a family. There was a growing sense that everyone deserved "little consumerist pleasures."[26] In *Waiting for Lefty*, this shift is deftly captured in Florrie's first line to her brother: "I gotta right to have something out of life. I don't smoke, I don't drink. So if Sid wants to take me to a dance, I'll go" (SP, 17). Tellingly, the official economic category of "standard of living" was by this time measured by the ability to buy consumer goods.

For millions of consumers, commodities were made increasingly seductive; more importantly, consumers expectations grew with increasing purchasing power. In *Waiting for Lefty*, even the sober and hardworking Miller is dazzled by his boss' opulent office. It is something he never dreamed existed "outside the movies," an idea which Fayette immediately picks up on:

Fayette: Yes, I wonder if interior decorators and bathroom fixture people don't get all their ideas from Hollywood. Our country's extraordinary that way. Soap, cosmetics, electric refrigerators—just let Mrs. Consumer know they're used by the Crawfords and Garbos—more volume of sales than one plant can handle.
Miller: I'm afraid it isn't that easy, Mr. Fayette.
Fayette: No, you're right—gross exaggeration on my part. Competition is cut throat today. Markets up flush against a stone wall. The astronomers had better hurry—open Mars to trade expansion.
Miller: Or it will be just too bad! (SP, 13)

This exchange clearly identifies what is at stake; the dream is not easily realized, but there is no indication, even after Miller refuses to spy, that it is false. The fault lies in dishonest, inhumane business practices—making poison gas and war—rather than in the dream of abundance.

In *Waiting for Lefty*, it is, of course, Edna's real and justifiable concern for the health of the children that prompts her threats. But as early as 1900, Thorstein Veblen had noted that the line between need and want is often thin, that the same commodity can function *both* as necessity and as superfluity; goods with true useful value in daily life may at the same time possess "a secondary utility as evidence of relative ability to pay."[27] As one example, food is often substituted as a symbol for other hungers, social, psychological, and emotional. In Odets' plays, his characters eat not only from physical hunger, but from spiritual and emotional hunger as well. Thus, they are what they eat, but they also eat what they want to become.

Edna's use of fruit as a means for comparison to the bosses contains Odets' commentary on the complicated, multiple functions of the commodity in a consumer society. Their lack of fruit confirms their low social standing and endangers their health. Certainly, one cannot deny the truth of her grievance that sickness and hunger are real and tangible results of their poverty. In the depression, poverty and ill health went hand in hand: "Families with a fully employed member had 66 percent less illness than those of the unemployed."[28] But Edna's bitter accusations speak more than frustration at ill health. There is also a sense of deeply held utopian expectations couched in consumerist language: "Everything was going to be so ducky! A cottage by the waterfall, roses in Picardy. You're a four-star bust!" (SP 9). Her bitterness arises in part from the comparisons she makes between her family's condition and that of the bosses, in part from her comparison of their circumstances to consumerist dreams conditioned by the culture of abundance. For Edna, not only is "this world . . . supposed to be for all of us!" but full participation in that world means participation in consumer culture, the possession of democratic ideals by possessing their representative commodities.

While her desire for healthful food seeks to meet a basic human need, the dreams Edna expresses of the cottage by the waterfall are no more romanticized than the desires Sid and Florrie express for velvet gowns, brandy and soda, and "fifty or sixty" dozen roses, even the simple desire for a place to sit together: "Beyond the bare minimum of physical survival, all needs are socially determined and it is arbitrary to divide them into those that are genuine and those that are not."[29] For Edna, the lack of fruit and the reduction of her life to "slavery and sleepless nights" (SP, 12) underscore her felt deprivations in comparison to reasonable social expectations. Indeed, the idea of social comparison connects Veblen's theory to the practice of advertising. Consumers find themselves lacking in comparison to others; commodities are a way to bridge the gap. In *Waiting for Lefty*, the secret desires of "Mrs. Consumer" are Fayette's bread and butter; her envy of the movie stars opens markets for his products.

It is also impossible to ignore Edna's citation of the newspaper as an authority. She absorbs from the paper not only the scientific information that vitamin C in orange juice can prevent colds but also the idea that in a "good" society, citrus should be available to everyone. Still, her appeal to the newspaper, a central vehicle for advertising in the developing consumer culture, places her concerns in a more ambivalent light; in fact, any audience of *Waiting for Lefty* must already be suspicious of the papers since the corrupt union leader has cited the same papers as evidence not to strike.

Odets' consciousness of mass media's ability to both seduce and tantalize consumers gave him the ability to distill large cultural shifts into a kind of documentary drama—though *Waiting for Lefty* heightens and simplifies issues for dramatic effect. Across the country, Edna and Joe's personal dilemma of scarcity amid abundance was repeated on a scale never before seen. The newspapers that offered inexpensive, mass-produced furniture to the working class on the installment plan also carried countless stories of evictions. The papers that ran exotic travel advertisements and promised readers a world full of easily available clothing, food, and commodities carried story after story about the government-sponsored destruction of agricultural "surplus" to hungry readers in 1933—millions of acres of cotton were destroyed, millions of pigs slaughtered to keep farm prices from dropping further. As Secretary of Agriculture Henry Wallace noted, this paradox was built into capitalism. Production beyond the capacity of the marketplace was useless to the system; only when it was tied to consumer's ability to buy commodities could such production signify a true culture of abundance. In *Waiting for Lefty*, a certain knowledge that plenty existed, coupled with bitter personal experience of scarcity, gave utopia a bitter taste; banishment from the Garden meant something only because the Garden seemed real and possible in the first place.

Waiting for Lefty was more than a bitter condemnation; it was a militant call to create a new world. The Stenographer in the "The Young Actor" scene quotes Revelation (21:1): "And I saw a new earth and a new heaven; for the first earth and the first heaven were passed away; and there was no more sea."[30] But as a number of critics have noted, this call to political action is more general than was standard in agitprop plays: "*Waiting for Lefty* says a great deal less about the actual taxi strike of 1934 than it does, by implication, about the general labor situation at the time."[31] Echoing Clurman's description of its opening night, Gabriel Miller suggest that the aim of Odets' play, in contrast to other agitprops, was more symbolic than specifically political: "*Lefty* is agitprop drama that resists identification with any specific time-bound problem."[32] Indeed, Odets' depiction of a strike that had taken place a year before made *Waiting for Lefty* different; it did not call for specific future political action as many did. For example, a piece called *Dimitroff*, written by Group members Art Smith and Elia Kazan, called for the release of specific political prisoners in Germany.

If vague, the call for action at the end of *Waiting for Lefty* is nevertheless insistent. Odets is not interested in the taxi strike as a particular labor action but rather as a symbol of protest against a system that denies abundance to many of its participants. As he admitted in an interview later in his life, the final decision to strike is only a local objective: "It is not enough to go out on strike and ask for better wages; it is much better to go out on strike and say 'This is a *beginning*.' . . . It will give you the chance, in a democracy, to find your place, to assume your place and be responsible for your growth and continued welfare and happiness in that place."[33] Odets' play is not "time-bound" because it calls for specific political action but rather because it could not have been written outside of a historical moment that juxtaposed the scarcity of the depression with the abundance of unprecedented production capacity—the whole play enacts what Sid calls "the 1935 blues."

At the end of the play, then, Keller's strike call is not simply for better working conditions but for a paradisiacal "new world," what Clurman called a "strike for greater dignity, strike for a bolder humanity, strike for the full stature of man" (TFY, 148). Certainly, the play does articulate the major concerns of the radical left—war, the increasing alienation of workers, poverty, and the uneven distribution of wealth—characterized with striking accuracy and economy. Furthermore, solutions to those problems are often couched in terms borrowed from Communist doctrine: the Stenographer tells the actor to read the *Communist Manifesto*, equating it with a loaf of bread (each costs a dime), Sid gives a long, personalized explanation of the economic basis of war, and Keller uses the Communist salute in his strike call. Nevertheless, what really separates *Waiting for Lefty* from other agitprops is its attempt to reconcile the material and physical desires of the characters with their sufferings. The characters suffer the indignities that come with poverty: Edna says, "[Money] is the subject, the EXACT SUBJECT! Your boss makes this subject. . . . He's giving your kids that fancy disease called the rickets. He's making a jellyfish outa you and putting wrinkles in my face" (SP, 12). Keller's glass eye is a reminder of horrible factory conditions; the actor's dilemma indirectly reflects Odets' own experiences as a would-be Broadway actor.

On the other hand, Odets' protagonists are more ambivalent about their position in society, indeed about their dreams, than their radical rhetoric suggests. Odets is also more explicit about his utopian beliefs, however romanticized, than other agitprops of the period. The Young Actor wants to get his foot in the Broadway door; like Odets as a young actor, he believes in the dream. Florrie expresses desires that would delight advertisers: "Don't you see I want something else out of life? Sure, I want romance, love, babies. I want everything in life I can get" (18). The culmination of the play, Keller's rousing speech, goads the drivers to action with both a condemnation of the current situation and a challenge to create the new world: "Tear down the slaughter house of our old lives! Let freedom really ring" (30). After Lefty is found dead, Keller explodes:

HELLO AMERICA! HELLO. WE'RE STORMBIRDS OF THE WORKING-CLASS. WORKERS OF THE WORLD. . . . OUR BONES AND BLOOD! And when we die they'll know what we did to make a new world. Christ, cut us up into little pieces. We'll die for what is right! put fruit trees where our ashes are! (31)

Keller's use of the fruit tree as a symbol for the longed-for new world is structurally and culturally significant, for it ties into Edna's desire for fruit as well as tapping into the utopian images inherent in Communist ideology.

Keller's willingness to sacrifice his body refigures into political action the Christian ideal of martyrdom. He acknowledges that the battle is fought on the battleground of the body; his "bones and blood" speech identifies the violence that follows from class conflict, echoing the remark made by Joe at the beginning that the cabbies are "the black and blue boys" (7). It demonstrates, too, that alienation, in addition to the psychological, has a demonstrable physical component manifesting itself in hunger, in physical pain, in sickness. But while the play places the blame squarely on the shoulders of a corrupt system, it retains at the same time the utopian vision of health and fullness upon which consumer capitalism was predicated, a utopian vision not unique to either a Christian or a Marxist position. Rather, it was also the way in which the developing consumer culture came to express itself. In the play, the topics of concern are hot meals, a place to sit with your beloved, and citrus fruit as much as specific and sweeping political action. For every Doc Benjamin who wants to work in socialized medicine, there is a Florrie who simply wants to have babies and to get everything she can; for every Miller who wants to work with an important chemist, there is an Edna who looks for her cottage by the waterfall.

What is at stake in much of *Waiting for Lefty* is increased material comfort: Odets recognizes that the testing ground of the new marketplace is the human body. Likewise, Keller's willingness to be cut into little pieces is more ironic in the light of Edna's withering remark to Joe that "any hackie that won't fight, let them all be ground to hamburger! . . . Only they don't grind me to little pieces. I got different plans" (11). So Keller's final plea for a strike, though moving and rhetorically powerful, is complicated by the ambivalent nature of the imagery it employs. The paradise Keller imagines is the same one that Edna reads about in the papers, full of fruit trees, but the only way to enter its gates is to sacrifice oneself for the material pleasures it promises, to be cut into little pieces. Ultimately, Odets' fiery political protest against the economic conditions of the depression cannot escape a lingering fascination with the developing consumer culture, which had adopted the utopian vision for its own. Odets' use of fruit imagery as a whole follows much the same pattern; it suggests a utopia, but a utopia caught between physical necessity and consumer desire.

"EVER SEEN ORANGES GROW? I KNOW A CERTAIN PLACE—": *AWAKE AND SING!*

Set in a lower-middle-class Jewish home in the Bronx—the Bergers live on Longwood Avenue, one of the streets where Odets lived as a child—Odets characterized his second play, *Awake and Sing!*, as a "struggle for life amid petty conditions." The play is firmly grounded in the Jewish experience of Odets' youth. Though Strasberg had criticized its ethnic limitations, the play nevertheless captured in compelling theatrical language the dreams and disappointments of an entire generation of immigrants. Alfred Kazin remarked that his experience of the play confirmed Odets' ability to speak for those seeking a better life in America:

Sitting in the Belasco, watching my mother and father and uncles and aunts occupying the stage in *Awake and Sing* by as much right as if they were Hamlet or King Lear, I understood at last. It was all one, as I had always known. Art and truth and hope could yet come together.[34]

In the play, the Berger family struggles to keep dreams of a better life alive. Ralph and his father, Myron, work in the depressed clothing business while the family matriarch, Bessie, struggles to maintain middle-class appearances and to keep Ralph from marrying an orphan girl. Jacob, Bessie's Socialist father, urges Ralph to break away from familial obligations and make it so "life isn't printed on dollar bills." But the claims of family are powerful, especially after the Bergers' daughter, Hennie, gets pregnant. Bessie arranges a marriage with the newly immigrated Sam Feinshreiber. Ultimately, Jacob sacrifices himself for Ralph's sake, deliberately falling off a roof at the end of the second act to give Ralph insurance money. In the third act, however, Ralph renounces the money, telling Bessie, "life's different in my head" (97). The play ends with his vow to work for Jacob's Socialist dream. Hennie, likewise, escapes Bessie's domination, leaving with the Berger's boarder, Moe Axelrod, for Cuba.

In the full-length plays that followed *Waiting for Lefty*, especially *Awake and Sing!*, *Paradise Lost*, and *Rocket to the Moon*, Odets remained ambivalent about the new abundance, intimating that the utopian visions with which he ends a number of his plays are at odds with the daily functioning of the marketplace. The ending of *Awake and Sing!*, for example, has been criticized as too hopeful for what has gone before, Hennie's abandonment of her child as evidence that the paradise she seeks with Moe is tainted by self-absorption, Ralph's awakening as implausible. John Howard Lawson denied that Odets had been rigorous enough in his analysis of social or economic conditions, calling the ending "an act of faith. It is not conflict, but the denial of conflict."[35] Odets maintained that people were upset by the implications of the ending rather than its dramaturgical flaws and would hold to this belief throughout his lifetime: "Young people can go through an experience and have their eyes opened, and determine from it to live in a different way."[36] The goal of *Awake and Sing!* was to show—as the Group had claimed when they changed the ending of Paul Green's *The House of Connelly*—that petty conditions and historical traps can be overcome, that life doesn't have to be printed on dollar bills.

If *Waiting for Lefty* took its structure from agitprop and the minstrel show, *Awake and Sing!* is firmly grounded in the American tradition of realism. Though influenced early by Ibsen and Shaw—and later by Strindberg and Chekhov—Odets' dramaturgy was as much seasoned by the stock companies with which he had apprenticed as it was by modern European theatre. Indeed, on the surface, it is sometimes difficult to characterize Odets' drama compared to that of his contemporaries. His plots are filled with standard devices of the well-made play: secret insurance payments, sudden revelations, family misfortunes, marital infidelities. The scope of his plays is sometimes small: *Awake and Sing!* never leaves the Berger living room, and *Rocket to the Moon* never leaves Ben Stark's dental office. Nor is Odets' dramatic vision particularly experimental. He never set out, as some of his contemporaries did, to shape a new American dramatic form. O'Neill tried a new form with virtually every new play; Susan Glaspell and Elmer Rice, among others, had experimented with expressionism; in *Processional* and other plays, Lawson had attempted to free drama into the rhythms of jazz; Maxwell Anderson reclaimed verse for the American stage in a series of historical dramas and one contemporary tragedy, *Winterset*; in the late 1930s and early 1940s, Thornton Wilder expanded his vision of drama into the cosmic, openly scorning the urban messiness of Odets' family dramas.

Odets' plays, though grounded in realism, nevertheless appeared as a new phenomenon in American theatre. In a world where "economics comes down like a ton of coal on the head" (SP, 71), Odets felt a need to give voice to the dispossessed and half-asleep, what he would call in *The Big Knife*, "the lonely junked people of our world" (57). The form of his plays, even their uncertain endings, therefore follow from his uncertain, yet sympathetic, reading of the world. *Paradise Lost*, for example, which baffled critics with its seemingly meandering plotline, its overdetermined symbolism (one of the characters, interested in banking, is dying of sleeping sickness; another capitalist is sexually impotent), and its strange non sequiturs, was Odets' attempt to encompass the whole of American experience into a play. While some saw the lack of structure in *Paradise Lost* as evidence of poorly digested Chekhovian influence, the play operates, as do most of Odets' later plays, by projecting romantic lyricism, a largeness of vision borrowed from Hugo and Whitman, into ordinary lives. His characters face deep and important struggles, but those struggles are couched in ordinary terms; they seek noble ends—connection, love, usefulness—but such goals are always manifested in simple, personal terms; they live in the objects that surround them.

Unlike the characters of O'Neill who, from *Beyond the Horizon* onward, seek to transcend the physical world with all its vicissitudes, Odets' characters take strength from it. It is their world to make better—for everyone. Thus, Odets' political and human sympathies, as well as his stock training and pressures from the Group, led him away from pursuing structural innovation the way O'Neill, Anderson, and other contemporaries had. Odets' plays, nevertheless, were innovative in their use of language, his dialogue fresher, more human than Anderson's heightened verse, more accurate and lyrical than O'Neill's attempts at rough common speech. O'Neill, Anderson, and Wilder looked to express big themes, to measure human existence against the backdrop of fate and eternity. Odets looked, on the other hand, to the smallness of "life amid petty conditions" in order to offer a vision of the world rooted in human connection. The sometimes overwrought speech (e.g., Sid's "Christ, baby, I get like thunder in my chest when we're together" in *Waiting for Lefty*) of Odets' uneducated characters—for there are no scholars in Odets plays, only yearners and romantics, amateur philosophers whose felt experience guides them toward their goals—is a verbal manifestation of frustrated hope. His characters want to break out, make a connection, talk their way into their lyrical vision; the dialogue works because the plays and their characters seek to transcend their world with language rooted in it.

Indeed, realism in a play like *Awake and Sing!* is not just a style of production but takes full manifestation in the material objects surrounding the Bergers. Food is everywhere in the play, carrying strong, often conflicting connotations: escape, salvation, fertility, success, or, on the other hand, failed idealism, debased consumption, alienation, and an uncritical complicity in the marketplace. In *Awake and Sing!* there are apples, halvah, duck, pastrami, chocolates, cake, chopped liver, and bread and jam onstage, as well as references to oranges, tangerines, chop suey, pickles, eggs, knishes, tea, coconuts, peaches and cream, raspberry jelly, and champagne—usually as figures of speech referring to economic matters. The play opens with the family at supper, another dinner is the setting for all of act 2, and there is a feast set out in act 3 for Jacob's funeral, prompting the Group's property man, Moe Jacobs, to remark to a *Herald-Tribune* reporter that "for him the play was 'one long meal'" (RLD, 279-280).

Awake and Sing! uses food and other consumer goods—such as the pair of "black and white shoes" Ralph longs for—to indicate personal and social ideologies, making even more explicit the problems of developing consumerism that Odets had explored in *Waiting for Lefty*. At the very beginning of the play, Bessie pinpoints the discrepancy between Ralph's desires and the family's needs: "You mean we shouldn't have food in the house, but you'll make a jig on the street corner?" (SP, 41). Ralph promptly turns the eating image on its head, characterizing his life as sitting around "with the blues and mud in your mouth" (SP, 42). Food is the most basic form of idealism, but an idealism that is configured differently for each of the characters. For example, when Sam gives Hennie a gift of candy, she mocks its cheapness: "Loft's weekend special, two for thirty-nine" (44). The commodity begins to unmoor from any fixed meaning in the culture and becomes associated with individual desires in different ways. She realizes that "commodities are not straightforward 'objects' but are rather progressively more unstable, temporary collections of objective and imputed characteristics" and chooses the meaning of the commodity in the light of personal desire.[37]

In fact, all the characters in *Awake and Sing!* invest their consumption with the ideological power of an entire belief system. Drawing on his memories of the food in his Aunt Esther and Uncle Israel's kitchen, dinnertime at the Bergers carries deep ideological meanings of home and family. For Bessie, the Sunday dinner she cooks in act 2 serves as an indication that the family is "respectable"—even though she admits that "I never saw conditions should be so bad" (61). Likewise, she uses invitations to the supper table to include or exclude people from the family circle. When Hennie announces her pregnancy, Bessie declares that the family meal will serve as a vehicle to get Sam to marry Hennie: "He'll come tomorrow night for supper. By Saturday they're engaged" (55). Conversely, Ralph's girl, Blanche, is excluded from the family by being excluded from meals.

Bessie's attempts to control the household by controlling consumption come into conflict with the alternative interpretations of consumption held by Ralph and Hennie, who use food as a symbol of a more romanticized utopia. The younger generation is more in tune with the promises of a consumer culture than the older; Bessie may be "naively delighted" (43) by Sam's gift of chocolates, but Hennie is able to recontextualize the romantic ideology Bessie (and Sam) assume is invested in the chocolates. Similarly, their boarder, Moe Axelrod, surrounds his food choices with a symbolic matrix that, while cynically expressed, is far more idealistic than Bessie's bourgeois practicality. To him, the lack of oranges indicates not only the tight economy but a sort of moral and social failure indicated by lack of participation in the consumer utopia: "No oranges, huh?—what a dump!" (49).

In *Awake and Sing!*, the most devastating cost to the participants in a consumer culture is a loss of idealism: what is promised is seldom delivered. Myron, a new Adam, wanders onstage at the end of the play, remarking to no one in particular, "No fruit in the house lately. Just a lone apple. Must be something wrong with me—I say I won't eat but I eat" (100). Here, the fall from the Edenic promise of abundance seems complete and irrevocable. Myron, beaten and cowed, shuffles around the house, quoting useless information from the paper, hoping to win the lottery, seeking refuge in the past. Abundance is clearly out of place in Myron's world; the only reward for his lifetime of hard work is the proverbial apple, which indicates banishment from the Garden.

Nevertheless, the conviction that America had been betrayed by the dream of material success is never without an optimistic counterpart in Odets' early plays. At the end of *Awake and Sing!*, Moe seduces Hennie with a utopian vision of "a certain place where it's moonlight and roses. We'll lay down, count stars. Hear the big ocean making noise. You lay under the trees. Champagne flows like—" (98). It is significant that Moe figures such an escape in consumerist terms; his vision is hedonistic and transformative. Indeed, one hears in lines to Hennie like "There's one life to live! Live it" and "Make a break or spend the rest of your life in a coffin!" (99) the kind of exhortations to personal transformation advertisers connected with the consumer goods. To buy a product—in this case, a "[t]en day luxury cruise to Havana" or "ritzy hotels, frenchie soap, champagne" (68)—is to buy a chance at paradise. Happiness is no longer measured by productivity but by consumption.

Moe stakes his future on the belief that redemption is possible: "Paradise, you're on a big boat headed south. No more pins and needles in your heart, no snake juice squirted in your arm. The whole world's green grass, and when you cry it's because you're happy" (99). He attempts to extricate the vision of utopia offered by consumer culture from the ideologies of the Calvinist work ethic, to enter the Garden on his own terms. Of course, critics have suggested that Moe and Hennie's leaving does not really change anything, that they are guided by dubious motives and act irresponsibly toward Hennie's baby. But even if valid, such objections ignore the profoundly utopian language in which Odets drapes their escape. Their leaving is an act of faith far more than one of reason; it is a compromise, a wager, or as Moe says, "one thing to get another" (100).

Even more idealistic than Moe and Hennie, Ralph applauds their decision to leave because he believes it mirrors his own plan to "fix it so life won't be printed on dollar bills" (97). He views their escape as an individual manifestation of his larger goal. Of course, the juxtaposition of his Socialist vision with the couple's consumerist paradise suggests underlying moral differences between the two visions of paradise. Nevertheless, Moe's dream is made to appear quite similar to Jacob's—and therefore to Ralph's—even if Moe's is more explicitly identified with individual consumption than social change. He asks Jacob early on, "Ever see oranges grow? I know a certain place— One summer I laid under a tree and let them fall right in my mouth" (50). Ultimately, Moe and Hennie's escape is idealistic and future-oriented. Even his nickname for her, "Paradise," is both ironic and earnestly romantic.

Others in the play also attempt to escape the confines of a narrow life. Jacob repeatedly seeks refuge in his records, a refuge tinged with the sadness of a lost idealism. Amid the Berger struggles, Jacob maintains his fervent, sentimental idealism, though as Odets notes in his character description he has "no power to turn idealism to action" (38). Jacob's fondness for his records—Caruso's recording of *O Paradiso* especially—indicates concretely the gap between the promised "paradise on earth!" (50) of which Caruso sings and the household where, as he says, "economics comes down like a ton of coal on the head" (71). He is forced in act 1, and again in act 2 to withdraw into the dreams his records symbolize, a withdrawal very similar to Myron's escape to the past. Indeed, Jacob disappears so often into his room that his music becomes a joke around the house.[38]

Jacob's dreams are fragile partly because they are invested in commodities that can be and are—in the climactic moment of the play—destroyed. The records' relationship to paradise is equivocal; Moe's and Bessie's mockery underscores the passivity of Jacob's utopian vision. However, the ideals Jacob finds in his albums are not intended by Odets as inherently ironic. Jacob's rhetoric is strong and sharp throughout the first two acts. Still, the fiery power of such lines like his remarks to Bessie "Marx said it—abolish such families!" (55) and "In this boy's life a Red Sea will happen again. I see it!" (72), is greatly tempered by his admission to Ralph that he only talked:

Look on me and learn what to do, boychick. Here sits an old man polishing tools. You think maybe I'll use them again! Look on this failure and see for seventy years he talked, with good ideas but only in his head. . . . you should act. Not like me. A man who had golden opportunities but drank instead a glass tea. (77-78)

Jacob uses his records much the same way he uses Ralph: as a shield against personal failure. If Ralph can, as Jacob says, "graduate from my university," his inaction will be erased by the action of his grandson, his passive consumption—of tea, of music, of books—transformed into political action.

Because *Awake and Sing!* invests material objects with idealism, the status of Jacob's records is an indication of Odets' lingering uncertainty regarding the marketplace. Certainly, it is common for human beings to place talismanic importance in a consumer good, especially in response to a failure of idealism. They become a place of refuge, a dream: "Sometimes it is not a glorious past that becomes the location of unfulfilled ideals but a glorious future. . . . [They are] temporal locations in which in which ideals can find protection from the possibility of contradiction."[39] Like Myron's longing for the days of Teddy Roosevelt, Jacob's imagination of a future "new world" is dislocated from the present reality in order to protect the fragile possibility of those ideals.

Jacob's inability to escape the marketplace is an indication of how clearly Odets recognized its pervasiveness in the daily lives of his characters. The physical presence of capitalism is an indisputable fact, for it is invested in the countless physical objects surrounding them. Thus, Morty and Bessie can point directly to the food on the table as evidence that they are well-off, while Jacob can cling only to a vague idealism that is itself invested in material objects. Morty tells his father, "Without a rich man, you don't have a roof over your head. You don't know it?" (72). As in *Waiting for Lefty*, the consumer culture in *Awake and Sing!* fights its battles on the physical as well as the ideological plane. Indeed, it is precisely because of this emotional and ideological investment in material goods that Bessie's violent smashing of the albums seems even more cruel and grotesque to an audience. The records are the last vestige of Jacob's idealism; her act symbolically shatters any utopia outside of consumer capitalism.

Awake and Sing! is ultimately Ralph's play, however. His decision to work to "fix it so life won't be printed on dollar bills" (97) is the culmination of Odets' search for a way out of petty conditions. Such a conviction—an untainted inheritance from Jacob's Marxist idealism that is starkly contrasted with the tainted inheritance, the insurance money—is an attempt not only to overcome the life that surrounds him but to step outside the marketplace in a way quite different from that of Moe and Hennie. His rejection of the insurance money is a rejection of Jacob's complicity in the marketplace; one of the precipitating events of Jacob's suicide is Ralph's disappointment in discovering that Jacob knew Bessie had tricked Sam into marrying Hennie.

The shift in Ralph's beliefs does not come suddenly at the very end of the play but rather is a gradual drift away from personal desires toward the kind of idealism Jacob espouses. In act 1, Ralph complains, "[A]ll my life I want a pair of black and white shoes and can't get them. It's crazy!" (42) but by act 2 admits that "All right, I can't get my teeth fixed. All right, that a new suit's like trying to buy the Chrysler building. You never in your life bought me a pair of skates even—things I died for when I was a kid. I don't care about that stuff, see" (66). Finally, in his last exchange with Bessie, he comes to Jacob's realization of the gap between real and the ideal, while maintaining the ability to translate the ideal into action that Jacob had lost:

Bessie: Ralphie, I worked too hard all my years to be treated like dirt. . . . Summer shoes you didn't have, skates you never had, but I bought a new dress every week. A lover I kept—Mr. Gigolo! . . . If I didn't worry about the family who would? On the calendar it's a different place, but here without the dollar you don't look the world in the eye. Talk from now until next year—this is life in America.
Ralph: Then it's wrong. It don't make sense. If life made you this way, then it's wrong! . . . life's different in my head! (95)

Ralph's idealism, unlike Moe's, is predicated on a movement *away* from consumer culture. Because life is different in his head, he believes by the end of the play that it is possible to gain a form of paradise without being buried by material goods: "Once upon a time I thought I'd drown to death in bolts of silk and velour. But I grew up these last few weeks. Jake said a lot" (96). It is in the contrast between these two visions of paradise, both depicted sympathetically in *Awake and Sing!*, that Odets demonstrates ongoing ambivalence about the culture of abundance. Moe and Hennie's consumerist utopia and Ralph's Marxist vision are intimately connected through images of fruit and other commodities, but the methods used to achieve them are diametrically opposed.

In most of Odets' Group plays, commodities are seen as vehicles for utopian desires; the successes of the culture of abundance are as central as the failures. If the system is, as Moe characterizes it, "all a racket—from horse racing down. Marriage, politics, big business—everybody plays cops and robbers," the price for participation is a surrender of idealism (71). But through Ralph's conversion at the end of the play and the similarity between Moe's consumer paradise and Jacob's Marx-

ist utopia, Odets offers hope for the new marketplace. Certain that commodity culture had already permanently transformed American life, Odets wanted to demonstrate in *Awake and Sing!* what the human costs of such a shift would be. The marketplace was not necessarily evil; the problem lay, rather, in the chances of full
participation without being smothered in goods as Ralph fears, devoured (Bessie
imagines that her life has been "sucked away" [85]), or becoming a commodity
oneself.

THE SWEET SMELL OF DECAY: *PARADISE LOST*

If *Awake and Sing!* was Odets' most fully articulated analysis of the struggle
for life amid petty conditions, *Paradise Lost* took a new direction; the image of a
disappearing Eden is used as a symbol for the disillusioned middle class. Though
Clurman noted, "The people of *Paradise Lost* are on a much higher plane of consciousness and their concern with the physical details of life are considerably less"
(B-G, 387), the plays contain parallels. Clara Gordon, a de-Jewishized Bessie Berger, controls the household by controlling food; she answers almost any question or
challenge with her tag line, "take a piece of fruit." As in *Awake and Sing!*, the tension within *Paradise Lost* heightens as the promise of abundance is undercut by a
gradual acknowledgment that plenty is not the necessary result of living in a productive world. Paul, a homeless man who arrives at the end of the play, sums up
Odets' lesson to the middle class: "You had a sorta little paradise here. Now you
lost the paradise. That should teach you something. But no! You ain't awake yet.
. . . You have been took like a bulldog takes a pussy cat! Finished!" (229). The violence of his simile marks the shift toward a natural world predicated upon violence,
a world where the consumers become the consumed.

The grim awakening of the Gordons is the dramatic action of *Paradise Lost*.
But despite his warning to the self-satisfied, Odets also offers a hopeful ending, in
which Leo Gordon responds to Paul by imagining a new Eden:

No! There is more to life than this! Everything he said is true, but there is more. That was the
past, but there is a future. . . . Truly, truly, the past was a dream. But this is real! . . . Oh, yes,
I tell you the whole world is for men to possess. Heartbreak and terror are not the heritage of
mankind! The world is beautiful. No fruit tree wears a lock and key. (229-30)

This ending, even more than Keller's exhortation in *Waiting for Lefty*, is idealized
in its vision of a "new world." Unlike Keller's clear acknowledgment that a physical sacrifice would be necessary, Leo's vision offers no indication of how to
achieve his utopia. His speech does not call for political action but looks to an
idealized future for redemption of present errors.

As they had with ending of *Awake and Sing!*, many critics felt the hopeful end
of *Paradise Lost* did not follow logically from the devastation that preceded it (Ben
Gordon is gunned down during a robbery; Julie, the other son, is dying of sleeping
sickness; their daughter Pearl has retreated to her room; Leo's partner has embez-
zled funds from the business, costing the Gordons both home and business). Michael Mendelsohn argues that "[it is] perhaps the most preposterous thing Odets

ever wrote. . . . it requires an impossible [suspension of disbelief] to accept it from
Leo Gordon."[40] Odets himself was open to the accusation that the ending was
tacked on to support a leftist ideology. Still, the fervent hope that someday paradise
would be regained is in fact what animates much of Odets' paradise imagery; perhaps such a vision is so vague in *Paradise Lost* because even by the mid-1930s it
was virtually impossible to imagine American culture outside of a consumer ideology.

If images of fruit in plays like *Waiting for Lefty* or *Awake and Sing!* are used to
indicate the idealized abundance of a free marketplace, the irony remains that it is
the temptation of fruit that ultimately evicts its residents from the Garden, for two
reasons. First, natural bounty becomes enmeshed in the food chain and in the vicissitudes of the marketplace; people must find a way to afford the food they need for
survival. Second, on a more abstract level, the mythology of the Garden is complicated by the ritual of subservience and self-destruction that gains access to it. Odets
suggests that to be able to consume freely requires one to sell oneself, either figuratively (e.g., Kewpie in *Paradise Lost*) or quite literally (Charlie Castle in *The Big
Knife*). Ideologically and practically, then, consumption requires sacrifice because it
requires participation in the marketplace.

In the earlier plays, food and fruit are relative goods; a wish for consumer objects such as Ralph's black and white shoes, though perhaps misguided, is benign.
But from *Paradise Lost* onward, Odets couples pleasant images of abundance with
darker ones; Eden fills with menace. Juxtaposing healthy and unhealthy images of
production, Odets suggests that the dream of plenty is out of reach. One of the
most powerful speeches in *Paradise Lost* shows the failure of abundance in the
depression reflected destruction of American idealism:

The bellyrobbers have taken clothes from our backs. We slept in subway toilets here. In Arkansas we picked fruit. I followed the crops north and dreamed of a warmer sun. We lived on
and hoped. We lived on garbage dumps. Two of us found canned prunes, ate them and were
poisoned for weeks. One died. Now I can't die. . . . Living on a boat as a night watchman,
tied to shore, not here nor there! The American jitters! Idealism! (*Punches himself violently*)
There's for idealism! (191)

Here Pike, the radical voice of the play, offers a striking contrast to the romantic
Emersonian vision offered by Leo Gordon at the end of the play. Leo's speech is
vague and visionary; Pike's specific and condemnatory. Fruit is no longer the product of a teeming natural world brought under benevolent control by technology but
a dangerous necessity, poisoned by the technology that cans it and the "bellyrobbers" who offer it for sale. Pike is excluded from the products of his labor; he feeds
off the waste products of industrialization.[41]

Though at times Pike seems as passive as the play's other characters, he has a
clearer vision of what is happening. He is merely "waiting for a whole world to
hang itself. Enough rope inchin' up to strangle all of us! In the meantime, look for
tough minded people" (198). There is scarcely in his worldview a romanticized
vision such as exists for Leo, Jacob, Ralph, Keller, or even Edna, a sense that the
fruits of labor can be better distributed, that plenty is available for all. Rather, Pike
is a constant reminder of a system that has betrayed the promise of abundance, in-

deed, the promises of democracy as a whole. A representative of American political idealism—his family has fought every war since the Revolution—Pike mocks the modern politician Foley, who theorizes that many people are tired because they don't get enough alkaline in their diets. Pike restates the contrast between acid and alkaline as a contrast between abundance and scarcity: "This is about the richest city in the world. A person starves to death in it every other day. Not enough alkaline. That's what it means! Hunger and degradation—eighty-twenty" (168).

Pike is surely one of the most complex characters in the play, "an expression of Odets' own amalgam of romanticism and radicalism."[42] More realist than romantic, he draws pictures of starving men and compiles statistics about unemployment, poverty, and disillusionment—an ongoing documentation of the failure of abundance. He also questions Clara's assertion, "Rich and poor—it's a natural condition" by recontextualizing the word "natural." He tells Clara, "It *is not natural* for men to starve while means to produce food are close at hand" (166). Like the destruction of agricultural overproduction while millions went hungry, Pike recognizes the bitter paradox of a culture of abundance in which many are unable to consume.

Pike does not participate deeply in the consumer world surrounding the Gordons. He tends furnaces and plays chess with the Gordons' son Julie. The coat the Gordons gave him is the first one he's owned in four years. By virtue of his difficult life (he lost his two sons in World War I), Pike realizes better than any other character the toll that participation in a market economy takes on individual lives. An exchange with Pearl near the beginning of the second act emphasizes the personal nature of the depression for Odets' characters, its effects even on those who imagine themselves immune:

Pearl: I'm homesick all the time. For what?
Pike: No one talks about the depression of the modern man's spirit, of his inability to live a full and human life.
Pearl: What?
Pike: I'm sayin' the smell of decay may sometimes be a sweet smell. There she is alone in her room with the piano—the white keys banked up like lilies and she suckin' at her own breast.
Pearl: You must be crazy! What are you talking about?
Pike: You. Your brother–
Pearl: Yes, I know. You think radical ideas will save us all. Just give the world its pound of bread! For my part, I discovered long ago the comic aspects of this so-called class war.
Pike: Yes, sixteen million unemployed is a pretty comic situation.
Pearl: Who cares about sixteen million? I'm interested in myself!
Pike: Let's *take* yourself. Where's your boy friend?
Pearl: Mind your business!
Pike: You liar and traitor to your own heart's story! (*suddenly whirling on Pearl, and gripping her by the arms*) You! Lay awake dreamin' at night. Don't you know it ain't comin', that land of your dreams, unless you work for it?.
Pike: I'm not sex starved, do you hear? I'm not! (199)

In this exchange, Odets crystallizes the chief concerns of *Paradise Lost*: the sterility and overweening self-absorption of the middle class, the failure of American idealism, the psychic and physical toll on ordinary people trying to participate in the dream.

In Odets, the physical bounty of the American Eden is reconstituted on a human scale, suggesting that the new economy depends upon people offering their bodies for the sake of production. Thus, Pike's vision of Pearl feeding on herself is one more indication of the violence outside. Disappointed in love, unwilling to participate in the "class war" she sees as comic, Pearl escapes (as Jacob does in *Awake and Sing!*) by playing her piano and hiding in her room. As Pike suggests, however, no rewards exist for those who do not participate in the marketplace. The "smell of decay" is the stench of rotting fruit, the waste of life-giving abundance. At the end of the play, when her "whole life," the piano, is sold like the rest of the Gordon's furniture, Pearl is devastated, isolated, wasted (222). Because she refuses to let herself be consumed, she dies on the vine.

Pearl's situation identifies another metaphorical complex woven into Odets' plays concerning the power of the female body as a source of production. As they were in advertising and Odets' personal life, in the plays women are directly identified with both the creation of natural abundance and the consumption of material goods. Pearl's assertion that she's not sex-starved seems almost a non sequitur until we recognize that in Odets, the biological acts of reproduction are intimately connected with the production and consumption of consumer goods. The struggle for a "pound of bread" is therefore transmuted into a larger struggle: for dreams, for love, for sex, for babies, for a full human life. Where others are starving, Pearl is "sex-starved"; instead of feeding off the abundance of Mother Nature, she lies there "sucking at her own breast," yearning for a world that no longer exists.

Odets' persistent references to female bodies as consumable goods are as much a product of misogyny as they are an examination of the paradise myth in the depression. Indeed, Brenman-Gibson's analysis of Odets' attitude toward women repeatedly emphasizes the nurturing possibilities he saw in the various women in his life. He looked to them, figuratively, to feed him, noting at one point in his life that the world was "like [a baby] blindly reaching out for a mother's swollen breast" and then transferring this image to his own preference for women with large breasts, whom he identified with "Cybele with her plenitude" (B-G, 180). This identification of nurturing with women's breasts finds its way into even his earliest plays, such as *Awake and Sing!* when Moe remarks to Hennie that when she gets married, she'll "get fat, big in the tangerines" (SP, 57). Moe's crude comment marks another connection between the nurturing fruit images that pervade the play, the productivity of the female body that characterizes a number of his plays, and the commodification of the body that almost always accompanies images of paradise in the later plays.

This image also ties in to Pike's vision of Pearl sucking at her own breast in *Paradise Lost*, underscoring the ambivalence of the nurturing breast in Odets' plays—and, as Brenman-Gibson notes, his life as well. She remarks that Bette Grayson, Odets' second wife, whom he characterized as having breasts "like great juicy melons," reminded him instantly of Cleo Singer, and she suggests that "Odets was relieved by this eager, admiring, and grateful child spectacularly adorned with the anatomy of a nursing mother" (B-G, 592-593). His fetishization of the female breast in his personal life would be easier to dismiss as an anomaly if it were not such a powerful cultural image—Steinbeck used it to great effect in his closing scene of *The Grapes of Wrath*—and also if it were not so inextricably woven into his plays. The juxtaposition of the hungry child and the mother who offers plenty harks back to images of abundance used in advertising in the first three decades of the 1900s as well as to the common mythology of the plenty of "Mother" Nature.

Still, however Odets' misogyny manifested itself in his personal life, in his plays the commodification of women is mirrored by the commodification of men, albeit in a somewhat different way. Sometimes the male characters are devoured, but more often they function as parasites upon the fecund natural world, a sort of nature gone awry. Sam Katz, Leo's business partner, is such a parasite, having bankrupted the business buying cures for his impotence. Even more significantly, the small-time gangster Kewpie sleeps with Ben's wife, Libby (whose body is characterized, typically, as "soft" and "juicy . . . like a mushmelon"[174]), despite the fact that he idolizes, even worships Ben. Nevertheless, by the end of the play, he confesses to Ben, "I'm in you like a tape worm" (204).[43] Like Pike's tainted fruit, the tapeworm indicates natural bounty that has become unmistakably "red in tooth and claw."

Thus, while Ben is increasingly disillusioned by daily work in an overproductive marketplace—he has gone from Olympic champion to selling useless "Mickey Mouse Drummer Boy" toys on the street corner, finding respite only in small consumerist pleasures, haircuts and manicures—Kewpie, who operates outside the legitimate marketplace, supports Ben's household through secret donations. Ben thus is not only bitten but devoured by the hand that feeds him; he is so beaten that he chooses to die passively in a hail of police bullets. Kewpie's vision is that of a debased utopia, one in which abundance is torn out of the world; the imputation of parasitical dependence is shifted to those who wait, like Pearl, for oranges to drop into their mouths: "You gimme worms, the whole bunch. . . . I don't stop to say it ain't my cake. I cut a piece without asking" (223). The Puritan ethic has degenerated from subjugation of the land to a subjugation of other people. Odets' view of the marketplace had darkened. Indeed, in most of his work after *Paradise Lost*, the conflicting visions of Kewpie and Leo compete for precedence.

"THOSE CARS ARE POISON IN MY BLOOD": *GOLDEN BOY*

After his first trip to Hollywood, Odets created *Golden Boy* as a vehicle through which he could examine popular culture within the broader culture of abundance. In his most allegorical mode, Odets attempted to articulate complex ideas through concrete images, to find the common cultural object and allow it to reflect deep meaning. Thus, in *Golden Boy* and later plays, popular culture becomes, like the fruit in the earlier plays, both a consumer good and the focal point for an entire ideological system. As Walter Benjamin had noted in the mid-1930s, the rise of consumer culture placed cultural goods in a new, increasingly ambivalent relation to their audience; the lines between popular and high culture blurred, and cultural objects circulated in the marketplace in a way never before seen.[44] Working as he did in Broadway and Hollywood and given his difficult experience with the Group, Odets had become extremely interested in the way popular culture fed (or choked) American democracy. Therefore, from *Golden Boy* onward, he increasingly utilized images of popular culture—popular music, film, automobiles, sports, gangsters, even the World's Fair—to examine the promises and failures of the American Dream at the most basic level.

Golden Boy is a play that moves quickly both in structure and in theme. Indeed, the primary impression created by the original performance was one of quickness. Brooks Atkinson described the play as "robust" and described Luther Adler's performance as Joe as having "the speed and energy of an open field runner." Even the sets by Mordecai Gorelik were "a mobile parade of scenery" (NYT, November 5, 1937). George Jean Nathan, never a fan of Odets, derided "the noisy express train that is his drama."[45] Nathan attributed this senseless movement to a Hollywood influence, an idea that persisted in other interpretations of *Golden Boy*. Even Brenman-Gibson argues that the play is "a prophetic paradigm of the unraveling of the American Dream, a world-image of redemption through Success . . . unthinkable without the Gun and the Machine" (466). Odets knew popular culture contained apt metaphors and images for his examination of the dream.

There is certainly some of Hollywood in *Golden Boy*. Odets had readily admitted in "Democratic Vistas in Drama" that the character of Joe Bonaparte was taken directly from the movie "gallery of American types." Film influence may also be present in the structure of the play; a number of critics have noted the unusually short scenes, each followed by the "filmic" stage direction, "fadeout." Of course, Odets' part-time residence in Hollywood was also taken as the source of the play's theme: the talented artist who sells out and thereby loses his talent. Nevertheless, despite the possibility of Hollywood influence, the sense of movement the play generates is integral to Odets' plan. The quick tempo directly reflects the themes of *Golden Boy*: the pressures on the artist in a capitalistic, competitive society and the fervent desire for instant popular and financial success fostered by the seductive images of popular culture. The play's director, Clurman, and designer Mordecai Gorelik worked to reinforce the image of the prizefight as the controlling metaphor of the play rather than making it merely its setting. Clurman noted that Joe's fight was everyone's fight—to become an individual in an increasingly impersonal culture.

Clurman's analysis points to the boxing ring as allegory rather than realistic setting, an idea that Gorelik picked up on in his design for *Golden Boy*. Gorelik took Clurman's concept of the "great fight" and made it a unifying principle: "It was as if each scene were set up in a prize ring, as if a gong rang for the start and finish of each scene, as if the actors came forward toward each other from the opposite corners each time."[46] In addition to reinforcing the fight metaphor, Gorelik used platform staging on tracks to make the transitions between the scenes more quickly and fluidly, to maintain the sense of forward movement of the play, and, to a lesser degree, to mirror the fluid effortlessness of film scene changes. He also intended the scene changes themselves to carry the sense of opposition between the two sides of Joe's dilemma; for example, Moody's office entered from the left, while Joe's home glided in on tracks from the right, like two boxers squaring off.

Speed drives *Golden Boy*, and nothing represents speed more clearly than the cars Joe covets. In his astute theoretical examination of the ideological myths of

American culture, Jean Baudrillard has suggested that the legendary American fascination with cars and driving is directly linked with a utopian ideal:

The way American cars have of leaping into action, of taking off so smoothly, by virtue of
their automatic transmission and power steering. Pulling away effortlessly, noiselessly eating
up the road, gliding along as if you were on a cushion of air, leaving behind the old obsession with what is coming up ahead, or what is overtaking you. . . . All this creates a new
experience of space, and, at the same time, a new experience of the whole social system.[47]

This new experience of the social system lives outside of history, constantly effaces
the past, and therefore re-creates a utopian belief at every moment, a sense reaf-
firming the idea that "America was created in the hope of escaping from history, of
building a utopia sheltered from history."[48]

   Baudrillard's suggestion of the automobile as one of the two technologies—the
other, significantly, is the cinema—that best exemplify the rootlessness, the eternal
"present" of American culture, echoes through the automobile images that pervade
Golden Boy. Odets, too, connects the idea of speed with a utopian version of the
world that exists outside of time. In the first act of *Golden Boy*, Joe confesses to
Lorna that "those cars are poison in my blood. When you sit in a car and speed
you're looking down at the world. Speed, speed, everything is speed—nobody gets
me!" When Lorna responds, "You mean in the ring?" Joe makes the connections
between his own career and the car unmistakable, "In or out, nobody gets me. Gee,
I like to stroke that gas!" (266). The car, like boxing, is a way to escape a painful
history that has been only partly mitigated by the pleasure of music: "People have
hurt my feelings for years. I never forget. You can't get even with people by playing the fiddle. If music shot bullets I'd like it better—artists and people like that are
freaks today. The world moves fast and they sit around like forgotten dopes" (264).

   Joe's feelings of aggression come partly from a difficult childhood, but Odets
is careful to indicate economic factors as well. In the first act, a restless Joe defen-
sively explains his reasons for choosing to fight:

Don't want to sit. Every birthday I ever had I sat around. Now's a time for standing. Poppa, I
have to tell you—I don't like myself, past, present and future. Do you know there are men
who have wonderful things from life? Do you think they're better than me? Do you think I
like this feeling of no possessions? . . . You don't know what it means to sit around here and
watch the months go ticking by! Do you think that's a life for a boy my age? Tomorrow's
my birthday! I change my life! (252)

The emphasis Joe places on time is significant because his reasons for boxing stem
from his projection of the past into the future. Anxious and afraid, Joe looks to the
boxing ring and the car to annihilate the slow ticking of the clock, to step outside of
time. But as Lorna comments, such an escape is predicated upon the violent denial
of human connections. Her early warning, "You sound like Jack the Ripper" (266),
becomes by the end of the play a damning conviction of Joe's alienation: "You
murdered that boy with the generous face. God knows where you hid the body! I
don't know you" (308).

By the mid-1930s, the automobile had become such a powerful icon of American culture that it was impossible to separate the object from the ideologies of popular culture associated with it. As such, it was ripe for allegory: "Dealing with a piece of Americana for which a common understanding existed, Odets did not have to force too many parallels outside the realistic context of the work."[49] Cars had become ubiquitous in American culture; Ford had produced over 15 million of his Tin Lizzies in two decades of production. In this sense, though ostensibly private, the car functioned as an extremely public commodity and embodied all that fascinated in modern American mythology: speed, efficiency, technology, and freedom. Odets thus consciously adopted the image of the car to heighten the conflict between Joe's idealism (represented by the violin) and the pressures of mass production and popular culture (represented by the boxing ring). Furthermore, unlike music's "forgotten dopes," the car is a public, identifiable symbol of one's place in the world. Possessing a car indicates participation in a consumer utopia, but *Golden Boy* suggests that it can also indicate complicity with a system that devalues the individual. Joe's dream of the speeding car offers the ironic promise of using a mass-produced (if expensive), popular commodity to move beyond the constraints of social and economic conditions, indeed, beyond history entirely.

In *Golden Boy*, Odets deliberately mined the relationship between democratic idealism and consumer capitalism, drawing a direct link between the mass production of consumer goods such as automobiles and the mass production and consumption of cultural goods such as movies or spectator sports. It is vitally important that the kind of car Joe wants is identified both by brand name and as the kind that Gary Cooper drives. Here, Joe's original desire for escape manifests itself in a concomitant desire for money and social recognition. Ultimately, he seeks something profounder than speed, namely, the sense that he is larger than life, looking down at the world, untouchable, unafraid. At one point, he found that release in music: "With music, I'm never alone when I'm alone. . . . I'm not afraid of people and what they say" (263). But with the car as "poison" in his blood, Joe moves beyond a desire for private peace into the realm of the public: "[D]own in the street . . . it's war! Music can't help me there" (264). That is, in order to be untouchable in the public sphere, larger than life, one has to be acknowledged as such; achievement in a competitive society can be measured only by its distance from the achievements of others.

Joe wants a car like a movie star's, not only for the car itself but because it reflects the image of a star. Gary Cooper holds special status in the marketplace, so that according to the logic of advertising, to possess his car is to partake in the aura of a movie star. Furthermore, as Baudrillard suggests, the image of a star produces the same sort of instantaneous utopian freedom that characterizes the speeding automobile: "Screen idols . . . are not something to dream about; they are the dream. And they have all the characteristics of dreams . . . above all, they have that power of instantaneous visual materialization (*Anshaulichkeit*) of desire."[50] Like the Deusenberg, Gary Cooper's image itself is a vehicle for escape; it lures Joe with the power of immediacy and the promise of inviolability. Odets connects popular culture to the idea of the American Dream. To be famous is to be rich is to be fast is to be free, or so Joe's fantasy would have it.

Hence, when Joe's boxing career accelerates, he is even more anxious for recognition: "Get me some main bouts in the metropolitan area. . . . And how about some mention in the press? Twenty-six bouts—no one knows I'm alive . . . you can't go too fast for me. Don't worry about autos" (277). Joe's impatience is born from the realization that the only rewards that accrue to a boxer are material goods and fame. Unlike music, there is no spiritual or social reward for winning in the ring; rather, everything is directed outward, as competition and self-aggrandizement; he acknowledges that "the whole essence of prizefighting is immodesty" (305). Soon, Joe's desire for recognition and untouchability—the twin pillars of fame—overwhelms him. He becomes a virtual machine, so that the purchase of the coveted Deusenberg is made possible by his being, like the car itself, "speedy as the wind" in the ring (254).

The means by which Joe succeeds is by necessity extremely public. His career as a boxer depends as much on the newspaper reporters who write about him and the "nine thousand" people who pay to see him fight as it does on his prowess in the ring. In fact, sporting events are not simply public events, but *popular* events in every sense.[51] The language and beliefs of sports have infused our culture on the deepest level. Odets is certainly aware of this in his other plays—baseball metaphors, for example, abound in *Awake and Sing!*, and the fact that Ben is an Olympic athlete in *Paradise Lost* is part of the indictment of the American Dream in that play. *Golden Boy,* however, is Odets' clearest expression of the cultural hero created—literally—by mass media attention.

By placing all his hopes on the search for fame and escape, Joe prevents the possibility of doing what is in his nature. In fact, Joe becomes increasingly aware of his own mechanization, though for most of the play he grudgingly participates in the process. He tells Moody and the gangster Fuseli that if they want to buy a "piece" of him, they can "cut it [i.e., him] up any way you like" (279). However, by the end of the play, he has become horrified by the final realization that Fuseli owns him: "You use me like a gun! Your loyalty's to keep me oiled and polished" (309). The reference to himself as a weapon for others reiterates what he says after his father rejects him: "Now I'm alone. . . . I'll show them all—nobody stands in my way . . . When a bullet sings through the air it has no past—only a future—like me! Nobody, nothing, stands in my way!" (299). The motion initiated by the dream ultimately must run its course. Once the bullet has been fired, there is no retrieving it; once in the speeding car, there is no turning back.

Odets also contrasts Joe's car with the horse-drawn fruit wagon his father drives. Mr. Bonaparte, throughout the play the perfectly wise, loving father who serves to remind Joe of his music, is completely at odds with the glittering world Joe seeks. Mr. Bonaparte stands for a tradition that exists largely outside the marketplace, a person for whom the populist spectacle of a prizefight is senseless violence: "If they wasa fight for cause or for woman, woulda not be so bad" (300). He is content to find his rewards in simple human connection; for him, the benefits of music are spiritual rather than economic. Thus in response to a suggestion that Joe won't be able to make a living as a violinist, Mr. Bonaparte responds: "A good life'sa possible. . . . Joe love music. Music is the great cheer-up in the language of all countries" (249).

By championing the local and the nontechnological, Mr. Bonaparte underscores Odets' doubt about the social usefulness of mass-produced commodities. Certainly, Joe holds a fascination with mass production technology; he confesses admiringly to Lorna that "they make wonderful cars today. Even the lizzies" (266). Still, automobiles are also shown to be an obvious threat, to the point where Gerald Weales points out the play's "ludicrous overpreparation for the death by automobile."[52] For example, in the first scene, Moody reminds Lorna that one of his former boxers "got himself killed in a big, red Stutz" (238); Moody also reveals that Joe "drives like a maniac" (276). However, for Joe's father, the danger is not merely physical but moral. The speed and fame Joe craves are a sort of predatory disease, a confirmation of Joe's statement that the cars are "poison" in his blood: "He gotta wild wolf inside, eat him up" (295).

Mr. Bonaparte sees in human connection the basis of meaning in life. Thus while Joe refers repeatedly to his desire to be free and untouchable, his father worries why Joe hasn't returned home. Mr. Bonaparte sees freedom in doing what one was born to do; Joe sees freedom in untouchability. Of course, Joe wavers from time to time. He reaches out to Lorna for redemption, but at the end of the play, overcome with remorse for killing his opponent in the ring, his only thought is escape. His final speech indicates how far Joe has traveled down the path of self-destruction. When Lorna urges him to find "some city where poverty's no shame— where music is no crime!—where there's no war in the streets—where a man is glad to be himself," Joe responds: "We'll drive through the night. When you mow down the night with headlights, nobody gets you! You're on top of the world then—nobody laughs! That's it—speed! We're off the earth—unconnected! We don't have to think!! That's what speed's for, an easy way to live!" (316).

Joe is indeed "unconnected." His pursuit of the slick dream of the sports hero and the Deusenberg made him a commodity, unconnected to anything human. He realizes this when he tells Lorna, "I murdered myself. . . . Now I'm hung up by my fingertips—I'm no good—my feet are off the earth!" (315). Like the mythical Antaeus, Joe has lost the strength-giving connection. He finally understands the danger of his desire. The isolation of popular success, metaphorized in the isolation of the car and the boxing ring, has left him incapable of creating a new connection, and thus his last lines serve as a premonition of their suicide by car—there is in reality no "easy way to live." It is only at the end of the play and only through the earthbound character of Mr. Bonaparte and Joe's brother Frank—a union organizer who "fights" so that he is "at harmony with millions of others" (318)—that Joe is able to reconnect: "Come, we bring-a him home . . . where he belong" (321) .

"IT'S A LEGITIMATE BUSINESS": *ROCKET TO THE MOON*

Odets' next play, *Rocket to the Moon*, continued his retreat from overtly political drama into a more generalized examination of American life, yet he carried over patterns of imagery and dramaturgical structure that make this play's connection to the first five unmistakable. On the surface, it focuses on Ben Stark, a dentist who hopes to wake himself from his midlife torpor by pursuing an affair with his secretary. His wife and her father serve as foils to Ben's quest for renewal, the father seeking to possess Cleo, the secretary, himself. In the third act, forced to choose between the two men, Cleo refuses both, leaving alone at the end of the play. Despite its mundane subject matter, however, this play moves outward to encompass larger issues; it is a middle-class drama, but a middle-class drama set against the backdrop of the depression and the increasing frustration of a fading idealism.

Cleo Singer, the central female character in the play, is Odets' most intriguing heroine, naive, immature and ignorant, yet idealistic and ultimately free. As with other Odets heroes and heroines, Cleo is associated generally with production and creation, but more importantly and specifically with the natural abundance of fruit, an association that is ambivalent at best. On the one hand, she is the only character who can in some way still offer the promise of abundance. Indeed, she is the one character with youth and vitality in a play about middle-age crisis and frustration, the only one who can "make [Ben] a living man again" (350), who wants to have "babies, three or four. . . . I'm healthy enough to have a dozen!" (374), who refuses a marriage of convenience to seek a "whole full world, with all the trimmings" (417). Ben has fallen asleep in his marriage; Belle, his wife, is unable to bear children, and her father, Prince, is old and unproductive; his only enjoyments seem to be making money on the market and listening to music, both passive pleasures. As Cleo tells him, "You've lived your life. I think you're good, but you're too old for me" (417).

On the other hand, by associating Cleo with the natural world, Odets puts her in the position of a commodity that *must* be consumed in order to have value in the marketplace. She is repeatedly objectified by characters who envy her power. For example, Frenchy calls her "Juicy Fruit" and "Angel Skin"; Prince tells her, "You're a girl like candy, a honeydew melon—a delicious girl" (369), and comments to Ben that she has "womanhood fermenting through her veins" (370). Even Cleo herself (in an image that looks back to both *Awake and Sing!* and *Paradise Lost*) tells them at the end of the play, "No man can take a bite out of me, like an apple and throw it away" (411). Cleo ultimately resists her own commodification, but her only answer, like Moe and Hennie, is to seek Paradise elsewhere. When Prince questions her choice not to marry him, "You'll go down the road alone—like Charlie Chaplin?," she responds lyrically:

Yes, if there's roads, I'll take them. I'll go up all those roads until I find what I want. I want a love that uses me, that needs me. Don't you think there's a world full of joyful men and women? Must all men live afraid to laugh and sing? Can't we sing at work and love our work? It's getting late to play at life; I want to live it. . . . none of you can give me what I'm looking for, a whole full world, with all the trimmings! (416-417).

Her act is one of rejection rather than assertion, an attempt to locate abundance outside of a world where she is expected to serve as either a mistress to Ben or an ornament to Prince.

The play intrigued and disappointed reviewers; many found it a hackneyed love story out of keeping with Odets' sharp social criticism. Brooks Atkinson, one of the few who liked it, nevertheless remarked that it "expires in a state of loquacious confusion . . . nothing much has been accomplished or clarified." Still, Atkinson remained a fan, remarking that the play was "torn out of the quivering fabric of life. Mr. Odets has a special genius for portraying footless characters who are imprisoned within the shell of economic circumstances and personal desires" (NYT, January 23, 1938). Others were less kind. George Jean Nathan remarked that "Clifford Odets continues to disappoint those critics who over-estimated him in the first place," and John Mason Brown called the first act "the finest Mr. Odets has yet written" but dismissed the play as "the most exasperating kind of failure."[53] The most common reason cited for the failure of the play was a familiar one: the ending seems falsely optimistic, the escape Cleo seeks impossible.

If the ending of *Rocket to the Moon* is sentimentally vague, and if its action is less overtly political than that of the earlier plays, the economic imperatives that drive the characters remain strong. For Odets, productivity—both the production of objects and the metaphorical creation of a good life—was shaped by the economic forces working on people in a market economy. Indeed, Odets' bitter characterization of the script of *Rocket to the Moon* as "veal chops" for the Group makes the connection between his own economic circumstances and the play clear; the characters in *Rocket to the Moon* are, like Odets himself, constrained by their participation in the marketplace. The naive dreams by which Cleo lives are in fact a direct reaction to a difficult economic situation. She remarks to Ben at one point, "My home life is fearful—eight in one apartment . . . I have all of the inconvenience of love with none of the pleasure" (373). Nevertheless, she vows to escape the narrow economic circumstances: "Would you laugh if I told you I want to be a dancer? Would you? Or an actress? . . . they won't hold me back" (373-374). Her exit at the end of the play, therefore, acknowledges the power of a consumer society even while attempting to escape.

Cleo's rebellion against her own commodification is posited as a creative act, an assertion of self in the face of an alienation. Unlike Joe Bonaparte, Cleo chooses to possess her own body rather that to allow it to become meat for the marketplace. Indeed, Cleo's belief in the natural goodness of the body as opposed to the marketplace becomes clear when she tells Ben conspiratorially: "I think happiness is everything. You can have a castle, and what have you got if you're not happy? An important person once told me Mr. Rockefeller—you know, that one, his father—he had a silver windpipe. With all that money! It goes to show you" (363). This image is a significant one for Odets' play, for it directly connects the idea of the body to the idea of the commodity. Rather than merely saying money cannot buy happiness, she latches onto a striking image of modern consumerism gone awry as the vehicle for her indignity. The idea of a piece of Rockefeller's natural body replaced by precious metal is as horrifying as it is unnatural, the Alger myth turned on its head. Thus, in her visions of cruises, fancy parties, and the coat that Prince gives her, the marketplace repeatedly reinscribes itself on her body. Cleo, aware of this tension, clings to her native idealism. When Prince tells her at the end, "I know your needs. I *love* your needs. . . . What do you have to lose?" Cleo responds, "Everything that's me" (416). Cleo's body is the contested ideological ground of *Rocket to the Moon*; it signifies the natural world so completely that Willy Wax, the loathsome dance producer, who describes himself as "a mechanical man in a mechanical era" (410), is bewildered by Cleo's fury at his advances.

Even more explicitly than Cleo's struggle for independence, Phil Cooper's difficulties are more manifestly economic than they are spiritual, moral, or emotional. Thus, even if Cooper's purpose in the play is to be a cautionary figure for Ben, the reasons for his despair are economic. Throughout the play, Cooper is at the brink of disaster; he is turned down for a loan, he cannot pay his rent, he is unable to pay the doctor's bills for his son's broken arm. He is unable to participate on even the most basic level in the society for which he went to war. A graduate of Columbia, he is nevertheless dependent on Ben's largesse to keep his practice. Things become so difficult that he is forced to sell his blood, the price of one pint equal to a month's rent:

Cooper: I decided to become a blood donor on the side.
Cleo (horrified): Oh, no!
Cooper: They pay well, thirty dollars a pint.
Cleo (in a low voice): A pint's a lot of blood, Dr. Cooper.
Cooper: A boy there gave fifteen times last year: a young fortune. He told me he lives on a plain diet, onions, and bread, no meats or anything.
Stark (after a pause): Phil . . . you mean it?
Cooper (bitterly): They didn't want me at first. But it seems I'm a type everybody needs. . . . I'm a very common type.
Stark: Phil, you don't mean that!
Cooper: Why not? It's a legitimate business, like pressing pants or cleaning fish (377) [54]

Here, the body has literally become a commodity; Cleo's Rockefeller image expands to encompass ordinary people in everyday life.

Though desperate, Cooper's is the voice of realism in *Rocket to the Moon*. His bitter realization that there is no paradise for him to look forward to— "If only they invented hydrants in the streets which give out milk and honey! . . . we'd be happier people. . . . Where can I sail away? To where?" (376)—is placed dramaturgically to interrupt Cleo's confession of love to Ben. The contrast shows an interrelationship between personal desire and economic stability, between idealism and realism. Throughout *Rocket to the Moon*, Odets contrasts functions within the marketplace—Cooper's realization that he is a "common type"—with rewards that apparently exist only outside it—Cleo's affirmation of the power of the "self." Or, as Cooper comments earlier in the play, "Who's got time to think about women! I'm trying to make a living!" (352).

Perhaps the clearest expression of Odets' belief that outside pressures come to bear on everyday human choices comes from Frenchy in act 3:

Who's got time for "love and the grace to use it"? Is it something apart, love? A good book you go to in a spare hour? An entertainment? Christ, no! It's a synthesis of good and bad, economics, work, play, all contacts. . . . it's not a Sunday suit for special occasions. . . . In this day of stresses I don't see much normal life, myself included. The woman's not a wife. She's the dependent of a salesman who can't make sales and is ashamed to tell her so. . . . the free exercise of love, I figure, gets harder every day. (404)

Love relationships in earlier Odets plays—Joe and Edna, Sid and Florrie in *Waiting for Lefty*, Ralph and Blanche in *Awake and Sing!*, Pearl and Felix in *Paradise*

Lost—are constrained by economic factors. Frenchy, who may be Odets' spokesperson in *Rocket to the Moon*, clearly articulates how the culture of consumption helps to form their choices.

Because life is pervaded by the marketplace, even the most mundane situations challenge characters to participate without losing themselves in the process. Though transportation images abound in the play—the rocket of the title, ships in the harbor, the cruise ships of which Cleo dreams, the "jalopy" that occupies Frenchy's free time, even the fanciful image of Aladdin's lamp that Ben uses to pacify Belle's desire for a vacation—Cleo is the only one who escapes. Ben, urged to take a rocket to the moon, never escapes his office. At the end, he decides to return to Belle, hoping faintly that his experience with Cleo has made him more aware of his life. The stifling atmosphere of the dental office amplifies the fundamental unproductiveness of most of the characters, calling into question the ultimate possibility of escaping modern life as Frenchy describes it. Cleo's exit is thus the sole hope of the play; she manifests Odets native idealism, his hope that the price for abundance needn't be so high.

"HERE'S THE FAIR—IT DON'T GUARANTEE ME MEALS"

Following the trend of *Golden Boy*, after *Rocket to the Moon*, Odets turned his attention more specifically to the influence of popular form of culture in his next play, *Night Music*. But despite consistent praise for the specific performances—Kazan as Steve Takis, Morris Carnovsky as Detective A. L. Rosenberger, and Jane Wyatt as Fay Tucker—the play was panned as pointless, self-indulgent, and wandering. Odets' fondness for this play, as well as the Group's dependence on the income from a successful run,[55] made the critics' responses especially frustrating. Odets fantasized a retreat into small, insular theatre:

My feelings were and are very simple. I felt as if a lovely delicate child, tender and humorous, had been knocked down by a truck and lay dying. . . . It was Boris A[ronson] who called the turn. He said "This show is very moving to me, a real artwork, but I don't think they will get its quality—it is not commercial." . . . I think now to write very inexpensive plays in the future, few actors, one set; perhaps hire a cheap theatre and play there. (TIR, 48-49)

Odets felt that the play, which attempted to show the aimlessness of American life just before World War II, was badly misunderstood.

Clurman, who directed it, saw in *Night Music* not only a discussion of a particular time and place but a complex argument that used the forms of American popular culture to expose its emptiness. He pointed out in a response to the critics that "the play stems from the basic sentiment that people . . . are haunted by the fear of impermanence in all their relationships; they are fundamentally *homeless*. . . . it is the 'melody' that pervades the play, " and suggests that "this play is nearest amongst Odets' plays to our conception of 'pure' entertainment" (NM, x-xiii). Following a failed 1951 remount of *Night Music*, Clurman wrote another article in its defense, arguing that "Odets takes for granted that . . . we all know that most of the slogans of our society are without substance in terms of our true emotions." However, without looking beneath the surface, American audiences could "find no meaning in a play that is as clear and simple as a popular song and in writing and characterization very rich."[56] Clurman's identification of *Night Music* with popular song—especially in the way they express common beliefs—is underscored by the romantic simplicity of the plot and the pervasive sounds of music throughout the play—Steve's clarinet, the musical score by Hanns Eisler, the singing crickets that give the play its title.

A fundamental paradox had troubled Odets since *Waiting for Lefty*—in Aronson's terms, how could a playwright gain a "commercial" audience with an "artwork"? As he had in *Golden Boy* and *Rocket to the Moon*, Odets attempted in *Night Music* to use popular forms to reflect a wide spectrum of American life. Ultimately, then, Clurman's characterization of the play as "entertainment" is not far from Odets' own conception, though many saw the popular forms without seeing the underlying political analysis. For example, Wendy Smith has noted how far the "fiery" Odets had come from *Waiting for Lefty* in just five years and argues that "*Night Music* was as mainstream in its aspirations as *Golden Boy*, but the earlier play challenged basic American assumptions about success in a way that the new one never did" (RLD, 395). The mood of *Night Music* is more diffuse and delicate than *Golden Boy*, less grim than later plays such as *Clash by Night* or *The Big Knife*, almost nothing at all like *Waiting for Lefty*. But there are complexities in Odets' use of the popular in *Night Music*; the mainstream and trivial are made unfamiliar, ambiguous, and indicative of larger social processes. Like images of abundance in the earlier plays, popular culture is used allegorically to characterize a nation caught between Depression and war, between hope and fear, between scarcity and abundance.

On the surface, *Night Music* is manufactured like a Hollywood plot, a typical "boy meets girl" romance. Also, because *Night Music* is the only play of his for which Odets also wrote the screenplay, it is easy to see Hollywood influence in the number of scenes, the shifting settings, the incidental music, and most apparently the way his principal characters meet. Steve Takis, a low-level employee of a film studio, is stranded in New York when the trained monkeys he is transporting steal a necklace from Fay Tucker, an aspiring actress. Steve's frustration and anger at his difficult life intensify during the play's twelve scenes, but through the beneficent offices of a detective assigned to investigate the theft, the two are happily united by the end of the play.

Nevertheless, as with *Golden Boy*, Odets' appropriation of the style and themes of the Hollywood movie was deliberate. He wanted to find a popular audience with the play, which is part of the reason *Night Music* is less overtly leftist than Odets' earlier plays. But against the background of an imminent war and the real or symbolic homelessness of most of the characters, familiar plot elements take on allegorical significance. The source of the play's themes and structure, popular culture is also the subject of its critique; *Night Music* measures the utopian visions offered by popular culture against the loneliness pervading American life during the "phony war." This was the essential point that contemporary newspaper reviewers had missed. For example, Wiella Waldorf in the *New York Post* remarked that the play was pointless: "For no particular reason, Mr. Odets . . . takes his leading trio on a visit to the World's Fair where they sit at the feet of Washington's statue and discuss life" (February 23, 1940). Waldorf's claim bears examination, for the scene at the World's Fair is the center around which the rest of the plot of *Night Music* revolves. It is the key moment in Odets' play where the unguarded optimism of a popular, technological culture meets the human victims of that culture.

A World's Fair—the New York version was contemporary with the first production of *Night Music*—is a manufactured piece of popular culture. In fact, it *must* capture the popular imagination, for it requires an enormous audience to exist at all. In addition, by 1939, the Fair had developed to the point where it had become a mass-produced spectacle, a bow to the marketplace produced by consumer capitalism and promoted through the popular media. Billed as "the People's Fair" and aimed, as the organizers phrased it, "to delight and instruct them," it nevertheless worked well within the structure of the new consumerism: "It was a Fair that from the very start viewed the people not only as observers but also as potential consumers of the products it displayed."[57] The Fair, therefore, was built for the marketplace at the same time it was built for "the people." Nevertheless, the visions presented in the exhibits could scarcely mask the hard facts of high unemployment and a looming war; to many, the Fair seemed out of place. Indeed, contemporary observers such as Garner Harding noted the irony that "of the 16 houses in the exhibit, only six 'meet the absolute minimum requirement of social usefulness in costing less than $10,000 apiece.'"[58] Exhibits such as the Futurama and the World of Tomorrow offered extravagant promises of the glorious plenty that consumer capitalism would provide and yet exacted a price from each person who wanted to catch a glimpse of that world. In fact, a 1939 Gallup poll established that the reason given by 63 percent of those who did not attend the Fair was that they couldn't afford it. Not only could "the people" not afford to buy what was offered, but many could not even afford to window-shop.

Odets therefore used a visit to the Fair ironically, as a way to question the cultural assumptions that underlie its very existence: the prevalence of widespread consumer capitalism, the usefulness of popular culture in meeting real, pressing social needs, the possibility of a "World of Tomorrow" in a world on the brink of war, the possibility for a home at all in a period characterized by homelessness. As Steve says, "They call this place the world of the future. . . . The world of tomorrow, don't they? It don't feel any different from than the present an' past, I couldn't get in here without the buck. . . . I don't respect that world of the future. Here's the Fair—it don't guarantee me meals" (161). As always, Odets brings the point back to the dignity and expectations of the common man; the utopian promise of the Fair is directly confronted by the economic hardship and spiritual malaise of the "millions . . . *tens* of millions" that Steve represents (162).

Widening the metaphoric basis of the play, Odets directly links the idea of the forgotten man to music, using the idea of harmony to underscore Steve's isolation. Steve, whose only pleasure comes from playing his clarinet and composing songs, takes issue with Fay's hopeful assertion that if crickets can sing, "We can sing through any night!" (160). He responds:

I'm a real harmony boy in my heart, if I get a chance. . . . What kinda life where you gotta compare yourself to crickets? *They're bugs!* I vamp around an' I vamp around an' nothin'

happens—you can't get a start. You're keepin' me there on a low A when I'm good enough
for a high C! *An' then came the war.* . . . An' that's what I'm good for. . . . that harmony boy
who mighta been! (180)

The ideal of harmony (which recalls Frank's assertion in *Golden Boy* that he is at
harmony with millions) is set against the vague promises of the World of Tomorrow and the darker certainty of American participation in the war.

While not explicitly connected to specific popular songs (as Odets would do
later in *Clash by Night*), the intimate relationship Odets senses between music and
the Fair is reflected by the fact that the immediate and overpowering sense of visi-
tors to the Fair was that it was "a festival of sight and sound—always sound. . . .
There were always bands, orchestras, and even, from some exhibits, the allure of
interior sound floating out onto the general grounds."[59] But such joyous music, like
the model homes that make up the World of Tomorrow, exists only within the con-
sumer-sanctioned confines of the Fair. Thus, Steve's notion of harmony is directly
at odds with the homelessness and isolation that beset all the characters, from the
three main characters to the loners gathered in the lobby of the Hotel Algiers and
the peripatetic men Fay and Steve meet in Central Park.[60] As in *Golden Boy*, music
exists to make a spiritual connection with others. The sense of being kept from
reaching his potential—stuck on a low A—only adds to Steve's sense of isolation.
Indeed, the play is permeated with wandering, loneliness, homelessness; Steve carries a suitcase around with him throughout. In addition to the Fair scenes, there are
eight different settings in the twelve scenes of the play, some outside, a number in
public spaces such as a restaurant, an airport, and a police station. No scene takes
place in a home; the closest they get are the run-down rooms of the Hotel Algiers.

The visit to the World's Fair is foreshadowed in an earlier scene of *Night Music*, when Steve encounters a homeless man named Roy Brown in Central Park.
Roy tells Steve that he is joining the army, but before he leaves, he wants to go to
the Fair—which for Roy is a magical goal, a symbol of success. It is significant,
therefore, that Odets immediately contrasts it to the threat of war; unable to afford
the Fair, Roy is certain that the army will take him immediately. This irony is fur-
thered in the scene at the Fair itself, when Steve sees Roy again, literally trapped by
the spectacle: "Now that I got in here, I can't find my way out" (172). Odets uses
Roy as counterpoint, a "specter of Steve's war thoughts." Thus, when Steve asks
Roy if he would like to have ice cream with them, Roy responds ominously, "That
don't mix with mustard. So long" (165). The reference to mustard gas underscores
Odets' conception of the Fair as a symbol of the dubious pleasures of consumerism,
offering pleasure to all, but at a steep price for most.

Odets, of course, was not alone is recognizing the ironies of the Fair at such an
uncertain historical moment. Some observers noted an odd sense of "anomie
amidst the optimism," but others were of the opinion that, as one writer for the *New
Yorker* put it, "the Fair would seem to be about as good a place as any to take refuge in when one wants to stop thinking about the world for a moment."[61] While
Odets is conscious of the pervasive sense of anomie, there is nevertheless a strong
thread of hope running throughout the play—even in its darkest moods. The trip to
the Fair does in fact represent a welcome escape from the realities that have con-

fronted Fay and Steve over the first two acts: her play has closed, he will likely lose his job, she is being pressured to return home to her parents, he has no home at all. After a visit from Fay's father and her ex-fiancé becomes a shouting match, Rosenberger offers to take Fay and Steve to the Fair to forget their troubles for a moment.

The fact that Rosenberger offers the tickets is a point in the Fair's favor, for throughout the play, he stands for the voice of calm, reason, and optimism, a father figure to the young people. As with Jacob in *Awake and Sing!* or Papa Bonaparte in *Golden Boy*, he tries to show Steve and Fay the power they have to change the future:

There are two ways to look, Mr. Takis—to the past or the future. We know a famous case in history where a woman kept looking back and turned to a salt rock. If you keep looking back on a mean narrow past, the same thing can happen to you. You are feeling mad. Why shouldn't you feel mad? In your whole life you never had a pretzel. . . . But your anger must bear children or it's hopeless. (189)

Rosenberger, though dying of cancer, goads and protects them—they are his future. It is in this sense that Odets admires the Fair; he, too, maintains an optimism that the "world of tomorrow" can be achieved. Indeed, Rosenberger's tag line sums up his character: "I am love with the possibilities, the human possibilities" (105).[62]

In the same vein, Rosenberger calls the Fair "Beautiful," suggesting that its true hope is not in its achievements—they are transitory—but in its possibilities. The Fair is thus represented in Odets' play as a sort of beautiful lie or dream, beguiling, seductive, but to this point unfulfilled. Nevertheless, like the utopian vision of plenty offered by consumer capitalism, it is also a goal to reach for; the Fair is truly lovely. One character warns them before they go, "Don't miss that Futurama—you'll get goose pimples" (157), and when they arrive, even the surly Steve is beguiled. He says, "This place looks like they sprinkled it with gold dust," to which Rosenberger adds ("*Admiringly*"), "You should see how it looks at night" (161).

Odets consciously tempered his criticism of the Fair as he reworked *Night Music* through several drafts. For example, in the typescript of the first draft, Rosenberger says, "It will be remembered as a tragic period when the Fair opened, an unfortunate year." Also, he rather than Steve is given the line about gold dust, to which Steve then responds, "Gold dust sprinkled on an October corpse" (LCA, 1939). These lines changed in the final script most likely because Odets was unwilling to repudiate hope in the face of the unfulfilled promises of the Fair and, by association, of American democracy. The ending of the play—Steve loses his job but gains Fay—is, in the manner of other Odets plays, lyrically optimistic but essentially vague. Fay and Rosenberg convince Steve that "your fight is here, not across the water. . . . your wonderful country never needed you more" (235-236). Some have suggested that the ending is saccharine and even dishonest, ignoring the deep problems raised in the play. Regardless of its dramaturgical flaws, the ending is very much in keeping with the guarded optimism that emerges in *Night Music*; indeed, the "Hollywood" ending can be seen as Odets' attempt to reconfigure the forms of popular culture into political theatre. Rather than using the high art of the theatre to condemn popular culture outright, Odets tries to couch his critique in a form that mirrors popular culture itself. Rather than abandoning hope, Odets suggests a progressive use for popular forms: to place the power of the future "in the hands of the people."

NOTES

1.   Carnegie's story of raising himself from spinner in a factory to command a huge steel empire is written as inspirational literature—the Gospel of Wealth—but Carnegie himself noted the social problems inherent in industrial productivity. He recognized that "[w]e assemble thousands of operatives in the factory, and in the mine, of whom the employer can know little, and to whom he is little better than a myth. . . . The price which society pays for the law of competition, like the price it pays for cheap comforts and luxuries, is also great; but the advantages of this law are also far greater still than its cost" (16). In "Andrew Carnegie and the Discourse of Cultural Hegemony" (*Journal of American Studies* 22.2 [August 1988]: 213-224), Alun Munslow has argued that Carnegie's rhetoric gradually developed into attempts to render harmless conflicting elements in the industrial order; thus, he recast poverty as a necessary precondition for wealth: "[T]he true hero was the poor boy, who through the pursuit of the Gospel of Success, was able to achieve wealth" (218). Political or class conflict was seen not as a fight within the society but as an insurrection against society.

2.   C. Wright Mills, *White Collar: The American Middle Classes* (New York: Oxford UP, 1956) 34.

3.   Tiziano Bonazzi, "Frederick Jackson Turner's Frontier Thesis and the Self-Consciousness of America." *Journal of American Studies.* 27.2 (August 1993): 163-164.

4.   Odets' fascination with the poetry of Walt Whitman indicates more than a passing interest in the development of the American frontier. Whitman was the poet of mid-19th-century American democracy who in his expansive, encompassing, and self-referential work attempted to record the breadth of experience and language suggested by the huge land and its peoples. Odets' brand of Whitmanesque idealism manifests itself throughout his work (in the sort of dialogue that Whitman characterized as "the slang or local song of the Manhattan, Boston, Philadelphia or Baltimore mechanic"), as well as in the hope he held for a national folk culture. Odets even named his only son Walt Whitman Odets.

5.   Christopher Lasch, *The True and Only Heaven: Progress and Its Critics* (New York: W. W. Norton, 1991) 93.

6.   Lasch, 68.

7.   Arthur Schlesinger Jr., *The Age of Roosevelt. Volume 1: The Crisis of the Old Order, 1919-1933* (Cambridge, MA: Riverside. 1957) 89. Mumford's book is an account of the historical development of technology from a sociological and scientific perspective. He argues that the failures of technology are manifest in the comparatively useless ends to which the harnessing of natural energy is put, vacillating between a condemnation of the contemporary system and a utopian argument for a planned system of technology that will free people from labor. It is significant that he ends the book with the forward-looking vision: "However far modern science and technics have fallen short of their inherent possibilities, they have taught mankind at least one lesson: nothing is impossible" (435). Technology thus becomes not the enemy of Eden, but its servant.

8.   T. J. Jackson Lears, *Fables of Abundance: A Cultural History of Advertising in America* (New York: Basic Books, 1994) 4.

9.   Lears, *Fables of Abundance*, 112.

10.   Lears, *Fables of Abundance*, 121. Lears' argument echoes Henry Adams' discus-

sion of the shift from a religious world view to a technological one. In the chapter of his 1918 book, *The Education of Henry Adams* (New York: Penguin, 1995) titled "The Dynamo and the Virgin," inspired by Adams' visit to the hall of technology at the 1900 Paris Exposition, he remarks, in his typically self-mocking tone, "To Adams the dynamo became a symbol of infinity. As he grew accustomed to the great gallery of machines, he began to feel the forty-foot dynamos as a moral force, much as the early Christians felt the cross." Adams contrasts the traditional European sense of power encapsulated in the cathedral and the Virgin with the American symbol of power, which elevated the dynamo from a machine to an entire worldview of mechanical productivity.

11. Lears, *Fables of Abundance*, 124.

12. Alice Marquis. *Hopes and Ashes: The Birth of Modern Times, 1929-1939* (New York: The Free Press, 1986) 120.

13. Lizabeth Cohen, "The Class Experience of Mass Consumption: Workers as Consumers in Interwar America," in *The Power of Culture: Critical Essays in American History* Richard Wightman Fox and T. J. Jackson Lears, eds. (Chicago: U of Chicago P, 1993) 141.

14. Cohen, 152. For a detailed analysis of the shifting contexts of consumption, see Ben Fine and Ellen Leopold's *The World of Consumption* (New York: Routledge) 1993.

15. We should be careful to note, with Jean-Christophe Agnew, that "standard of living" measurements are an indication that "historians have taken the world of goods for granted. . . . commodities have become the gauge by which allegedly more important historical developments are to be assessed" ("The Consuming Vision of Henry James," in *The Culture of Consumption: Critical Essays in American History, 1880-1930*. Richard Wightman Fox and T. J. Jackson Lears, eds. [New York: Pantheon Books, 1983] 80). Lewis Mumford in the 1930s suggested that a focus on commodities came at the expense of other measures of progress: "*[T]he higher the vital standard, the less can it be expressed adequately in terms of money* . . . and the more, therefore, will it tend to be expressed in terms of goods and environmental improvements that lie outside of machine production" (*Technics and Civilization*. [New York: Harcourt Brace, 1934] 398-399).

16. Pasi Falk, *The Consuming Body* (London: Sage, 1994) 159.

17. Richard Wightman Fox, "Epitaph for Middletown," in *The Culture of Consumption: Critical Essays in American History, 1880-1930*. Richard Wightman Fox and T. J. Jackson Lears, eds. (New York: Pantheon, 1983) 103.

18. T. J. Jackson Lears, "From Salvation to Self-Realization: Advertising and the Therapeutic Roots of the Consumer Culture 1880-1930," in *The Culture of Consumption: Critical Essays in American History, 1880-1930*, Richard Wightman Fox and T. J. Jackson Lears, eds. (New York: Pantheon Books, 1983) 19.

19. The emerging consumerism of the early 20th century pitted one side of a dual Protestant ethic—an Augustinian vision of personal transformation—in conflict with the other branch which depended on restraint and mastery over both self and world (Lears, "From Salvation," 47). Colin Campbell, in *The Romantic Ethic and the Spirit of Modern Consumption*. (London: Basil Blackwell, 1987), traces the historical development of the "Other Protestant Ethic" from the 18th century cult of sensibility to the Bohemian exultation of pleasure. He notes that the difference between utility and fantasy is the basis of the split between the Calvinist Protestant ethic and the Augustinian: "The former was identified as a preoccupation with sensory experience, with 'pleasures' regarded as discrete and standardized events, and in the pursuit of which there is a natural tendency for the hedonist to seek despotic powers. Modern hedonism is marked, in contrast, by a preoccupation of 'pleasure,' envisaged as a potential quality of all experience. In order to extract this from life, however, the individual has to substitute illusory for real stimuli" (203).

20. Gary Cross, *Time and Money: The Making of Consumer Culture* (New York and London: Routledge, 1993) 39.

21. Falk, 98-99.

22. R. Baird Shuman, *Clifford Odets* (New York: Twayne, 1962); John Gassner, "The Long Journey of a Talent," *Theatre Arts* (July 1949): 25-30.

23. Harold Cantor, *Clifford Odets: Playwright-Poet* (Metuchen, NJ: Scarecrow, 1978) 119; Gabriel Miller, *Clifford Odets* (New York: Continuum, 1989) 215.

24. Rita Barnard, *The Great Depression and the Culture of Abundance* (Cambridge: Cambridge UP, 1995) 19.

25. Cabell Phillips, *From the Crash to the Blitz: 1929-1939. The New York Times Chronicle of Modern Life* (London: Macmillan, 1964) 256.

26. Barnard, 23.

27. Thorstein Veblen, *The Theory of the Leisure Class: An Economic Study of Institutions* (London: Macmillan, 1908) 154.

28. Robert S. McElvaine, *The Great Depression: America, 1929-1941* (New York: Times Books, 1984) 80.

29. Fine and Leopold, 67-68.

30. "The Young Actor" scene was removed from the Modern Library (1939) edition of Odets' first six produced plays, though it did appear in his *Three Plays* (New York: Covici-Friede, 1935). Odets told Michael Mendelsohn that it was dropped from the later edition because it was "too untypical." Perhaps it was too radical for the Broadway version. Whatever the reason, the scene is consistent with the other scenes in its use of imagery and language.

31. Gerald Weales, *Clifford Odets, Playwright* (New York: Pegasus, 1971) 43. Odets himself testified to the House Un-American Activities Committee (HUAC) in 1952 that he had never been near a strike when he wrote the play. Weales, however, has given strong evidence that Odets used a number of factual incidents from the 1934 New York taxi strike as the basis for his play.

32. Miller, *Clifford Odets*, 169.

33. Michael J. Mendelsohn, "Odets at Center Stage," interview with Odets. *Theatre Arts* (May /June1963): 18.

34. Alfred Kazin, *Starting Out in the Thirties* (Boston: Little, Brown, 1962) 80-81.

35. John Howard Lawson, *Theory and Technique of Playwriting* (New York: Hill and Wang, 1960) 252.

36. Mendelsohn, "Center Stage," 17.

37. William Leiss, *The Limits to Satisfaction: An Essay on the Problems of Needs and Commodities* (Toronto: U of Toronto P, 1976) 82.

38. Weales suggests that Odets was being more ironic than it appears by using a piece of music that coupled images of paradise and prison: "It is such a double-edged symbol that one cannot help supposing—hoping at least—that Odets intended to let the records themselves undermine their value for Jacob. Such intricacy is too much for an audience in the theatre to grasp, but Jacob's vulnerability does not hinge on an aesthetic reaction to Bizet. . . . His records fail him because, like most dreams, they are fragile and Bessie can and does smash them" (*Clifford Odets*, 63-64).

39. Grant McCracken, *Culture and Consumption: New Approaches to the Symbolic Character of Goods and Activities* (Bloomington: Indiana UP, 1988) 107.

40. Michael J. Mendelsohn, *Clifford Odets: Humane Dramatist* (Deland, FL: Everett Edwards, 1969) 38.

41. Pike's characterization of the difficult life of the fruit picker is borne out by the history of the citrus industry in California. Its growth, aided vastly by the development of the transcontinental railroad, changed "the diet and nutritional emphasis of the nation"

(Gilbert G. Gonzalez, *Labor and Community: Mexican Citrus Worker Villages in a Southern California Community, 1900-1950.* [Urbana: U of Illinois P, 1994] 6). Utilizing a powerful nationwide advertising program, the industry had prospered by emphasizing consumption: "The orange became a symbol of health, vitamins, and nutrition, and as it did, year-round production increased, while improved marketing and distribution effectively placed the commodity within the main population centers across the nation" (20). Building its success on the backs of more than 750,000 Mexican workers, the growers kept wages low and conditions hard even as citrus shipments more than tripled in the twenty years between 1921-1922 and 1941-1942. The citrus industry became a "success story" that nevertheless revealed the dangers of an American consumerism that assumed production was easy and effortless. Problems in this Eden became clear when a June 1936 strike by the workers was violently suppressed by the grower's association.

42. C. W. E Bigsby, "*Awake and Sing!* and *Paradise Lost,*" in *Critical Essays on Clifford Odets,* Gabriel Miller, ed. (Boston: G.K. Hall, 1991) 161.

43. The homoeroticism between Ben and Kewpie is emphasized by other characters; when Ben and Kewpie reconcile after an argument, Libby questions acidly, "what's this, a love duet?" (SP, 178). Other obvious instances of homoeroticism in Odets are found in the characters of Fuseli and Roxy Gottleib in *Golden Boy,* but perhaps most notably in *The Big Knife,* where terms of feminine endearment are common among the men in the play, who call each other "sweetheart," "boyfriend," and "Ella" throughout. It is interesting to note that often these homoerotic connections are based upon parasitism, as in the case of Kewpie and Ben and Fuseli and Joe Bonaparte, suggesting that by virtue of providing—being the source of nourishment—the "host" becomes a feminized commodity. Thus Fuseli, "a queer" (SP, 292), can speak of buying "a piece" of Joe and Tokio, his trainer, tells everyone that "If you want the goods delivered you have to treat him delicate, gentle—like a girl" (255).

44. Walter Benjamin, "The Work of Art in the Age of Mechanical Reproduction," in *Illuminations,* Harry Zohn, trans. (New York: Schocken, 1969) 219-253.

45. George Jean Nathan, *Encyclopaedia of the Theatre* (New York: Alfred Knopf, 1940) 292.

46. Quoted in John Gassner, *Theatre at the Crossroads* (New York: Holt, Rinehart, Winston, 1960) 310-311.

47. Jean Baudrillard, *America,* Chris Turner, trans. (New York: Verso, 1988) 80.

48. Baudrillard, *America,* 80.

49. Gassner, "Long Journey," 30.

50. Baudrillard, *America,* 56.

51. See David Q. Voigt, "No Sex Till Monday: The Fetish Phenomenon in American Sport," in *Objects of Special Devotion: Fetishes and Fetishism in Popular Culture.* Ray B. Browne, ed. (Bowling Green, OH: Bowling Green U Popular P, 1982) 115-135.

52. Weales, *Clifford Odets,* 128.

53. Nathan, *Encyclopaedia,* 288; John Mason Brown, *Broadway in Review* (New York: W. W. Norton, 1940) 176, 178.

54. The thirty dollars also suggests the thirty pieces of silver paid to Judas. Cooper is both the betrayer and the betrayed, however, an example of what consumer culture requires for participation. It is also significant to note that while Cooper talks about living in the park and eating grass if Ben doesn't allow him to postpone rent payment and plans a diet of onions and bread, as soon as Ben says he will wait until the end of the summer, Cooper leaves for a shave in the barbershop downstairs. Consumerist pleasures are difficult to escape, even in hard times.

55. Wendy Smith notes that it wasn't just Odets' imagination that saw the salvation of the Group as his responsibility. She cites an unsigned paper generated within the

Group titled "An Analysis of the Problems," which viewed "Odets once more as the Group's potential savior." She goes on to quote the paper directly: "'The successful production of *Night Music* opens the opportunity of reorganizing the Group to ensure its future existence as a Group" (RLD, 394).

56. *New Republic*, April 30, 1951.

57. Warren Susman, *Culture as History: The Transformation of American Society in the Twentieth Century* (New York: Pantheon, 1984) 214-215.

58. Quoted in Susman, *Culture as History*, 223.

59. Susman, *Culture as History*, 212.

60. Max Horkheimer and Theodor Adorno have argued that, like consumer capitalism, the very idea of a World's Fair is predicated upon the idea of abundance, in fact, of "discardability" ("The Culture Industry: Enlightenment as Mass Deception," in *The Dialectic of Enlightenment*, John Cumming, trans. [New York: Continuum, 1972] 120). It appears and disappears, changes shape, molds itself to consumer expectations and ideals. The visit of Fay and Steve to the Fair acknowledges this fact: "In a few days they'll close it all. . . . the season's over" (NM, 160).

61. Robert A. M. Stern, Gregory Gilmartin, and Thomas Mellins, *New York 1930: Architecture and Urbanism Between the Two World Wars* (New York: Rizzoli, 1987) 727; Clifford Orr, "Around the Fair: Momentary Refuge." *The New Yorker* 15 (September 19, 1939): 55.

62. It is significant that Rosenberger's first names are Abraham Lincoln. In his journal in 1958, Odets wrote, "Lincoln did some tricky and sly things but I doubt, from my reading, if he ever did an inhuman one. He is human, strangely human. And it is true, I think, that he showed me the folly of the extreme left position. It is a place for goading but not for construction" (LCA, dated February 12, 1958). Odets' admiration for Lincoln is reflected in *Night Music* by Rosenberger, whose moderate urging of Steve and Fay is far less radical than that of characters in his earlier plays. What is also important is Odets' use of political populism to connect national myths with his argument. In the play, a huge statue of Washington on Constitution Mall at the Fair reminds the characters of the idealistic beginnings of the Republic. Washington promised "bread and apples for every man, a flower for his girl" (179), but Odets delineates the discrepancy between idealism and realism when Steve says, "The world of the future! I'd like to meet this Mr. Whiskers. He don't know I'm living, Uncle Sam" (178). At the end of the play, Rosenberger quotes Washington's "the preservation of the sacred fire of liberty . . . is in the hands of the people" as a call to arms.

Chapter 4

Odets and the Dwindling Political Theatre, 1940-1954

CLASHES BY NIGHT: THE END OF THE GROUP AND THE BEGINNING OF THE WAR

After *Night Music* failed, Odets withdrew in discouragement from the Group for much of 1940, drifting between New York and Hollywood, working sporadically on various plays—one on Woodrow Wilson, another about a group of homeless men, and a third about a violent love triangle (which would eventually become his first non-Group play, *Clash by Night*). The Group itself was in uneasy hiatus, without a secure plan for the fall season. The old conflict between Clurman and the actors intensified as the year progressed and no clear solution to pressing problems appeared. At the same time, the escalating war in Europe compounded the tension and despair—the growing certainty of American involvement exacerbated arguments among Group members who favored different courses of action. On May 10, Germany invaded the Low Countries, and by June 14 troops were in Paris. The quick German victories pressed the grim realities of the war more forcibly upon the Group, fighting its own war; Clurman noted that "the outside world in its crack up appeared to justify the sense of breakdown within me" (TFY, 270).

Against this backdrop, the Group, without Odets, gathered in June to forge a workable plan. They scheduled one show for the fall of 1940, Irwin Shaw's *Retreat to Pleasure*—a play strangely out of keeping with Group artistic and temperamental standards (RLD, 407). By September, Clurman proposed more radical changes: a reorganization of the Group that would, in effect, make it a producing organization along the lines of the Guild. Only those actors who could be used in *Retreat to Pleasure* would be cast and paid; others would be released. The actors were outraged at Clurman's proposal. Odets, too, was unhappy with Clurman's highhandedness, yet was unwilling to remain with the Group if the underlying problems of the theatre—political and economic—were not addressed. The failure of *Night Music* had clearly signaled the beginning of the end, not just for Odets' participation in the Group but for the Group itself.

Throughout the year, Odets, too, was struggling to reconcile his desire for personal achievement with his position in the Group. As a substitute for work and a way to combat lethargy—he refers to himself in June as a "sunken cathedral of a person" (TIR, 189)—Odets began to keep a regular journal, the only time he ever did so. The diary reveals an increasing struggle to reconcile personal and dramaturgical questions with political ones. Though Odets remained politically committed, overall his private writings detail the shift away from overtly political concerns to a concern with the larger issue of "form" that he had begun to explore in *Night Music*. This conscious concern with finding the proper means to express his ideas certainly reflects anxiety over the loss of the Group, but it also indicates a maturation in Odets' dramaturgy. His Group plays had been propelled by an energy borrowed from his surroundings, an almost visceral response to the depression and its effect on people. As Clurman noted,

He would say that he had written his first plays because he had seen his schoolmates, whom he had always thought cheerful good fellows, turn into either tasteless masses of nameless beef, or become thin, wan, sick ciphers. He wanted to explain what had happened to them, and, through them, express his love, his fear, his hope for the world. (TFY, 118)

But by 1940, Odets recognized that his innate ability to connect with people, his facility with language, and his passion could undercut his working habits, drawing him away from a steady devotion to work. Often, he admonished himself in his journal to work harder, more honestly; he pondered how he could reconcile his innate romanticism with a detached discipline: "There is something vastly self-destructive in the essential nature of the romantic, but when he is a good artist he builds a form to gird him in, to prevent the scattering of his life—his art teaches him a way of life and he lives it!" (TIR, 172). The Group and the depression had given him as much of a framework as his early plays needed. The trained actors were the discipline for his passion; the deprivations of the depression lent focus to his lyrical protests. His post-Group plays, however, were a new challenge, a struggle to find the new forms that would allow him to develop outside the Group context.

The first play that challenged Odets' new sense of form was *Clash by Night*. In the journal, he chronicles its development from its beginnings. Envisioning the play as "brutal," one that "has to do with the need for a new morality, with a return . . . to voluntarily imposed and assumed forms in a world of democracy where there are no forms" (TIR, 240-241), Odets saw the form of the play mirroring the social and political mood of mid-1940 America. Thus, his idea of form involved both dramaturgical structure and codes of behavior. It was a regulating force, a sense of direction in a world consumed by unrestrained appetite: "There is no dynamic in life or art without form: paradoxically, the prison cell is what gives the freedom!" (TIR, 344).

With the Group on the verge of dissolution, Odets' struggle for "form" was a struggle to find a context in which his work could be meaningful—not just commercial—to a larger culture. He was worried that the Group's difficulties reflected a larger failure of culture in America. Clurman remembers a conversation with

Odets in 1940, as they walked down Broadway; Odets asked, as they surveyed the decay of the once great theatres, "Is it possible for anything good to come out of such an environment?"[1] His anxiety was exacerbated by a stay in Hollywood in which he completed the screenplay for *Night Music*. His journal entries condemn the "constant toadying" required by the movie business, the way real life "is subordinated to device, cliché, and plot movement—to the supermechanism" (TIR, 263). Under pressure from producer Al Lewin, the script changed drastically in Hollywood; for example, ethnic differences, important in the play, are elided in the screenplay: the Greek-American Steve Takis becomes Steve Edwards, while Rosenberger becomes Detective Tobin (LCA, no date). The film was never produced, and by the end of his "season of learning" in Hollywood, anxious about the developing political situation in Europe, Odets was thrilled to return to *Clash by Night*.

The war had influenced the plays Odets had been working on. The Woodrow Wilson script, for example, was intended to answer to increasingly adamant calls for American intervention. He specifically criticized Robert E. Sherwood, whose *There Shall Be No Night* had just opened, for writing a theatrical "call to arms." Sherwood's play, which won the Pulitzer Prize for 1941, addressed the Soviet invasion of Finland, celebrating those engaged in the fight for democracy.[2] *There Shall Be No Night* reached the stage when America was deeply divided about the war and came down firmly on the side of intervention. On the other hand, Odets' ideological pacifism—he long remained sympathetic to the Soviet cause, outraged by the betrayal of ordinary people by political leaders, and firmly convinced that the war was capitalism at its most brutal—drove him to show the United States headed down a well-traveled bloody path.

America had been inching closer to war since the 1939 Soviet-German nonaggression pact. By mid-1940, Americans held few illusions about Hitler's goals; his quick subjugation of Poland, Belgium, and Holland, the German march into Paris, and the beginning of air raids of London in August made it clear that American involvement was imminent. In June, Congress approved $4.5 billion for defense; by the end of the year, that appropriation had more than doubled. But the clearest indication of American involvement in the war was Roosevelt's 1940 transfer of warships to Britain in exchange for naval bases and the Lend-Lease Act of March 1941, which made more equipment available for Britain's defense. The adoption of the first peacetime draft in American history, approved in September 1940, advertised that America would fight if provoked; without a formal declaration of war, this was the closest America could come to involvement in the conflict.[3] Nevertheless, isolationist sentiment remained strong in certain circles. The 1940 presidential election, in which Roosevelt sought an unprecedented third term, divided the country even further. Despite the fact that his opponent, Wendell Willkie, had endorsed the agreement with Britain, the campaign focused upon the question of which candidate would be best able to keep the country out of war. Roosevelt vowed the United States would not enter the war unless attacked; Willkie declared that Roosevelt was already committed. In November, however, voters sided with Roosevelt, sending him back to the White House with a clear majority in both popular and electoral votes. If Roosevelt was indeed committed to involvement, the American people were beginning to approve of that commitment.[4]

The probability of war increased throughout late 1940 and early 1941, sparked by a series of events in both Europe and Asia: a September 1940 economic and military alliance forged between Germany and Japan, the German invasion of the Soviet Union in May 1941, and the sinking of a number of American ships by German submarines in the summer of 1941. In the Pacific, Japanese control of China and increasing advances against European outposts had put Roosevelt on guard. America responded by employing economic sanctions against the Japanese, which were expanded in July 1941 to include the oil Japan needed to fuel their planes. The situation deteriorated; by November, the Japanese were planning the attack on Pearl Harbor that forced the United States into war.[5]

Clash by Night, written against the backdrop of these events, takes on their gloomy mood. On the surface level, the play is constructed as a vicious love triangle in which a jealous husband, incited by a weak but malevolent Fascist, murders his wife's lover rather than lose her. On a deeper level, however, the play continues the larger examination of "American life" that had begun with *Golden Boy, Rocket to the Moon*, and *Night Music*. In fact, Odets' play was less overtly political than many others of the Broadway season: Sherwood's *There Shall Be No Night*, Lillian Hellman's *Watch on the Rhine* (1941), Maxwell Anderson's *Candle in the Wind* (1941), or John Steinbeck's stage adaptation of his novel *The Moon Is Down* (1942)—all of which dealt specifically with the threat of Nazism to freedom at home and abroad—or Howard Koch and John Huston's *In Time to Come* (1941), a biographical drama about the last years of the Wilson presidency. Odets' political stance was less concerned with the possibilities of war than with the American attitudes that allowed war to become a possibility. No wonder, given the galvanized political climate in December 1941, that the underlying themes of the play were missed by reviewers. When *Clash by Night* opened less than three weeks after the attack on Pearl Harbor, Odets' antiwar play was lost in the political exigencies of the moment. In one of the more positive newspaper reviews, Brooks Atkinson noted that the first act had "some of the best literary work any one has done in the modern dramas" but that the last half is "maundering and wordy," the theme "commonplace" (NYT, January 11, 1942).

As *Night Music* had been, *Clash by Night* was an attempt to articulate the political by means of the personal, to show how an inherent American lack of "form" led to the ensnaring of human beings in violence; the hot, dull Staten Island setting becomes a microcosm—though not an allegory—of the kind of personal abdication that allows despotism to gain power. In this sense, *Clash by Night* manifests the ongoing concerns about American life fostered in Odets by the Group. Taking its title from the final line of Matthew Arnold's "Dover Beach," it examines the superficial attitudes that Odets felt led to the surrender of individual will to the collective (Fascism) and eventually to unspeakable violence. As in Arnold's poem, facing a world of ignorance and violence, the only hope is individuals who are "true to one another."

The initial abdications in the play are Mae Wilinski's refusal to treat her husband Jerry honestly and respectfully and his inability to behave maturely in relation to her. Prodded by inchoate desires for something greater, she takes up with Jerry's friend, Earl, a movie projectionist who remains unconnected to anything throughout the play. The most risible character is Jerry's uncle Kress, an outspoken Fascist who urges his nephew to murder from behind a mask of kindness. Only two characters are clear-eyed enough to see the connections between individual responsibility and social action within the play. Joe and Peggy, in many ways the ideological descendants of Ralph Berger and Leo Gordon, vow to escape from the cycle of false promise and avoided action, though as others have noted, their presence scarcely relieves the dark mood.

Part of the irony of *Clash by Night*'s lukewarm reception was mirrored in Odets' own changing attitudes toward the war. Despite his distrust of political maneuvering at home and abroad, Odets had always opposed Hitler (*Till the Day I Die* was one of the first anti-Fascist plays to be produced on Broadway); by late 1940, he was increasingly convinced that America had a moral and political responsibility to stop the German dictator. *Clash by Night*, then, gingerly treads a middle ground between the abhorrence of war as a sucker's game perpetrated by capitalism for profit and the desire for democratic nations to maintain decency and idealism in the world. The dark tone of the play reflects Odets' belief that America had lost its idealism, its clarity; he wanted to echo the wartime ambivalence and fear of the entire country in his doomed love triangle. However, three weeks at war, American audiences were already shifting into a different mood, one that left Joe and Peggy's indictment of the system far behind.

The production of *Clash by Night* was fraught with difficulty. Though embittered by his *Night Music* experience, in late 1940 Odets reluctantly offered *Clash by Night* to his company. Hoping that his new play might allow for the Group's reorganization, Odets approached Lee Strasberg to direct the play under its banner. Odets wanted Clurman to restructure the Group as a collective, with Strasberg as co-director. Otherwise, if the Group went commercial, he wrote "([F]or me for one) the movies for us! I will not live and work in a Broadway theatre which dictates conditions which I despise" (TIR, 251). But by December, *Retreat to Pleasure* had failed, Clurman had virtually abandoned the Group, and Odets and Strasberg were left to stage *Clash by Night* independently, with Billy Rose as producer. Indeed, the connection to Rose underscored the frustration with the commercial model the Group had challenged from its inception. Rose insisted upon such a large share of the profits that there would be little left for the Group. Finally, he insisted that the Group's name be removed from the playbill and influenced casting to the extent that only two Group actors, Lee J. Cobb and Art Smith, ended up in the production.

The Group officially shut its doors on May 18, 1941, months before *Clash by Night* reached the stage. Clurman penned an elegy in the *New York Times* declaring that the Group failed ultimately because "there can be no institutional product without an institutional foundation." After ten years of struggling against Broadway practice, the Group was forced to abandon its increasingly quixotic dream. Even more importantly, with the Group officially dissolved, Odets was an independent playwright for the first time. Now more than ever dependent upon the whims of the marketplace for success, Odets had to tread even more carefully the tightrope between profit and personal expression. The commercial and critical failure of *Clash by Night* forced Odets to again rethink his relationship with Broadway. He looked for a period of "creative repose": "I wanted to shake out of my system the disappointments of two successive commercial failures in the theatre" (NYT, July 25, 1948). As before, when times grew difficult in the theatre, Odets turned to Hollywood; this time he would stay for five years.

"THEY WOULDN'T TAKE ME FOR ANYTHING": THE WAR YEARS

Odets left for California in 1942 to write a film about the life of George Gershwin for Warner Brothers. Working steadily, he forged a dense, but completely unworkable, 900-page script titled *Rhapsody in Blue*. Though he offered to cut the script on his own time, Jack Warner immediately fired him, calling another writer in to finish. A film of the same name was released in 1945; Odets received no screen credit for it, but the director, Irving Rapper, claimed that some of Odets' original script had been used.[6] Of course, such borrowing was in keeping with standard studio practice of farming out drafts from one writer to others, cobbling together scripts from the efforts of various people, and awarding screen credit arbitrarily. Indeed, the lack of final control over the screenplay—along with the lack of a clear or fair system for determining screen credit—was one of the key issues that had driven the screenwriters to unionize in the 1930s. Odets himself claimed that he had refused credit for scripts rewritten by others after he left Hollywood: "Rather than share credit for what they churned out between gin-rummy games, I decided to pass up fame and keep my self-respect" (NYT, August 27, 1944). In fact, throughout his career, he worked on what he called "dozens" of screenplays—including *It's a Wonderful Life, Notorious, Blockade*, and others[7]—though he accepted or was given credit for only seven: *The General Died at Dawn* (1936), *None but the Lonely Heart* (1944), *Humoresque* (1946, with Zachary Gold), *Deadline at Dawn* (1946), *Sweet Smell of Success* (1957, with Ernest Lehman), *The Story on Page One* (1959), and *Wild in the Country* (1961).

In late 1942, Odets returned to New York briefly, where he was contracted by the Theatre Guild to work on *The Russian People*, the first adaptation of Soviet writer Konstantin Simonov in the United States. Set in a village occupied by the Germans, the play exalts Russian courage in fighting the occupation, offering the American audience a glance behind the lines. Nevertheless, though the play was advertised as a virtually documentary depiction of the Soviet struggle, most American reviews of the play saw it as sentimental, uneven, and confusing. Coming as it did during the German assault and the always-tenuous alliance between America and Russia, the production proved to be more important for political goodwill than for any artistic reasons; its main purpose was to raise support for the Soviet cause. Odets later called it "such a bad play" that he wanted to disavow connections with it, claiming that he was prevented by a Soviet government order from making substantial changes to Simonov's original. Constrained as he was by the Soviet order, Odets didn't write the script so much as transpose the original into "clear and vital theatrical English."[8] Most of the adaptation Odets did on the play tended toward characterization, making specifics out of generalizations.

The adaptation had another short-term benefit for Odets: renewed contact with the Guild. The next year, he worked on an adaptation of Franz Werfel's *Jacobowsky and the Colonel*, but director Elia Kazan was unhappy with Odets' version.[9] The script, completed by S. N. Behrman, opened in March 1944 to modest success. Despite his work with the Guild, Odets' inability to write a full-length original script until 1948 emphasizes how deeply the closing of the Group offices—and his repeated trips to Hollywood—had affected him. After the Group's dissolution, the adaptations filled his need for a political and socially relevant reason to write; they also placed him once again at the center of Broadway theatre. In some sense, war plays like Simonov's and Werfel's held an analogous position to the Popular Front leftist plays of the 1930s. Both reached out to wide audiences in support of a common cause, and both hoped to create a union between the theatrical event and the lives of the participants.

However powerfully Odets had given voice to the discontents of his generation during the depression, however much he was the man of the 1930s, the war found him cast aside. Branded as a "premature anti-Fascist" (a euphemistic label given to many radicals and Communists from the 1930s) Odets was turned down for work in the Office of War Information as a writer of morale-boosting plays or films. Odets had rallied to the war cause, even dutifully registering for the draft in the fall of 1940. However, he was prevented from active duty because of his bad eyes and an arthritic condition in his foot. The irony that the war against Fascism could not tolerate those who had been prematurely opposed to it or that outspoken supporters of the Soviet Union—American allies—would not be allowed to serve made the war years, as he said, "a difficult time. . . . They wouldn't take me for anything" (NYT, February 20, 1949). While others from Hollywood (e.g., Frank Capra in his 1942-1945 *Why We Fight* series) and Broadway (Sherwood's speechwriting for Roosevelt) who didn't serve in combat found ways to put their particular talents to use in service of the war effort, Odets was kept from the only active service he was able to offer. Others with leftist leanings were also excluded: Capra himself fired a number of writers who were under investigation by HUAC, and the screenwriter Philip Dunne was denied security clearance to work with John Ford on his war documentaries.[10]

Excluded from service, Odets felt alienated and confused. His inherent distrust of war was complicated by his desire to be needed. He recognized that the draft was a sign of an ideological force galvanizing the entire country; difficult times were forging important social and political bonds:

[The draft] has brought all young men between the ages of twenty-one and thirty-five together. They look at each other in a different way, feel related, are less restricted with each other. . . .This feeling of togetherness is very important in the lives of living men; it is a feeling that a capitalist state never gives, except in times of emergency . . . which explains the real attractiveness of war for men—joining together to fight a common enemy!" (TIR, 320)

For Odets, who had lost the Group, another set of comrades fighting against a common enemy, exclusion from the war effort isolated him even further.

Broadway was quick to adapt to political events. War plays flourished in the early 1940s—though they by no means made up a majority of those produced, nor were they always successful. As Brenda Murphy has commented, most of them "represented the Allies' fight against Hitler as a clear contest between the forces of good and the forces of evil in which the soldier's moral choice had no shades of gray."[11] Nevertheless, the number of plays (many by prominent playwrights) either set in the war or using the conflict as a backdrop shows how powerfully World War II shaped American theatrical consciousness. The 1942-1943 season brought Maxwell Anderson's *The Eve of St. Mark*, Phillip Barry's *Without Love*, and a number of London transplants; the 1943-1944 season debuted, in addition to the Behrman adaptation of Werfel's play, Moss Hart's successful *Winged Victory*, Anderson's *Storm Operation*, and Lillian Hellman's *The Searching Wind*. While these plays were of mixed quality and efficacy, their prominence on the Broadway stage demonstrated an intimate connection between the political situation and Broadway theatre.

The 1944-1945 season, though it premiered over sixty new shows, had only a handful of plays dealing with the war, and many of those used the war as backdrop for comic or dramatic action increasingly unrelated to the war effort. As the devastation on both fronts dragged to a close, audiences became less interested in watching the horrors of war replayed onstage than they were in escaping into other fare. Two of the biggest comic hits of the 1944-1945 season were the escapist *Harvey* and *I Remember Mama*. The season also marked the debut of a new force in American drama, Tennessee Williams, whose play *The Glass Menagerie* earned plaudits for Williams and for its star, Laurette Taylor. America was preparing for the postwar period. By the 1945-1946 season, a number of plays chronicled the struggles of soldiers readjusting to American life, most notably, Ralph Nelson's *The Wind Is Ninety*, Arthur Laurents' *Home of the Brave*, Robert Ardrey's *Jeb* (about the racial discrimination facing many black soldiers following the war), Maxwell Anderson's poorly received *Truckline Café*, and Robert E. Sherwood's first play in five years, *The Rugged Path* (set during the war but dealing largely with postwar issues).

While Broadway worked its way through the war prosperously and patriotically, Hollywood produced its own brand of patriotic propaganda. The commercial film industry had mobilized with the rest of the country, and soon a spate of war films flooded the theatres. Perhaps more importantly, the studios and the government had come to a tacit agreement about acceptable forms, assuring both "predictability and profit."[12] Odets returned to Hollywood in 1943 and would soon offer his own screenplay in support of the war, an adaptation of Richard Llewellyn's *None but the Lonely Heart*. The rights to the novel had been purchased by RKO at Cary Grant's insistence; Odets was brought in to transform the novel's callow, working-class protagonist into a character worthy of Grant's star image. Initially, Odets was stunned to hear the role was intended for Grant— "I asked if anyone *read* this book. It seemed no one had"—but Grant himself had chosen Odets to write the screenplay and later insisted that Odets direct the film.[13] The two would remain lifelong friends.

None But the Lonely Heart is among the most polished of Odets' film scripts; it is doubtless the most like his plays. As director, he had relative control over the entire process. The movie—unlike many films produced during the war, which followed a relatively set formula that elided class and racial differences to promote consensus—is concerned with class difference and the search for a full human life.[14] At the same time, it is a war movie, articulating Odets' deep conviction, first expressed in *Waiting for Lefty*, of the necessity of fighting for a good life and his growing fear, expressed most critically in *Clash By Night*, that his contemporaries had abdicated the fight. The film loosely follows Llewellyn's novel, tracing the life of Ernest Verdun Mott (Grant), who, as the opening voice-over tells us, "searched for a free, a beautiful and noble life in the second quarter of the twentieth century" (BFP, 263), The film opens upon Ernie's return home to London. Indeed, this is the first Odets play set outside of the New York area, and though the dialect often seems inauthentic (perhaps as much Grant's fault as Odets'), the themes are recognizably Odetsean. Unwilling to participate in an economic system that forces one to be either the devourer or the devoured, Ernie has made a life of odd jobs and wandering, disconnected even from his ailing mother (Ethel Barrymore). He refuses to help run her secondhand store: "She don't know they milk the cow that stands still. Wants me in that silly dusty business of hers, squeezing pennies out of paupers. No thanks!" (273).

The main part of the movie follows the growing relationship between Ernie and his mother. Ernie, rooted in home and store, still feels trapped in a mercenary game. A number of scenes demonstrate his innate sympathy for the impoverished people who come into his shop. When his mother reminds him that there are millions worse off than they, Ernie responds, "Peace. That's what us millions want—without having to snatch it from the smaller dogs. Peace—to be not a hound and not a hare. But peace with pride and a decent human life, with all the trimmings" (302).[15] Only human connections keep him from leaving again. He befriends Harry Twite (Barry Fitzgerald) at Armistice Day services at Westminster Abbey (Twite lost his son in World War I; Mott, his father). At the same time, he is involved in complex relationships with two very different women. The first, Aggie, is an artist, a cellist whom Ernie has known all his life. She understands and loves him and makes no claims upon him. The second, Ada, is a cashier at the local arcade.

None but the Lonely Heart interrelates themes of homelessness and responsibility with the economic questions that had always fascinated Odets. Fearful of his mother's poverty, Ernie joins up with Jim Mordinoy, a small-time gangster (reminiscent of Fuseli in *Golden Boy*), hoping to make her life more comfortable. For Odets, "decent human life" is still in part measurable in material possessions. The first thing Ernie does with his newfound wealth is to get his mother's house wired for electricity, and, prodded by an advertisement—"Why let mother slave away?"—he buys her a refrigerator. But as always, the refrigerator is an ambiguous good; it is a real benefit to those who can afford it, admired by almost all the neighbors who come to see it; however, its price is high. Once in the game, Ernie feels he must continue to run with the "hounds," though he hates Mordinoy (who refers to himself as "a machine") and is torn by guilt. In one particularly violent episode, Mordinoy's gang ransacks and robs Ike's shop, beating Ike and his employee. At first Ernie stands by quietly but eventually jumps in to protect Ike, alienating Mordinoy and setting the stage for his own fall. His mother dies, and Ada leaves him for Mordinoy.

At the end of the film, then, Ernie is alone again. This time, however, he has a vision. Hearing the ominous sounds of airplanes overhead, he tells Twite: "What a go—what a rum go it is! Where's the decent human life the books tell us about? When's the world coming out of its midnight? When's the human soul getting off its knees?!" When Twite suggests that "the world finds something if it needs it bad enough. But sometimes it takes a war," Ernie vows that he will "[f]ight with the men who'll fight for a human way of life" (330-331). Like the romantic characters from Odets' plays who vow a better life through human effort, the movie ends with Ernie's resolve to participate in the struggle. Though *None but the Lonely Heart* is set before the start of World War II, it clearly supports the struggle against fascism. Mordinoy's assault on Ike is a particularly pointed condemnation of the machine-like Nazi brutality against the Jews. While not jingoistically patriotic, Ernie's closing vow nevertheless reflects the dominant concerns of wartime liberals, who looked to a postwar period in which (as Archibald MacLeish, deputy director of the Office of War Information, said) "something admirable, something of human worth and human significance" would be created.[16] Even during the war, Odets' concern is with those people for and by whom it was fought.

None but the Lonely Heart was not a box office success, though it was selected by the National Board of Review as one of the best English-language films of the year and garnered a number of Academy Award nominations. Barrymore won an Oscar for her portrayal of Mrs. Mott. Still, the film has had many admirers for both the screenplay and Odets' direction. James Agee in *The Nation* remarked that, despite some sentimentality, what really showed through in Odets' direction were his "faith and love for people. . . . Odets was more interested in filling his people with life and grace than in explaining them, arguing over them or using them as boxing gloves." Pauline Kael praised him for bringing off some "hard-earned effects with an élan that recalled Orson Welles' first films" in "an extraordinary debut film." The French filmmaker Jean Renoir, who befriended Odets in Hollywood, called it "a masterpiece." But *None But the Lonely Heart's* failure at the box office forced Grant back to comedy and cut Odets' directing career short. As Kael commented, "It is an indication of the movie industry's attitude toward talent that Odets only got one other chance to direct—fifteen years later."[17]

Odets would receive credit for two other films before returning to Broadway with *The Big Knife*, a play that viciously attacked Hollywood minds and morals. *Humoresque* (Warner Brothers, dir. Jean Negulesco, 1946) is a melodrama starring Joan Crawford and John Garfield in which a struggling violinist (Garfield) is aided by a wealthy socialite (Crawford). An intense affair ensues, but when the relationship complicates his work, the violinist chooses music over love. At the end of the film, she commits suicide by walking into the ocean, while the musician plays a concert. Despite themes that seem characteristically Odetsean—the struggling violinist mirrors *Golden Boy*—perhaps the most striking element of the movie is the nonstop wisecracking of pianist-comedian Oscar Levant, a friend of Odets' who plays Garfield's friend in the film. Levant's joking (much of which he claimed was ad-libbed rather than scripted by Odets) and Garfield's intensity enliven what is for the most part a conventional, if tautly written, melodrama.

The other film Odets wrote in the 1940s was *Deadline at Dawn* (RKO, 1946), directed by Clurman. The script, which Clurman says Odets wrote for him "as a favor," based on a 1944 William Irish novel, traces the efforts of a sailor to clear his name of a murder charge before he must return to his base. Aided by a beneficent, philosophical cabdriver, a quirkily Odetsean character in the line of Gus in *Paradise Lost* or Rosenberger in *Night Music*, the sailor and his girl (Susan Hayward) struggle unsuccessfully, until the cabdriver confesses to the murder in order to help the sailor. Sprinkled with Odets' quirky dialogue and character—for example, the cabbie has a habit of beginning his sentences with "Statistics show . . ."—it is a generally undistinguished, if enjoyable, film. Clurman himself called it "of no importance" but noted that it had proved "moderately profitable."[18] Still, some critics have noted that the dialogue in this film rings with Odetsean sympathy for the common people: "Odets created a verbal world of his own, with inverted word order, lilts, and nuances that captured a sincere "authenticity" for the worlds that the neighborhood characters inhabited.[19]

What Odets thought about the film is unclear; he rarely talked about his scripts specifically, but he did believe that his work for film had helped him as a writer, as he would say in an interview in the early 1960s:

Let them stand for what they are. They are technically very adept. I have learned a great deal from making and shaping these scripts. . . . It's professional work; I'm a professional writer. And I'm never ashamed of the professional competence which is in these scripts. I have never downgraded human beings.[20]

Odets would continue to vacillate about the possibilities of meaningful film work up until his death. He left the industry in the late 1940s because of the blacklist but by 1957 had returned for good.

ODETS, THE NEW AMERICA, AND THE COLD WAR

In late 1945, America was preparing for a stable postwar period different from any before. First, the war had brought to an end 1930s-style leftism; driven by patriotism and a need for security, the country had drifted right. Threats of foreign invasion had prompted the internment of hundreds of thousands of Japanese-Americans on the West Coast, and the passage of the Smith Act in 1940 initiated strong peacetime antisedition powers to suppress suspected subversives.[21] Roosevelt himself asked the Federal Bureau of Investigation (FBI) to probe political opponents as early as 1940. After the war, such measures manifested themselves in the excesses of the Cold War, as fear of Communism dominated American consciousness. In addition, Republicans gained control of both the House and Senate in the 1946 midterm elections, effectively killing what progressivism remained from the New Deal.[22] One of the most telling signs of leftism's postwar eclipse was the struggle of organized labor. Unions had grown stronger—and more liberal—during the war, striking often and successfully for better wages and working conditions. In 1944 and 1945 there were almost 5,000 strikes involving over 2 million workers. By 1945, CIO membership was at an all-time high of almost 15 million. Yet by the late 1940s and early 1950s, unemployment and conservative postwar legislation began to limit union power. The Taft-Hartley Act, passed over Truman's veto in 1947, required union leaders to sign non-Communist affidavits and allowed states to prohibit closed union shops.[23] Labor, long the bastion of leftism in America, was on a collision course with management, and over the course of the next decade many unions sacrificed larger visions of the left—civil rights, universal health insurance, and federal aid for education—for private gains, including cost-of-living increases and better benefits for members. The social collectivism of the 1930s turned toward achievement of the individual dream in the postwar years. In addition, the war against Fascism and the fear of Communism's spread had created even in liberals a fear not only of totalitarianism but also of the "mass," who represented "the dangerous and irrational impulses within every individual and every society."[24]

If the country as a whole was moving right, Odets had drifted some of the way with it. Though he remained liberal and never lost the fervent romanticism that had driven him during the 1930s, his work from the war onward reflected a growing understanding of what it meant to work within the consensus-seeking structures— economic and political—that shaped postwar America. He remained in Hollywood for extended periods and began a family. He had married an actress named Bette Grayson in 1943, and they had two children, Nora (born in 1945) and Walt (born in 1947). From the mid-1940s through the 1950s, Odets worked periodically (and often unhappily) within the confines of the studio system. Still, he continued to speak out against a society that urged people to acquire more and more—the economic boom of the 1950s would explode all notions of what was possible within consumer capitalism—without offering moral or spiritual balance. Even more importantly, the radical beliefs that had formed the backbone of progressive leftism and that had catapulted him to fame in the 1930s would come back to haunt him in the late 1940s and 1950s.

Economically strong, natural resources intact, with an industry hungry for profits and a large workforce eager for employment, the United States had emerged from World War II an even more dominant economic, military, and political power than it had been in 1941. Domestically, things were changing quickly as well. An unprecedented baby boom in the years immediately following the war, coupled with a building boom in the suburbs and the largest migration in American history—over 2 million African-Americans moved from the deep South to northern cities during the 1940s and another 3 million came in the next twenty years[25]— radically altered the demographic structure of American cities. Many African-Americans had moved north to take advantage of high-paying work during the war and had stayed, hoping that racial conditions would improve in the postwar period. Progress was slow, however; race riots exploded in several urban areas in the late 1940s, as minorities who had served valiantly in the war returned home to find themselves still second-class citizens. In the rapidly developing suburbs, whites often resorted to violence to keep their neighborhoods segregated. Racial tensions in the North nevertheless remained better than conditions in the South, where Jim Crow laws were used to deny African-Americans access to jobs, education, and the vote.

At home and abroad, increased power meant more responsibility; Americans, though fearful, were increasingly committed to aggressively protecting democracy throughout the world. Until 1949, the United States was the only country with an atomic bomb and a demonstrated willingness to use it. Also, between 1948 and 1952 it had helped to rebuild Western Europe by giving $13.34 billion in aid through the Marshall Plan, aid both political and humanitarian; it aimed to shore up areas many feared vulnerable to Communism. In March 1947, President Truman boldly declared American intentions to "support free peoples who are resisting attempted subjugation by armed minorities or by outside pressures . . . [and] assist free people to work out their own destinies in their own way."[26] This "Truman Doctrine"—which was partly formulated to "scare the hell out of the American people"—helped to widen the already growing rift between the United States and the Soviets, who were building a security zone of puppet governments around their borders.[27] The Cold War had begun in earnest; it would dominate the political and cultural landscape as powerfully as the depression and the war had done.

The Cold War influenced domestic and foreign policy, entertainment, the media, and everyday life in profound ways. By early 1946, Stalin had taken a decidedly anti-American stance, blaming "monopoly capitalism" for the war and suggesting that the spread of Communism was the only way to avoid future wars. When twenty-two people were arrested in Canada on suspicion of spying for the Soviets, the fear of Communist infiltration forced Americans, both in the government and out, into a state of high alert. Though there was fear in the administration that an overtly anti-Soviet policy would bring about war, by 1949 American worries about Communism were strong enough for Congress—which had refused all peacetime alliances since 1778—to join the North Atlantic Treaty Organization (NATO), a new alliance with Western European nations that "treated an attack against one as an attack against all." By 1951, American forces had been committed to NATO in Europe.[28]

Elsewhere, the victory in China of Mao-Tse -tung in October 1949 made fear of worldwide Communist domination even more a threat; "containment" became the goal of American foreign policy. By early 1950, America was involved in a police action to stop Communist aggression against South Korea. In 1949, the Soviets, working with information obtained through espionage, had successfully tested a nuclear device. By late 1952, American scientists working at the Los Alamos laboratory had developed a hydrogen bomb with a force 1,000 times greater than the atomic bomb dropped on Hiroshima. The Soviets successfully tested a similar bomb in 1955.[29] The new nuclear age, holding the possibility of the most destructive war in human history, overshadowed the prosperity of postwar America.

The idea of "containment" also affected domestic affairs. The National Security Act (1947) established the Central Intelligence Agency (CIA) and the National Security Administration and increased spying on Communists by the FBI. Communist paranoia began to manifest itself in the worst Red Scare since the 1920s. Investigations of communist activity in the United States had taken place during the late 1930s and early 1940s; for example, Congressman Martin Dies of Texas had headed HUAC since the mid-1930s, and had briefly investigated film and theatre, but little direct action had been taken. In 1947, however, with Republicans in control of Congress, J. Parnell Thomas of New Jersey became the ranking member of the committee. Riding the rising tide of anti-Communism, Thomas stepped up his investigations of the film industry as a hotbed of radical activity. These investigations were deliberately public; the film industry was an obvious, almost tailor-made target. In May 1947, Thomas held a series of hearings in Los Angeles, targeting labor unions (including the Screen Writer's Guild) and Communist front organizations. Fourteen "friendly" witnesses testified to pervasive Communist influence in Hollywood, giving Thomas enough fodder to issue forty-three subpoenas for people to appear in front of HUAC.

Rumors circulated in Hollywood about who would be called to Washington; not surprisingly, Odets' name was prominent among them. He was not immediately called, however, possibly because the committee wanted to focus on current members of the Communist Party. Of the forty-three initial witnesses, nineteen were suspected radicals or Communist Party members; the rest were "friendly." The latter group, including Jack Warner and Gary Cooper, testified first in Washington, explaining how subversive content found its way into films and naming possible Communists in the industry. Odets' screenplays were mentioned as subversive by at least two witnesses: Lela Rogers, mother of Ginger, testified that *None but the Lonely Heart* was filled with Communist propaganda. Jack Warner was more circumspect, relating how he had to remove a line from an unnamed movie (*Humoresque*) in which one character upbraided another for being born rich. He did, however, name Odets and other writers as Communists, though many of those he named were not.

After the friendly witnesses had testified, ten of the other nineteen—later dubbed the Hollywood Ten—were called.[30] Claiming protection of the First Amendment, the ten (plus an eleventh, Bertolt Brecht) pugnaciously refused to answer questions about political allegiance and were declared in contempt of Congress on November 24, 1947. A number of people felt that the Ten had approached the issue unwisely; rather than openly declaring party membership and forcing the committee to admit that such membership was not illegal, they had squandered their public support in outbursts that had no effect on Thomas and his committee.[31] Though their strategy was to seek appeal to the Supreme Court on the basis of the First Amendment, their appeal was denied, and all Ten were sentenced to federal prison in June 1950. The same day—despite public promises to the contrary— movie executives issued a statement that would change the lives of Odets and hundreds of others over the course of the next decade: "We will not knowingly employ a Communist or a member of any party or group which advocates the overthrow of the government of the United States." The blacklist had begun.

Though at first opposed to HUAC's tactics, the film industry had capitulated when its financial backers insisted upon a blacklist; big-business opposition to Communism in American foreign and domestic policy had filtered down to the film industry. Privately, Odets noted that one of the complicating factors of the blacklist was the status of the writer in Hollywood: in "[a] private industry, companies hire workers to manufacture their product. Legally it is their right to hire whom they choose. Free speech does not enter as an issue. Discriminatory activities do enter (All is complicated by the fact that directors, writers & actors think of themselves as artists & not workers & trade unionists)" (LCA, dated December 1947).[32] Odets believed that "trade union mass action" was the most effective way to protest the blacklist. However, given the political climate, it is unlikely that a strike would have worked, even if one could have been organized in the face of mounting para-noia within the industry.

Following the convictions of the Ten, outrage mounted in leftist circles, though many felt a sense of impotence in the face of the increasingly implacable anti-Communism of HUAC and public opinion. A week after the blacklist was an-nounced, Odets responded publicly in a letter to *Time*. He condemned the commit-tee and denied party membership: "Shut my big unamused mouth if I don't think the Thomas Committee is a disgrace to the United States." He went on to attack what he saw as the real un-American problem, "the hopelessly vulgar and neuroti-cally superficial trash called the Hollywood film," and claimed that the supposed propaganda in his films was in fact human and honest: "I get damn tired of hearing crackpots here and in Washington constantly ascribing anything really human in films to the Communists alone. Why do they keep giving the Devil all the good tunes?"[33]

Combining his disgust for the committee with his disaffection for Hollywood, Odets laid out the terms for battle that would consume his life over the next few years. By 1948, perhaps because of the blacklist, he had returned to Broadway and was working on a new play about the film industry, at first titled *A Winter Journey* but later *The Big Knife*. As he explained to an interviewer, the "big knife" of the title is "that force in modern life which seeks to cut people off in their best flower. . . . I have nothing against Hollywood per se. I do have something against a large set-up which destroys people and eats them up" (NYT, February 20, 1949). Claim-ing that he used Hollywood as a setting because he knew it better than any other "company town," Odets centered the action on the life and death of an idealistic actor, Charlie Castle, who has been corrupted by the system. Trapped between a long-term contract and the love of his wife, Charlie in the end chooses suicide to free her from the burden of his past sins.

The Big Knife, directed by Strasberg and starring John Garfield, opened on February 24, 1949. It was Odets' first play on Broadway in almost eight years—eight years that had seen the war come and go, the decline of the left and the rise of HUAC, and the arrival of two major American playwrights, Tennessee Williams and Arthur Miller. Several groundbreaking plays had been performed: Brecht's *Galileo*, Miller's *All My Sons*, Williams' *A Streetcar Named Desire* and *Summer and Smoke*, and Jean Girardoux's *The Madwoman of Chaillot*. Odets was no longer at the center of the American theatre (though his reappearance was enough to spark $200,000 in advance sales). Indeed, comparing *The Big Knife* to Miller's *Death of a Salesman*, which ran at the same time, critics saw Odets' play as structurally weak and overwrought in tone. Kappo Phelan suggested that Odets "walk four blocks up the town to learn how the American paradox (tragedy) is to be handled without social, ethical or artistic pretensions."[34] Many others saw hypocrisy in its attack on Hollywood, accusing Odets of biting the hand that fed him.

Despite the lukewarm success of *The Big Knife*, however, Odets threw himself into the theatre scene more vigorously. He began drafting a new play, *The Country*

Girl, which he would direct as well. The play, which Odets wrote to be a hit, is a sharp study in psychology, taut and more tightly plotted than any other Odets play. Odets would later called it "a good show," though not his best work. *The Country Girl* centers on a young director who takes a chance on an older, alcoholic actor. The tension mounts when it becomes unclear whether the actor will stay sober, or whether his wife, used to her husband's dependence, will subconsciously drive him to self-destruction. In the end, the actor triumphs with the cooperation of both director and wife. Regardless of what Odets thought about *The Country Girl*, the production, with Uta Hagen, Paul Kelly and Steven Hill in the leads, was almost universally praised. John Mason Brown welcomed Odets back into the Broadway fold: "No one interested in the theatre can fail to take an almost personal satisfaction in the success which, with *The Country Girl*, has again come to Clifford Odets, and come because of his having deserved it."[35] It ran seven months.

Bolstered by his success, in early 1951 Odets volunteered to teach an introductory playwriting class to a group of students at the Actor's Studio. One of his students recalled years later Odets' generosity and teaching skills, even beneath the shadow of impending HUAC testimony.[36] In one sense, Odets was trying to restart the work he had done in the 1930s with the Theatre Union and elsewhere. As he remarked in an essay in the *New York Times*, "[T]he talent and quality of the men and women in the class, the content of their plays, shows the real health and striving for our country" (NYT, April 22, 1951). Having drifted for years without the Group, Odets was building the foundations of a new theatrical life. Early in 1952, he directed a well-received revival of *Golden Boy*, starring Garfield, at the American National Theatre and Academy (ANTA).

Odets' success was part of the powerful Group legacy that continued through the 1950s. The Actor's Studio, a conservatory founded 1947 by Elia Kazan, Cheryl Crawford, and Bobby Lewis, had by 1949 become Lee Strasberg's training school. The Group style that had developed Odets as a writer was now one of the mainsprings of American acting. Strasberg's "Method," apotheosized in Brando's electrifying stage and screen performances as Stanley Kowalski in Williams' *A Streetcar Named Desire*, would dominate Broadway and Hollywood for years to come. Kazan became one of Broadway's most powerful directors after a series of hits: *A Streetcar Named Desire*, Thornton Wilder's *The Skin of Our Teeth*, Miller's *All My Sons* and *Death of a Salesman*, and others. Similarly, though political drama was a less conspicuous part of the 1950s theatrical landscape, Odets' continuing influence—even on Miller, the most outspoken political playwright of the period—was apparent.[37]

"NO PARTY TO BELONG TO": ODETS' HUAC TESTIMONY AND ITS AFTERMATH

In 1951, HUAC investigations of the film industry resumed after a three-year hiatus. Over that time, the blacklist had expanded, fueled by the virulent rhetoric of anti-Communists like Wisconsin senator Joseph McCarthy—who in 1950 claimed to hold a list of 205 known party members in the State Department. No one was safe; writers, actors, directors; and in time, teachers, professors, scientists, army officers, and government officials (especially those connected with the New Deal) would be tarred with the brush of Cold War fear. A number of highly publicized trials served to fix Communism as treason in the public mind; Communist Party leaders were convicted for disseminating revolution under the Smith Act in 1949, State Department official Alger Hiss was convicted of perjury, and nuclear spies Ethel and Julius Rosenberg were sentenced to death for espionage in 1951.[38]

Against this gloomy backdrop, a number of Hollywood people on the blacklist or graylist (those yet to clear their names) were called before the HUAC. Besides Odets, Group members J. Edward Bromberg, Elia Kazan, John Garfield, and Lee J. Cobb testified, as did Lillian Hellman, Michael Blankfort, Edward G. Robinson, Arthur Miller, and Paul Robeson. Some named names; some defied the committee. Garfield refused to testify and was blacklisted; he died of a heart attack shortly afterwards. Bromberg died from the pressure, too; Odets spoke at his funeral, condemning the "tricks and twists of shameless shabby politicians banded into yappy packs" who had caused Bromberg's "death by misadventure."[39] Kazan at first refused to testify but decided the costs, personal and professional, of not testifying were too high—especially because he had broken with the party in the 1930s. Before he faced the committee again, Kazan talked with Odets, telling him, "I don't have any respect for their program. I do have respect for the truth and the effect that it would have if it were spoken."[40] Odets agreed, and Kazan gave testimony naming Group members who had been Communists.

The public nature of the investigation made it natural for the committee to pursue celebrities; Odets had been high on its list since 1947. He testified in executive session in April and then publicly on May 19-20, 1952, giving hours of sometimes defiant, sometimes conciliatory testimony in which he lectured the committee but also named members of the Group "cell."[41] Odets freely admitted his party membership, telling the committee he had joined "in the honest and real belief that this was some way out of the dilemma in which we found ourselves" but that he had left because "I could only write out of my own experience. I couldn't be given a theme and handle it. It was not my business. It meant to me, if I may say it in this way, a loss of integrity." Ultimately, what Odets disliked about Communism—besides its aesthetic arrogance—was its secrecy, its unwillingness to "move in the open." Nevertheless, he asserted "there was nothing less possible in Hollywood" than inserting revolutionary propaganda into a film.[42]

Despite his condemnation of party tactics—much of the testimony deals with the aborted 1935 Cuban fact-finding mission—Odets' testimony aggressively supports liberalism as much as it condemns Communism, declaring their inherent connections: "I have fought for civil rights and civil liberties, again when it seemed to be taking the Communist Party point of view" and stating his conviction that even the Supreme Court was split about whether Communism aimed to overthrow the government.[43] In his personal shift toward a temperate liberalism, which had been taking place since the late 1930s, Odets never denied Communism's appeal, for in the absence of a "liberal-labor party" he felt he had "no party to belong to":

I found myself frequently on platforms with Communists that I did not know about then but evidently are now known Communists. Many of these people have some very good tunes.

They have picked up some of our most solemn and sacred American tunes and they sing them. . . . I have never wittingly, since these early days, joined or spoken on an exclusively Communist program or platform. I see that one must do one of two things: One must pick one's way very carefully through the mazes of liberalism and leftism today or one must remain silent. . . . the little I have to contribute to the betterment or welfare of the American people could not permit me to remain silent.[44]

The ambivalent nature of Odets' confession is perhaps best indicated by the reaction of the committee itself. Though they invariably thanked "friendly" witnesses, they did not thank Odets.[45]

Odets felt that his testimony "showed the face of a radical"; others, noting the inescapable fact that he named names, saw him as a traitor. Kazan and Clurman both later insisted the reactions broke Odets' spirit; as Kazan said, "naming his old comrades deprived Odets of the heroic identity he needed most, I don't believe he was ever again the same man."[46] Even outside the Group circle, Odets' testimony shocked many. Blacklisted screenwriter Jules Dassin recounted Harry Kurnitz weeping when he discovered "the poet of the working class" had capitulated: "Harry was not even a left guy. He was a middle guy, but decent. He said, 'Clifford.' . . . and began to cry. We all did."[47] Brecht was more sympathetic, suggesting that Odets write a play about it for his own good.

Those who named names had motivations as individual as the witnesses themselves. As Dalton Trumbo, one of the Hollywood Ten who later publicly denounced Communism, noted about the period,

No one on either side who survived it came through untouched by evil. Caught in a situation that had passed beyond the control of mere individuals, each person reacted as his nature, his needs, his convictions, and his particular circumstances compelled him to. There was bad faith and good, honesty and dishonesty, courage and cowardice, selflessness and opportunism, wisdom and stupidity, good and bad on both sides; and almost every individual involved, no matter where he stood, combined some or all of these antithetical qualities in his own person, in his own acts.[48]

Odets' own reasons were complex and personal. First, like Kazan, he believed there was something dubious about Communist secrecy, which prevented honest political debate. Second, his personal life was in turmoil. He and his second wife had divorced in 1951; Odets was worried about financially supporting his two young children—though he did not return to Hollywood until three years after his testimony. Certainly, Odets had been deeply affected by four years of political pressure and incrimination, knowing that, as he said in one speech in 1949, "if I speak here on Sunday I may be without a job on Monday."[49]

Whatever the reasons for Odets' testimony, the post-HUAC period marked a serious falling off in the volume of his work. Kazan argued that when Odets lost respect, he lost his impetus for work. Though Odets found the reactions to his testimony as difficult to swallow as the practices that had prompted it, he tried to answer them with his next play. He began working on the play, a moral fable about Noah and his family on the ark, in the summer of 1953 and completed it by mid-1954. The play follows the family from Noah's call to build the ark through the flood and to the reestablishment of the human community after the waters recede. Far less fervent than any of his previous plays, *The Flowering Peach* drew criticism from leftists such as Mordecai Gorelik who saw in it Odets' apologia for the HUAC testimony. "There is idealism just in survival," says one of the characters, a line that seemed to indicate Odets' desire for ease and comfort rather than fighting for what he believed in. Odets himself recognized that "I couldn't have written *The Flowering Peach* twenty years ago" but saw the shift as growth rather than abdication: "[W]hen you start out, you have to champion something. . . . But if you still feel that way after ten or fifteen years, you're nuts. No young writer is broad" (NYT, December 26, 1954).

The Flowering Peach opened on December 28, 1954, with Menasha Skulnik as Noah; it received split notices from the critics. Some, like Walter Kerr, found it repetitive, but Brooks Atkinson named it one of Odets' best plays: "it has emotional depth and a feeling of apprehensiveness; in its rueful acceptance of everyday life, it preserves some of the heritage of the race. There is something universal about it" (NYT, January 9, 1955). Though the play was not financially successful, the Pulitzer Prize jury found *The Flowering Peach* strong enough to nominate it for the season's best drama, though their decision was overturned by the Advisory Board, which gave it to Tennessee Williams' *Cat on a Hot Tin Roof*. No one—not even Odets—knew of the jury's recommendation until after Odets' death in 1963, but clearly Odets' talent had not been destroyed by Hollywood or HUAC. Nevertheless, though he would plan numerous other plays over the next nine years, filling file folders with notes, outlines, and character descriptions, *The Flowering Peach* was the last play Odets ever finished.

NOTES

1.   Harold Clurman, *All People Are Famous* (New York: Harcourt Brace Jovanovich, 1974) 265.
2.   Sherwood's overtly political goals for his play are made clear from the fact that following the fall of Finland, he rewrote the play to reflect the German invasion of Greece. There is a hint of envy in Odets' criticism, for Sherwood had achieved popular success with political plays for years, while Odets struggled to live up to the revolutionary promise of *Waiting for Lefty*. Sherwood's work for Roosevelt as a speechwriter was another indication of Odets' distance from the power structures of American democracy. Odets had written to Roosevelt in early 1939 offering his services as a speechwriter in the 1940 election (and offering to write a "pro-Roosevelt" play). Roosevelt's polite reply did not mention the offer.
3.   Michael E. Parrish, *Anxious Decades: America in Prosperity and Depression, 1929-1941* (New York: Norton, 1992) 367, 370, 465. The influx of government money stimulated the economy to the point where the depression had begun to disappear by 1941. Odets' plays from *Clash by Night* on therefore lost the economic focal point of the depression, and shifted to the larger concerns of mid-century American life: war, peacetime prosperity, nuclear anxiety, and the dangers of lost idealism.
4.   Parrish, 467-472.
5.   Parrish, 472-476.
6.   Gabriel Miller, *Clifford Odets* (New York: Continuum, 1989) 144.

7.   While individual contributions to screenplays are difficult to attribute, there is evidence that Odets contributed a good deal to the early part of *It's a Wonderful Life*. In his biography of Capra, Joseph McBride notes that two of the credited screenwriters, Albert Hackett and Frances Goodrich, deliberately borrowed one of Odets' early scenes, and that Capra himself retained "the scene of George as a boy saving his brother, the dance and moonlight walk, and the romantic rivalry over Mary" (512). There is no clear evidence about what part of Odets' work remained in the final cut of *Notorious*. Michael Mendelson notes that a shooting script for *Blockade* lists John Howard Lawson and Odets as coauthors, though only Lawson received screen credit, suggesting, perhaps, that this is one of the films for which Odets refused to take credit.

8.   Gerald Weales, *Clifford Odets, Playwright* (New York: Pegasus, 1971) 151-153.

9.   Harold Cantor, *Clifford Odets, Playwright-Poet* (Metuchen, NJ: Scarecrow, 1978) 107n. Kazan suggests that it was Guild director Lawrence Langner who disliked Odets' work.

10. Lary May, "Making the American Consensus: The Narrative of Conversion and Subversion in World War II Films" in *The War in American Culture: Society and Consciousness During World War II*, Lewis A. Ehrenberg and Susan E. Hirsch, eds. (Chicago: U of Chicago P, 1996) 78. May goes on to note that the tension between the government and the filmmakers' desire for freedom sometimes resulted in censorship. For example, John Huston's *Let There Be Light* was censored by the OWI for showing the psychological effects of war.

11. Brenda Murphy, "Plays and Playwrights, 1915-1945" in *The Cambridge History of American Theatre, Volume II: 1870-1945*, Don B. Wilmeth and Christopher Bigsby, eds. (Cambridge: Cambridge UP, 1999) 326.

12. Clayton R. Koppes, "Regulating the Screen: The Office of War Information and the Production Code Administration," in *Boom and Bust: The American Cinema in the 1940's*, Thomas Schatz, ed. (New York: Scribner's, 1999) 272.

13. Gerald Peary, "Odets of Hollywood," *Sight and Sound* 56 (1986-1987) 61.

14. Robert B. Ray, *A Certain Tendency of the Hollywood Cinema, 1930-1980* (Princeton: Princeton UP, 1985) 113; May, 79-82.

15. Ernie repeats Cleo Singer's declaration in *Rocket to the Moon*. Odets often borrowed lines from his plays for other plays or screenplays, though often those lines are put in characters' mouths decidedly different from the original. In *Deadline at Dawn*, for example, a philosophical cab driver seems much like Rosenberger from *Night Music*, with his benevolent philosophical musings on city life, but he in the end turns out to be the murderer his friends are searching for. In the same way, one of Twite's lines in *None but the Lonely Heart*—"life is a queer little man"—is appropriated by Smiley Coy, one of the corrupt studio executives in *The Big Knife*.

16. Alan Brinkley, "The New Political Paradigm: World War II and American Liberalism," in *The War in American Culture: Society and Consciousness During World War II*. Lewis A. Ehrenberg and Susan E. Hirsch, eds. (Chicago: U of Chicago P, 1996) 314.

17. James Agee, *Agee on Film, Volume 1* (New York: McDowell Obolensky, 1958) 128; Pauline Kael, *For Keeps* (New York: Dutton, 1994) 638; Jean Renoir, *My Life and Films*, Norman Denny, trans. (New York: Atheneum, 1974) 261.

18. Clurman, All People Are Famous, 153.

19. Paul Buhle and Dave Wagner, *Radical Hollywood: The Untold Story Behind America's Favorite Movies* (New York: The New Press, 2002) 341-342. Buhle and Wagner cite George Lipsitz's *A Rainbow at Midnight: Labor and Culture in the Cold War*. (Urbana: U of Illinois P, 1994) and Bernard F. Dick's *Radical Innocence: A Critical*

Study of the Hollywood Ten. (Lexington: U of Kentucky P, 1989) to support their claims that Odets, even in Hollywood, maintained his instinctive ability to capture "the uncertainty and restlessness that seemed to seize a population coming out of depression and war" (341).

20. Edward Murray, *Clifford Odets: The Thirties and After* (New York: Frederick Ungar, 1968) 87-88.

21. James T. Patterson. *Grand Expectations: The United States, 1945-1974* (New York: Oxford UP, 1996) 57.

22. Brian Waddell, *The War Against the New Deal: World War II and American Democracy* (Dekalb: Northern Illinois UP, 2001). Waddell argues that the domestic liberalism of the New Deal was transferred to the international sphere through programs such as the Marshall Plan, effectively marking "an end to domestic activism" (145).

23. Patterson, 42, 52.

24. Brinkley, 322.

25. Brinkley, 315.

26. Patterson, 128.

27. Waddell, 146. Senator Arthur Vandenberg suggested to Truman that the only way he would be able to get support for international aid to Turkey, Greece, and other countries would be to raise the specter of world communism. American foreign policy used fear to create an anti-Communist consensus.

28. Patterson, 117-120, 167.

29. David Halberstam, *The Fifties* (New York: Fawcett Columbine, 1993) 98-99.

30. The Hollywood Ten included seven screen writers—John Howard Lawson, Dalton Trumbo, Albert Maltz, Ring Lardner, Jr., Alvah Bessie, Lester Cole, and Samuel Ornitz—one director (Edward Dmytryk), and two producers (Adrian Scott and Herbert Bieberman). Brecht, as a foreigner, did not feel entitled to protection under the Constitution and opted for obfuscatory testimony in which he denied membership in the Communist Party and discounted Marxist influence on his writing. He left the country immediately afterward, eventually settling in East Germany.

31. Otto Friedrich (*City of Nets: A Portrait of Hollywood in the 1940s* [Berkeley: U of California P, 1986]) quotes Lardner as saying that none of the Ten had anticipated going to jail; they had support from a large group of Hollywood people called the Committee for the First Amendment. Others, such as Leon Kaplan, M-G-M's chief counsel, believe that if the studio heads had actively fought the blacklist, "none of this would have happened, or it would have happened on a very reduced scale" (Victor S. Navasky, *Naming Names* [New York: Viking, 1980] 145).

32. Ironically, these notes are scribbled on the back of an invitation from the Vice Consul of the U. S. S. R. to a reception in honor of the 30th anniversary of the October Revolution.

33. *Time*, December 1, 1947.

34. Quoted in Murray, 181.

35. *Saturday Review*, December 9, 1950, 26.

36. Benjamin Appel, "Odets University," *Literary Review* 19 (Summer 1976) 470-475.

37. Gerald Weales, "Clifford's Children: or It's a Wise Playwright Who Knows His Own Father," in *Critical Essays on Clifford Odets*, Gabriel Miller, ed. (Boston: G. K. Hall, 1991) 261-273. Weales traces connections between Odets and Miller through Kazan's work with the two younger playwrights. He specifically sees connections between *Awake and Sing!* and *The Glass Menagerie* as well as between *Paradise Lost* and *Death of a Salesman*. Weales also connects Odets to Lorraine Hansberry, Sam Shepard, and David Mamet.

38. Ellen Schrecker, *Many Are the Crimes: McCarthyism in America*. (Boston: Little, Brown, 1998) 176-78, 190-200, 233.

39. Friedrich, 382.

40. Elia Kazan, *A Life* (New York: Knopf, 1988) 462.

41. Among the Group members he named were Kazan, Bromberg, Tony Kraber, Phoebe Brand, Art Smith and Lewis Leverett—all of whom had been named by others. He denied Garfield's membership. After he was spurned by many on the left, Odets had a bound copy of the entire 300-page transcript made and tried to convince his friends to read it, believing that in its entirety, it showed "the face of a radical."

42. Eric Bentley, *Thirty Years of Treason* (New York: Viking, 1971) 501, 517, 530.

43. Bentley, 527. Odets is speaking about the 1949 Smith Act trial of Communist Party leaders in the United States. By a vote of 7-2 the Supreme Court upheld their convictions.

44. Bentley, 531. One of the platforms upon which Odets had sat with Communists was the Fine Arts panel at the March 1949 Cultural and Scientific Congress on World Peace which he chaired with Arthur Miller and Dmitri Shostakovitch. The Congress itself was declared by HUAC to be a Communist front organization.

45. Clurman, All People Are Famous, 162.

46. Kazan, 134. He describes a scene immediately following the testimony in which Odets and Kazan were confronted by a group of people on the street who relayed their disgust at Odets' testimony. Odets was silent in the face of this confrontation, as Kazan saw it, "distressed not because of hurting other people but because he'd killed the self he valued most" (135).

47. Patrick McGilligan and Paul Buhle, *Tender Comrades: A Backstory of the Hollywood Blacklist* (New York: St. Martin's, 1997) 218.

48. Quoted in Bentley, xxi.

49. Address to the Cultural and Scientific Congress on World Peace, March 27, 1949 (LCA).

Chapter 5

"A Real Artist of the People": Odets' Post-Group Plays

"SUAVE AND SWANK JUNK": THE POETICS OF KITSCH

Odets' early Group plays articulated the promises and failures of the American marketplace largely through a language of abundance; his later plays, however, shift to a focus on images of popular culture as the expression—however distorted—of the people's voice. Ralph Willett has commented that "however corny the images of beauty and contentment circulated by popular culture, they at least provide a language through which the inarticulate can express their desires. Odets' respectful use of the clichés of popular song and film is a measure of his authentic sympathy for the classes he writes about and of his identification with their yearning hopes."[1] Odets, always fascinated with popular forms, insisted they could be turned toward progressive ends. For example, he argued in "Democratic Vistas in Drama" that film was the art of the people, with cultural and political power rooting far deeper than its superficial form. Widespread acceptance made film and other mass media ideal vehicles—as advertisers well knew—for reaching audiences with their messages. For example, following World War II, television boomed even more rapidly than radio had in the 1920s. In 1948, there were only twenty-eight stations in the country and 172,000 television sets; by 1955, 32 million sets were in use, and by 1960, almost 90 percent of households had one.[2] With his longing for connection to a large group of like-minded people, Odets naturally gravitated toward the reach and scope of popular forms. His best work was built upon an expression of American's common experience.

However sweet this dream, Odets was conscious throughout the 1930s and 1940s that a folk culture uniting people in common artistic and social endeavor was far from reality. As early as *Golden Boy* and *Night Music*, he had depicted popular culture as a flawed vehicle for the promises of democracy. Such sharp criticism continues in Odets' post-Group plays. For example, the bloody climax of *Clash by Night* takes place in a movie projection booth; Jerry Wilinski strangles his adulterous friend Earl while "a typical Hollywood 'product'"—described by one character as "Suave and swank junk" (226-227)—plays onscreen. Indeed, Odets weaves into his late plays—*Clash by Night*, *The Country Girl*, and *The Big Knife*—a skeptical examination of popular culture that continues his career-long examination of the American marketplace. More often than not, he condemns popular culture for its simplistic forms and false promises. Just as consumer capitalism preached plenty while denying basic desires to many of its participants, Odets suggests, popular culture promised uplift and artistic pleasure but delivered only clichéd blandishments to an increasingly narcotized public.

Odets' tightrope-walking ambivalence toward popular culture also reflects an ongoing discussion that pervaded American intellectual life from the 1930s onward. Since the rise of radio and the popularization of sound film in the late 1920s, culture had been increasingly enmeshed in a process of artistic reproduction and commodification that made it difficult to separate uplifting forms of art from culturally debilitating ones, and even more difficult to avoid the changes new technologies would bring. As Gus Michaels warns the Gordons in *Paradise Lost*, "Television's coming in, sure as death" (SP, 161). Odets dramatizes his society's anxieties about the place of these new cultural forms in American democracy.

The cultural object—play, film, popular song, World's Fair, radio program, television program—is inextricable from the economic system that produced it. Recognizing that "[m]odern advertising is born with one foot in the world of goods and the other in mass culture,"[3] Odets shows this connection, depicting how the marketplace increasingly shaped both form and content, both the production and reception of cultural objects. Furthermore, as a number of critics of the 1930s, 1940s, and 1950s argued, popular forms elided gaps between high and folk culture, blending everything into a "midcult" manufactured for and by popular consent and cemented in place by prevailing economic structures.[4] In 1938, about the same time Odets wrote "Democratic Vistas in Drama," an art critic for the *Partisan Review*, Clement Greenberg, argued that mass production techniques, universal literacy, and a demographic shift to urban centers had resulted in the development of an (popular) ersatz culture he derided as kitsch.[5] For Greenberg, true art was necessarily elitist because it challenged accepted notions; any attempt to popularize art invariably adulterated it, resulting in a weak, commercialized imitation: "Kitsch, using for raw material the debased and academicized simulacra of genuine culture, welcomes and cultivates this insensibility [to the values of genuine culture]. It is the source of its profits. Kitsch is mechanical and operates by formulas. Kitsch is vicarious experience and faked sensations."[6]

For Greenberg, kitsch parasitized the forms of avant-garde art without a concomitant progressivism in content, imperiling the avant-garde through cheap repetition. Furthermore, while concerned about the effects on audiences, he worried even more about the development of artists. Because kitsch contained within its form a predetermined emotional response, it was immediately accessible to the popular audience and therefore profitable. This potential, Greenberg suggests, placed enormous pressures on writers to "modify their work under the pressure of kitsch, if they do not succumb to it entirely."[7] The result was a kind of contamination in which the impurities of kitsch poisoned whatever remained of true art. For example, the methods of advertising, which depend on quick recognition and emotional identification, tend toward kitsch. In this view, technology makes popular art something to be bought and sold, cultural commodities stained a priori by their intimate connection with mass production, until they become what Leo Lowenthal called in 1950 "manipulated consumer goods."[8]

If, as their detractors argued, mass media elided the difference between high art and kitsch, they also elided the personal differences among consumers of popular culture. As the products became standardized, the responses did as well; the individual melted into the mass. This process was seen as self-perpetuating, a demonic machine whose continual operation was more important than the product it generated. Dwight MacDonald, more open early in his career toward the regenerative possibilities of popular culture, by 1950 had declared that "the Lords of kitsch sell culture to the masses. It is a debased, trivial culture that voids both the deep realities (sex, death, failure, tragedy) and also the simple spontaneous pleasures. . . . The masses, debauched by several generations of this sort of thing, in turn come to demand trivial and comfortable cultural products."[9] The individual mark of the aesthetic had been superseded by the mechanisms of production and consumption.

Not all writers about popular culture decried its effects. Gilbert Seldes, for example, located the origins of popular art in the American democratic tradition, arguing that much of American high art was an elitist project, virulently critical of the average person. Drawing a direct line from the Age of Jackson through Whitman and Emerson, Seldes argued that while the mass media often failed to achieve their goals, and while they were shot through with commercialism, there was nevertheless hope for the "popular arts," as he called them: "[P]ersistence of change reflects the one emotion all Americans hold in common . . . the future is theirs to create. It is a confession that the present is not perfect and an assertion that nothing in the present can prevent us from changing for the better."[10] Nevertheless, Seldes' optimistic assertion is undercut throughout the rest of his essay by a partial dismissal of the achievements mass media had made. Thus, even the defenders of popular forms of culture were forced again and again to admit to the paucity of "real" culture in mass media, arguing instead—as Odets did in "Democratic Vistas in Drama"—for their seemingly unlimited potential.

Theodor Adorno, a sharp critic of mass culture, nevertheless suggested in 1954 that the commercialism of mass media was perhaps more a matter of degree than of kind:

It would be romanticizing to assume that formerly art was entirely pure, that the creative artist thought only in terms of the inner consistency of the artifact and not also of its effect on the spectators. Theatrical art in particular cannot be separated from audience reactions. Conversely, vestiges of the aesthetic claim to be something autonomous, a world unto itself, remain even within the most trivial product of mass culture.[11]

Odets and the Group had struggled with this quandary; theatre was a social art dependent on a real and powerful connection between the stage and the audience. The difficulty—onstage and in the studios—was how far the writer had to budge to meet that audience.

Odets' fervent romanticism gave him deep sympathies with Seldes' democratic view. Still, as his work on Broadway and in Hollywood attests, the opportunity to reach a large audience placed pressures on the mode of production itself, creating an interchange of anticipation and expectation between artist and audience, playwright and company, screenwriter and producer. Indeed, Walter Benjamin had argued in 1935 that systems of mass production had radically changed the way in which art was created, or rather *produced*: "To an ever greater degree the work of art reproduced becomes the work of art designed for reproducibility."[12] Benjamin seemingly applauds this emancipation of art from ritual, arguing that a more political orientation offers hope for social change. But the politicization of art brings a deeper danger of mass control, since along with modes of production, it changes the audience as well; individuals see themselves as part of a mass, or, worse, are part of a mass without realizing it. In Benjamin's view, this sort of social control is the aesthetic counterpart to Fascism; rather than fostering democratic change by expressing the will of the people, it defuses political action through artistic expression: "Fascism sees its salvation in giving those masses not their rights but instead a chance to express themselves."[13]

Benjamin's analysis articulates the mixed feelings Odets exhibited toward his plays and screenplays. Of course, the mass media and the theatre operate in different ways, the former by highly efficient reproduction and the latter by the far more inefficient repeated singular event; it is perhaps disingenuous to compare them. As Odets recognized, theatre was the least effective—and on Broadway, probably the least democratic—way to create a truly popular art. But his bouncing back and forth between Hollywood and Broadway makes such comparisons inevitable; furthermore, his own writings invited them. For example, by characterizing film audiences as imitative and credulous in "Democratic Vistas in Drama," he participates in the blanket critique of mass culture of the late 1930s and early 1940s "whereby the fat cat, capitalist 'lords of kitsch' set about ventriloquizing an inert and prefabricated mass of consumers."[14] At best, in the essay, Odets claims that the "people" need to be challenged with an accurate look at their world; at worst, he refuses them autonomy to resist the narcotic power of popular culture.

Odets does not interest himself in the differences between work as a playwright and work as a screenwriter in "Democratic Vistas." The contrast between the debased movie world and the theatre is one of intention rather than method. However, his analysis is not disingenuous. In fact, Odets' plea for a new, socially committed, and popular drama ends with an affirmation of the nobility of the masses: "A writer of talent could begin a great career that way—as 'celebrator and expresser.' Great audiences are waiting now to have their own experiences explained and interpreted for them." For Odets, the politically democratic must be reconciled with the culturally and economically democratic; popular art must speak to and for the people. It is this responsibility of the artist to the people—an attitude that characterized all of Odets' work from the Group onward—that gives his plea a ring of authenticity.

"Democratic Vistas" is one example of how in the late 1930s inclusion of anti-Fascist fellow travelers in the Communist Popular Front had encouraged left-leaning intellectuals to embrace (however tenuously) the political potential of popular culture, while remaining distant from the masses for whom it was intended:

Even in the broadened cultural base of the Popular Front period, intellectuals could still see themselves as missionaries, offering the masses an alternative folk culture (or through the social agency of Hollywood Popular Fronters, a "progressive" film culture) that was more germane to their interests than what was seen as the debilitating political effects of commercial popular culture.[15]

Beginning with the Soviet-German nonaggression pact, however, arguments against popular culture increasingly identified such culture with the dangers of Communism, suggesting that only Communists, who had weak intellects and bad taste, could find popular culture useful.

Rooted in the social upheaval of the 1930s, the political arguments against popular culture reached their apex in the Cold War. Disenchantment with Stalinism fueled the belief that popular culture could only be a dangerous form of social control. Accordingly, following the war, there was a virtual rewriting of American intellectual history (led by MacDonald and Bernard Rosenberg) that argued that the true tradition of American arts was elitist and noncommercial. They valorized those artists who tried to operate outside the cultural marketplace, who refused the pressures of the "people" to produce a certain kind of art, and who were seemingly immune to economic pressures. But Andrew Ross notes that "this is a claim . . . that depends on forgetting the enormous efforts of the thirties, when intellectuals *en force* devoted themselves, in however imaginary a fashion, to the task of politically creating a culture that would be both national and popular."[16] Odets' dream of a democratic, collective art—his "Charlie Theatre"—was increasingly out of step with the times.

During HUAC investigations into Communist influence in the film industry, fears of popular culture as social control surfaced again. Odets, the Hollywood Ten, and others were accused of hijacking scripts for their Communist propaganda, though ironically, "the one area in which Hollywood's Communists had very little impact was in the films they made. . . . the producers controlled the final product."[17] The committee's motives were complex (and often questionable), but its stated goal was to protect audiences from "subversive" content. Fearful of what secret messages might do to unsuspecting mass audiences, the investigations—first of the Dies committee in the late 1930s, then the blacklist of the 1940s and 1950s—in effect defined art as what was morally inoffensive and politically mainstream: the popular by negation.

The film industry had attempted for years to ward off investigations and outside censorship by self-policing. The Motion Picture Code (MPC), adopted in 1930, was a direct outgrowth of the long-standing belief that art had direct, measurable effects on audiences. It aimed, in essence, to control behavior by controlling aesthetic content:

It has often been argued that art in itself is unmoral, neither good nor bad. This is perhaps true of the *thing* which is music, painting, poetry, etc. But the thing is the *product* of some person's mind, and that mind was either good or bad when it produced the thing. And the thing has its *effect* on those who come into contact with it. In both these ways, as a product and the cause of definite effects, it has a deep moral significance and an unmistakable moral quality. . . . In the case of the motion pictures, this effect may be particularly emphasized because no art has so quick and so widespread an appeal to the masses. It has become in an incredibly short period, *the art of the multitudes.*[18]

As HUAC would, the MPC places responsibility upon the "good or bad" mind of the individual who creates, rather than the viewer of the movie, institutionalizing the critique of mass culture as an irresistible force. The MPC, designed to keep the government out of the film industry, unwittingly gave HUAC investigators moral and political ammunition for their attacks.

Once the fear of subversive effects was established, the debate centered on what constituted "bad" content. HUAC's conservatism demonstrated that in the hostile political mood of the times, any liberal content was liable to charges of Communism. Though some of those investigated were in fact Communists, others were accused of fostering subversion with politics that ten years earlier had been mainstream New Deal liberalism. It is not surprising, then, that Odets, the clarion voice of the leftist 1930s, was among those against whom the backlash was directed. The price these workers were paid for their leftist attachments was, in part, the threat of economic and political destruction; most of those named by the committee lost their jobs. The blacklist was more than just an economic sanction, however. Symbolically, the threat to remove connections between artist and audience, preventing the "infection" of a large number of people with subversive ideas, confirms the committee's fear of the popular arts and suggests that, even among conservatives, a belief in—or fear of—real social change through popular art had never disappeared.[19]

Odets' conflicting testimony in front of HUAC underscores the difficulty of separating the political effects of popular culture from the economic conditions of its production. In his personal files, there is a copy of a speech that was apparently prepared—but never delivered—by Odets to the committee:

Not poor myself, I am convinced by every feeling, the experience & thoughts of my not-especially-endowed life, that capitalism must in the name of everything human & sacred be replaced by socialism. . . . the great struggle in the world today, so painful & tormenting, so confusing, is about this one subject: shall human values make the economics or shall economics make the values? I am proud, even defiant to stand where I do. This is my statement. (LCA, undated)

The fact that Odets never delivered this statement highlights his personal insecurities, as well as larger economic and political pressures placed on writers. Blacklisted, Odets would never have been able to reach the people he wanted to reach; still, he remained unwilling to cooperate fully with the committee. Certainly, Odets' ambivalent HUAC testimony gives evidence of the popular artist's place in the midcentury political climate. Nevertheless, it is the plays that best evince Odets' growing distrust of popular culture, as well as his ongoing romantic yearning for a full democracy, life with all the trimmings.

"THE ANTI-PICNIC FACTS": *CLASH BY NIGHT*

Odets' critique of the effects of popular culture was greatly tempered in *Night Music* by his romantic optimism. But in *Clash by Night* (1941), the mood becomes ominous, the critique of popular culture almost completely damning. Opening a few weeks after Pearl Harbor, *Clash by Night*'s tension mirrors the political climate into which it was born. Newspaper reviewers were quick to sense the shift that Odets' attitudes had taken, and few were more pleased by the new grimness than they had been with the optimism of *Night Music*. Even with generally high praise for Tallulah Bankhead as Mae and Lee J. Cobb as Jerry, the reviews were far more negative than Odets or his producer Billy Rose (who promised the play would win the Pulitzer Prize) could have anticipated. John Anderson of the *Journal-American* called *Clash by Night* "one of Mr. Odets' worst plays, a rambling, episodic, lurid, and rather pretentious drama," while Burns Mantle deplored its "unsympathetic, uninteresting subjects" and noted that it is "completely unrelieved in mood and tone." The reviews caught the increasing frustration with the unfulfilled promises of American life that had driven the play.

An article Odets wrote for the *New York Times* in 1942, "Genesis of a Play," excerpts journal entries tracing the development of *Clash by Night*. One early entry, for example, suggests that "[p]art of the theme of this play is about how men irresponsibly wait for the voice and strong arm of Authority to bring them to life" (NYT, February 4, 1942). Thus, in the title and themes of the play there is evidence of Odets' continued concern with the dilemmas of American culture: individual freedom without social responsibility, abundance without participation, morality without humanity, appetite without understanding. There is in Odets' conception of the play, in fact, a connection between these appetites and the tendency he speaks of to submit to authority unquestioningly, for unthinking complicity in the economic and cultural marketplace parallels an unthinking complicity in the political marketplace. As critical of the prevailing order as *Awake and Sing!*, *Clash by Night* demonstrates how the foundations of democracy are undercut when the responsibilities of the individual are subverted into the quest for material goods. The critique of popular culture that Odets began in *Golden Boy* and *Night Music* finds its most vitriolic expression in *Clash by Night*.

The play opens with Mae and Jerry Wilinski, seven years married, sitting on their porch with friends Joe and Peggy. While the others are absorbed in watching the moon rise, Mae is occupied with visions of escape: "An old song was running through my mind (*singing softly*) 'I'm the Sheik of Araby, this land belongs to me. At night when you're asleep, into your tent I'll creep. . . . 'Anyone remember that song?" (CBN, 4). Memories of this and other popular songs return to Mae throughout the play, assuming increasing emotional importance. More importantly, they provide her with a language to express her desires and fears. When Joe and Peggy leave, Mae tells Jerry why Joe ought to marry Peggy: "She happens to be very much in love with that self-centered gent. She wants him to creep into her tent and he won't" (15). Born from a popular song, Mae's idea of love offers escape and excitement to contrast with the boredom of her life with Jerry. Her use of the song also contrasts Jerry's wide-eyed wonderment at the beauty and distance of the moon and stars with Mae's familiarity with popular culture. Mae's song expresses unfulfilled desires, a sense of longing, and half-articulated hopes. In that sense, it is like the folk tune that Jerry's father plays on his concertina: "It's a Polish song. . . . about the little old house, where you wanna go back, but you can't find out where it is no more, the house" (10-11). Music in this play has subtly shifted, from Poppa Bonaparte's "great cheer-up" in *Golden Boy* toward the language of the dispossessed and disaffected.

Mae's preoccupation with the mythologies expressed in popular culture is also reflected by her reaction to Jerry's friend Earl, a film projectionist who embodies for Mae the desires excited in her by the movies. Even if his job is, as he says, "good pay but dull work" and he suggests that "they're not happy, those movie people, none of them," Mae nevertheless expresses her longing for the "money, cars, and chauffeurs" that to her signify the exotic life of the films (27). The sixty dollars a week that Earl earns in the booth is a small fortune compared with the scratching and saving she must do with Jerry. It is also significant, then, that the night in which Jerry confronts them, they have been to the "amusements"— amusement is precisely what Mae desires. Her cynical irritation with Jerry, a carpenter on the WPA projects, emphasizes desperation with "life on the installment plan" (94): "You talk too much Jerry. You jump on everything like it's a plank and you're gonna saw it in half" (6). The first act, therefore, sets up a contrast between the bright, almost utopian promises of a vague land where the Sheik of Araby creeps into your tent and the hot, small Staten Island home where Jerry and Mae live with their crying baby, barely making ends meet.

Perhaps the clearest delineation of the contrast between real and ideal comes in act 1, scene 2, at an ocean pavilion. Amid a score of contemporary references to news events, sporting events, popular music, and politics, Earl begins his crude seduction of Mae. The background of this scene, including the seemingly irrelevant tangents, is more important than the actual seduction, for it indicates the scope of the problem as Odets saw it, the connection between popular culture and social responsibility. Indeed, the plot of *Clash by Night* is nothing original. It concerns the development of a love triangle over the course of a long hot summer and culminates in the violent death of one of the participants. But the way in which Odets frames the seduction within the context of 1941 America, against the background of a popular culture that fills lives on the verge of war with false images of bliss, deepens Odets' "triangle play" into an analysis of American idealism.

In the pavilion scene, contemporary references abound: Father Coughlin, the Giants, the songs "Mexicali Rose," "The Beer Barrel Polka" and "Avalon," and the rhumba, in addition to references to Steinbeck's *Of Mice and Men*.[20] Such references don't merely ground the play in the familiar; they offer a departure point for the play's dark mood. Certainly, the audience was expected not only to recognize the references to popular culture but also to react to the juxtaposition of the play's dark foreboding with "happy" popular songs. To an extent, they did. For example, Charles Gentry of the *Detroit Evening Times* remarked when the play opened its pre-Broadway run that *Clash by Night* had "poetry, social significance and a timeliness which is amazing" (October 28, 1941). Odets worked outward from a core of specific references to a general indictment of the culture's false promises. Mae's bewilderment at the power of popular songs, expressed most clearly in her comment to Earl about the song "Avalon," recalls the utopian visions that filled Odets' earlier plays: "It gives me the jim-jams . . . always gets me. I used to sell sheet music in the dime store. A place called Avalon. . . . no worries there, sort of flowers in the winter, I don't know how all that stuff gets in a song, but it does. . . . Well, keep smiling! I don't blame Jerry for what he is" (75-76).

Mae's adoption of "Avalon" to express her bewilderment, like her use of "The Sheik of Araby" as a shorthand expression of discontent, demonstrates the visceral power of popular culture. Language is co-opted by the popular song and the advertising slogan; it slides into romantic cliché. Likewise, Mae's "keep smiling" refusal to consider the consequences of searching for the chimerical "Avalon" dooms her escape attempt to failure. In fact, all the characters wander through the play without a sense of direction; thus, Mae characterizes Earl as "one of those who needs a new suit or a love affair, but he don't know which" (80). To add this sense of purposelessness, Odets uses the action of constant drinking throughout the play. From the first scene on the porch to the final scene where a drunken Jerry kills Earl, alcohol figures prominently in *Clash by Night*. It is another narcotic, another attempt at escape. As Earl puts it, "That's why I drink this varnish, lady—to get unborn" (103-104). Odets had made a similar connection in *The Silent Partner*, where the baker Corelli says of popular culture: "Many workers is such dope fiend—baseball and boxing dope fiend, movie dope fiend" (LCA, dated 1936).

The success of *Clash by Night* depends on the success of the popular culture critique. Gabriel Miller, for example, finds the play flawed because the use of popular culture is fundamentally undeveloped:

[T]he gimmick only suggests that Odets' play is not much more meaningful than the average film, or the cited popular songs, "The Sheik of Araby" and "Avalon." The attempted criticism of popular culture is ambitious, but the terms of the charge are not fully explored in this play. . . . Because Odets has established no adequate connection in the play between the personal and the social, his sudden attack on the popular culture is as vague as his treatment of economics, fascism, and war.[21]

Miller's analysis, while in part true, nevertheless undervalues Odets' participation in the larger debate about popular culture as not only a symptom of the American malaise but also a contributing cause. The popular reflected a powerful belief system of a great number of people. For Odets (and HUAC), the popularity made it meaningful, but also dangerous.

Unlike intellectual critics of popular culture, Odets does not condemn it as inherently flawed, stained by easy accessibility; rather, he warns those who buy its promises unthinkingly. In the key passage of the play, Joe, who has stood aloof from the adulterous trio, tells Peggy:

We're *all* afraid! Earl, Jerry, Mae, millions like them, clinging to a goofy dream—expecting life to be a picnic. Who taught them that? Radio, songs, the movies—you're the greatest people going. Paradise is just around the corner. Shake that hip, swing that foot—we're on the Millionaire Express. Don't cultivate your plot of ground—tomorrow you might win a thousand acre farm! What farm? The dream farm! Am I blue? Did you ask me if I'm blue. Sure, sometimes. Tricky Otto comes along, with a forelock and a mustache. Then he tells them why they're blue. "You been wronged," he says. "They done you dirt. Now come along with me, Take orders park your brains, don't think, don't worry; poppa tucks you in at night!" . . . And where does that end? In violence, destruction, cripples by the carload! But is that the end for us? No, sweetheart, not while a brain burns in my head. And not because we're better than them. But because we know the facts—the anti-picnic facts. Because we know that Paradise begins in responsibility. (217)

Like Leo Gordon, Ralph Berger, or Agate Keller, Joe's statement is a call to arms, but unlike the earlier plays, Joe's call is born from fear rather than hope.

Miller is partly correct in arguing that Odets has not prepared the audience for Joe's strong and specific attack on popular culture toward the end of the play with other explicit criticisms. But there are implicit criticisms throughout the play. No audience could be unaware of the utopian promises of the American Dream that are the targets of Joe's criticism, just as they would recognize the popular songs used earlier in the play (or the ones parodied in his speech) and the ongoing debate about the uses of popular culture. Odets' play is shaped so much from the common stuff of the world that it seems mundane and petty—the dreary Staten Island setting irritated a number of critics—but the underlying premise is utopian. Odets' call, through Joe, is not to annihilate popular culture but to recognize its power and understand the social ramifications of that power. He calls for individual responsibility toward the social, rather than individual surrender to the mass implied by Kress' Fascism. Thus, a well-grounded person such as Abe, Earl's fellow projectionist, can dismiss the films he screens as "propaganda for the bug house" (227) and focus instead on his work and family, "Make a plan. Have respect—do your work with respect" (230). Only then can the paradise promised by the American myth and shaped by the forms of popular culture be achieved.

"THIS WHOLE MOVIE THING IS A MURDER OF THE PEOPLE"

If *Clash by Night* concerned itself with the utopian dreams of individuals within a social order, Odets' next two plays, *The Big Knife* (1949) and *The Country Girl* (1950), are at once both more removed from, and more entwined with, such concerns. Many have suggested that by the time *The Big Knife* was written, Odets was trapped in Hollywood "in a system to which he finally could envisage no alternative. And the images of popular culture, which had expressed the youthful dreams of the depression era, were no longer drawn upon when the theme became decay and exhaustion in middle age."[22] To be sure, specific references to popular culture decline in the later plays—popular music, for example, virtually disappears—and while Odets' work is never free of contemporary references, they don't serve the same central purpose in these two plays as they had in the earlier ones.

Nevertheless, the characterization of Odets as a Hollywood "lackey" ignores the complexities of his dual career as well as his expressed ambivalence about both the theatre and film industries. *The Big Knife* and *The Country Girl*, in fact, marked the beginning of a six-year return to Broadway. Furthermore, analysis of either play is incomplete without an understanding of the relationship between them. Even more important is an understanding of the relationship among the plays, popular culture, and Odets' Hollywood career. These two plays are, in one sense, Odets' attempt to allegorize his own life against the backdrop of the American Dream, to do what he once wrote in his journal, "I will reveal America to itself by revealing myself to myself" (B-G, xiv).

First produced in 1950 and directed by Odets, *The Country Girl* was received by the newspaper reviewers as some of his best work. John Chapman of the *News* called it "tight, taut, and trim" (November 11, 1950); Kenneth Tynan noted that the London production was "quite an important evening in the English theatre."[23] Though Harold Clurman dismissed it as "lightweight Odets" (*New Republic*, December 11, 1950), Brooks Atkinson called it "the best play Odets has written for years. Only *Awake and Sing!* stands above it in the lexicon of his career" (NYT, November 19, 1950). Overall, it was hailed as a triumphant return to the theatre for a writer who had been lured from the stage for Hollywood and whose previous play, *The Big Knife*, had been dismissed as a bitter self-reproach at selling out to the film studios. It is ironic, then, that such praise (except from Clurman, who knew Odets better than the others and who had given advice during the development of *The Country Girl* came for a play that Odets held in low regard.

Odets was not pleased with *The Country Girl* mainly because he had written it specifically with the box office in mind: "I set down deliberately to write a success."[24] Writing a play to make money was not new for Odets; the pressures placed upon him by the Group forced him to consider financial questions as well as artistic ones. *Golden Boy*, for example, was written specifically for money. Odets recognized the differences between the two, however; in *Golden Boy* he had found a popular form for his examination of the American Dream that he hadn't in *The Country Girl*. Nevertheless, he was unable to dismiss his "theatre piece" entirely:

It does have about it a certain kind of psychological urgency, because if you are creative, things do creep in despite the conscious impulse. For instance, there crept into that play a central problem of my own life. And this did give a certain urgency and heat to much that went on in the script. I didn't *mean* for that problem to come out; I cannily and unconsciously disguised it. But that is unconsciously what came out in the writing of that play.[25]

Still, Odets found it ironic that the least ambitious, the least socially oriented of his plays was among the most popular. He had once more gained access to the audience he always wanted but this time with a play he felt said nothing really important.

The Country Girl is tightly structured, a compelling psychological study of the interdependence between the aging alcoholic actor Frank Elgin, his younger wife Georgie, and the theatre director Bernie Dodd. It is deep in characterization, integrated in feeling and form, and moves toward a convincing ending with a sense of purpose. Elgin's breakdown and rehabilitation and the shifting relationship between Bernie and Georgie are compelling, and there is a never a sense of unreality or falsity about the theatre scenes. Nevertheless, there is a slick feeling to the play that supports Odets' claim that it was manufactured from the outside in, and only as the play was being written did any depth of feeling enter. As if in confirmation, shortly after *The Country Girl* was produced on Broadway, Odets wrote an essay in the *New York Times* (April 22, 1951) titled "Two Approaches to the Writing of a Play"—about the same time Odets was working with his young playwrights from the Actor's Studio. He had once again been thinking about the crucial relationship of form to content, and in the essay, he delineates the method he used in *The Country Girl* and the method by which he normally wrote:

In the first case, the writer sits down to "fabricate," without personal affiliation or personal relatedness to the material; he is reporting an objective event, performing a technical operation or what you will, but fabricating he is. The second writer, with equal technical grasp of his medium, begins always with the premise of expressing a personal state of being.

Odets felt that "fabrication" like *The Country Girl*, however skillful, could never quite reach the highest level of creative work. For him, form always followed the expression of personal states of being.

Apart from the tacit criticism of his own play and its reception, there is also in *The Country Girl* and the essay an implicit criticism of the theatre industry itself. Furthermore, his indictment of the theatre parallels the criticism of the film industry he had given in *The Big Knife*. In that play, Charlie Castle, the compromised film star, asks, "Don't they slowly, inch by inch, murder everyone they use? Don't they murder the highest dreams and hopes of a whole great people with the movies they make? This whole movie thing is a murder of the people" (70). While "false" theatre is obviously not as dangerous as the "murderous" consequences of a dishonest movie industry, Odets suggests that, just as Hollywood appropriates the dreams of America to make money, theatre is easily trapped within a mind-set that makes a play a commercial rather than an artistic entity. Like kitsch, commercial theatre appropriates the forms of true art to mask its inferior content; it is inherently dishonest. As an industry, then, theatre is capable on a large scale of the kind of falseness inherent in a "manufactured" play.

Still, in spite of the fact that "the creative and deeply felt play is the exception rather than the rule with us, and our theatre the poorer for it," Odets remained unwilling to abandon Broadway. The indictment of theatre in *The Country Girl* is less vehement than his criticism of Hollywood in *The Big Knife*. For example, Bernie tells Georgie at the end of *The Country Girl*, "I'm interested in theater, not show business. I could make a fortune in films, but that's show 'biz' to me." When Georgie responds, "What do you call this play, Literature?" Bernie is forced to acknowledge the parallels between the two industries: "That's true: it's show business trying hard to be theater" (TCG, 103). Still, Bernie's admission of the true nature of the show he is directing does not deny the fact that there is something useful in it, for the young playwright Unger and for Frank, especially. Bernie believes that "[a] man like Elgin, giving his best performance—he has the magic to transform a mere show to theater with a capital T!" (103).

There is a chance at redemption in *The Country Girl* that never surfaces in *The Big Knife*, as is readily seen in a comparison of their final lines. In *The Country Girl*, Georgie says, "Wrestle, Bernie. You may win a blessing. But stay unregenerate. Life knocks the sauciness out of us soon enough" (124). On the other hand, the final words in *The Big Knife* are Marion's "Help! . . . Help!! . . . Help!!!," a screaming that the stage direction indicates "*does not stop and will never stop in this life*" (TBK, 77). The final line of *The Country Girl* also had personal meaning for Odets: "It is one of my favorite lines, 'wrestle and you may win a blessing. In my life I don't 'wrestle' enough. Perhaps an ease of expression of a fluid emotion or simply a fear of losing others' affection if I persisted and pushed" (LCA, dated July 21, 1953). Giving this line to Georgie at the end of the play makes even stronger the connections implied by Odets' setting his play in the theatre. For him, art was a struggle with strong forces, of which the desire for acceptance or affection is one of the most powerful.

Odets' assertion of hope at the end of *The Country Girl* is paralleled in the hopeful ending of his *Times* article. Writing about his playwriting class, Odets asserts, "No theatre need worry for its future while such young people are working and waiting in the vestibules of our common life." The idea of a common life, the collective experience that recalls his work with the Group, is contrasted to the mechanistic, isolated, profit-oriented film industry he pillories so mercilessly in *The Big Knife*. In fact, theatre is held out to Charlie in *The Big Knife* as the only possible source of hope; his wife, Marion, tells him (in virtually the same words Clurman would later use to Odets), "The theatre can still give you a reasonable living." Charlie responds caustically, "The theatre's a stunted bleeding stump. Even stars have to wait years for one decent play" (15), but *The Big Knife* nevertheless offers a lingering belief in theatre as liberating social art. Though there is the dangerous possibility that theatre will grow false in seeking money, the creative individual working for the common good always possesses the possibility of redemption. Odets' criticism of the theatre is thus made not from despair, but from a hopeful belief of the possibilities inherent in the medium.

On the other hand, the film industry is depicted throughout *The Big Knife* as a parasitic form of popular culture that uses the social myths for private ends and thereby devalues them. The voice of conscience in the play, Hank Teagle, tells Charlie:

I don't want Marion joining the lonely junked people of our world—millions of them, wasted by the dreams of life they were promised and the swill they received! *They* are why the whole world, including us, sits in the middle of a revolution! Here, of course, that platitude carries with it the breath of treason. I think lots of us are in for a big shot of vitamin D: defeat, decay, depression, and despair. (57)

The film industry is unredeemable; it denies the very connections it claims to create. Charlie's marriage is failing, he has an affair with his best friend's wife, and he is involved in the cover-up of a fatal accident in which he was involved. He becomes isolated and despairing, crying out to Marion: "Look at me! Can you face it? Look at this dripping fat of the land? Could you ever know that all my life I yearned for a world and people to call out the best in me? How can life be so empty? But it can't be. It can't! It's proven—statistics and graphs prove it—we are the world's happiest" (72). Charlie's disbelief expresses for Odets the entire American ethos: the mindless waste of talent and social impulse in the pursuit of money. The kitschdom of Hollywood wears the form of utopia, but the shell is hollow. Like Joe Bonaparte, Charlie chooses suicide over disconnection.

Marion's plea for help underscores the isolation Odets felt was inherent in the industry, the difficulty the individual faced in creating something useful in a culture where only conformity was rewarded. As Odets was aware, the moral pressure to conform obviates any chance at individual expression; as Charlie says in *The Big Knife*, "Free speech is the highest priced luxury in the country today" (11).[26] Nevertheless, it is not necessary to accuse Odets of bad faith or greed in his early encounters with Hollywood to understand the vitriol of *The Big Knife* in his later career. As he delineated in "Democratic Vistas in Drama," he was excited about the potential audience that film could reach and about the possibilities of disseminating a positive social message to millions of people. But as Michael Denning has pointed out, "[T]he great paradox of film and broadcasting" is the fact that only huge sums of capital can create a truly widespread culture.[27]

Odets—like Charlie, the Steinbeckian "fat of the land"—felt trapped in an industry that could not be swayed by other than economic interests; even the most "radical" films of the radical 1930s were not particularly so. For example, Colin Schindler notes that the film version of Steinbeck's *The Grapes of Wrath* (dir. John Ford, 1940) was anticipated with inordinate worry that it would cause unrest around the country. But Schindler suggests that the film was transformed into something more religious rather than political in tone, far more optimistic than Steinbeck's novel, especially its final appeal to the people: "We're the people that live. Can't nobody wipe us out. Can't nobody lick us. We'll go on forever, Pa. We're the people." The democratic appeal to the people is here wedded to the economic machinery of the popular culture industry: "[Producer Daryl] Zanuck was interested in the triumph of the common man because it was his patronage upon which Twentieth Century's prosperity was founded."[28]

In two articles written for the *New York Times* about his work in Hollywood—the first titled "Writer Tells Why He Left Hollywood" (July 25, 1948) and the second titled "In Praise of a Maturing Industry" (November 6, 1955)—we get perhaps the clearest encapsulation of Odets' vacillation about popular film. The first article explains his leaving for Hollywood in 1943 as a reaction to the poor reception of *Night Music* and *Clash by Night*. He speaks of his pleasure and education during his work writing and directing *None but the Lonely Heart*, but suggests that further attempts to make another "human motion picture" were rebuffed because "none of it fitted into recognizable Hollywood schemata." Odets sharply criticizes the Hollywood mentality that "desire[s] to make every movie as accessible as chewing gum, for which no more human maturity of audience is needed than a primitive pair of jaws and a bovine philosophy"; nevertheless, he is ultimately unwilling to forgo entirely the "dream of a Renaissance to come."

Still concerned with the idea of "how our American cultural world is to move on with human health," Odets places his hope once more in the theatre, where, despite those who seek profits, "the search for the reality of the age (whatever that is!) may still be spread upon our stage." There is in the 1948 article, then, the criticism of popular culture that reappears in *Clash by Night* and *The Big Knife*. Hollywood is damned, not because of its dependence upon technology but because technology has been co-opted by commodity capitalism. What could have been democratic has become Fascistic; as Charlie says in *The Big Knife*: "Don't you see them pushing man off the earth and putting the customer in his place?" (18).

However, the production of three more Broadway plays (plus revivals of *Night Music* and *Golden Boy*, the latter of which Odets directed) in the years between

1947 and 1955 and the trauma of testifying in front of HUAC in 1952 make it a different Odets who writes about the film industry in 1955. Coming after years of theatrical work, his 1955 article (written after Odets had seen the film version of *The Big Knife*, which he liked very much) can't be quickly dismissed as self-justification for being in Hollywood. In the article, he argues that "American film-makers are turning more and more to screen subjects of realism and importance. . . . Moviemakers are aware of the problems of the world and its people." Odets suggested in a later interview that this was because the large studios had broken up after the war, allowing independent producers to work on more interesting projects.[29] By the end of his career, then, Odets had formed an uneasy truce with the film industry, though he never surrendered (either on Broadway or in Hollywood) the goal of creating a people's art. In these plays, Odets attempted to elucidate a connection between popular culture and American life. He tried to show how popular forms both embodied the American Dream and betrayed it, how the democratic ideal of a people's art was problematized by a commodity capitalism that measured everything in terms of financial success.

"I'LL TELL YOU A MYSTERY . . .": *THE FLOWERING PEACH*

Odets' last play, *The Flowering Peach*, seems out of place in his dramatic chronology. It is set outside contemporary times and in distant lands; it lacks the political fervor of his early plays or the bitterness of his post-Group plays. Nevertheless, in important ways, the play serves as a fitting bookend to his work. Covering the story of Noah and his family before, during, and after the flood, the play harks back to *Awake and Sing!* in its depictions of a loud, boisterous Jewish family bound together by struggle and love. It has a maturity beyond most of the Group plays and a humor virtually absent from *The Big Knife* and *The Country Girl*. Indeed, many contemporary commentators found it to be among his best plays. Brooks Atkinson called it "beautiful. His finest [play] in fact" and noted that Odets is not setting himself up "as an oracle. He does not pretend to have the magic formula" (NYT, December 29, 1954). John Gassner remarked that *The Flowering Peach* appeared to be the personal testament of a rueful man content to accept contradiction and shortcomings in man and the world.[30]

Certainly, *The Flowering Peach* is less strident than Odets' earlier plays. Odets remarked, "I couldn't have written *The Flowering Peach* twenty years ago. As you grow older, you mature. The danger is that in broadening, you may dilute your art. A growing writer always walks that tightrope" (NYT, December 26, 1954). But for all the dissimilarities from his earlier work, Odets offers enough similarities in *The Flowering Peach* to mark it clearly as his own. For example, he again examines the theme of responsibility, which had concerned him in *Clash by Night* and afterward. Noah, called to build the ark, fears ridicule: "I don't want it! I'm too old everybody should laugh in my face. . . . Pass me by—Pass me by. Please" (TFP, 11). The family, too, was drawn from the same middle-class Jewish life that inspired the Bergers. Odets, in fact, used his Uncle Israel, in whose kitchen he had spend many of his best childhood days, as the model for Noah. The defiant son, Japheth, borrows idealism and strident longing from Ralph Berger and Steve Takis.

But perhaps the most striking characteristic of *The Flowering Peach* is that it marks a return to allegorical visions of plenty that dominated the earlier plays. The main tension in *The Flowering Peach* exists between Noah and his youngest son, Japheth. They disagree about how the world is to be used, how imperfect people are supposed to fit into God's perfect plan. Before he is knocked unconscious by Noah and dragged onto the ark, Japheth refuses to board. He chooses rather to die in the coming flood, declaring, "Someone . . . would have to protest such an avenging, destructive God!" (19). Japheth's reasons for resistance are made clear in a speech to Rachel; looking down at the roads crisscrossing in the valley, Japheth exclaims, "Those roads down there! The patterns they make! They're not cobwebs, those roads, to be brushed away by a peevish boy! Those roads were made by men, men crazy not to be alone or apart! Men, crazy to reach each other! Well, they won't now" (49-50).

The sense of community that Japheth sees in the roads is in direct conflict with Noah's divine mission to take the family out of the world and begin again. In one sense, the conflict depicted in the play mirrors the increasing tensions of the Cold War. The possibility of world annihilation increasing with the invention and testing of ever more dangerous weapons of mass destruction—the play premiered the year after America's first successful test of the hydrogen bomb, and after the Soviets revealed that they had the atomic bomb—allows a reading of *The Flowering Peach* that is both literal and allegorical. Japheth's outrage is the outrage of the leftist romantic against the blind power represented by Noah. Noah wins the first part of the conflict by getting Japheth on the ark, but the troubles resume when Japheth tries to get Noah to see that putting a rudder on the ark is not disrespectful to God: "God didn't tell you to invent the hoe and the rake and yet you did! . . . God doesn't want the respect of a slave upon its knees!" (68-69). When the ark threatens to sink, the old man finally capitulates, and everyone aboard undergoes a transformation. As Japheth says, "I have a strange feeling that God changed today" (74). Complete surrender to God's will embodied by Noah's autocratic manner eventually becomes a joint responsibility between human action and divine guidance. Odets is thus able at the end of the play to suggest that human life requires human action and commitment to others: "It's in man's hands to make or destroy the world" (85).

At the end of the play, the ark has safely landed, the conflict is seemingly resolved, and though the world has been destroyed, it has also been re-created. Even Japheth remarks that "the world looks washed" (82). Nevertheless, the question remains about what kind of world has been created. Early on, for example, Noah told Japheth that he should take a wife because "the new world will need babies, bushels and bushels of babies." Though Japheth counters with "And what about the bushels of babies who will die in the flood?" (29)—a question the play never satisfactorily answers—the use of the word "bushel" to indicate human beings equates human beings with a product of the natural world but also a product produced for consumption. Still, there is a shift by the end of the play. When the ark lands, the human beings aboard it have become both the producers and the consumers of the natural bounty; there is a balance, an easiness of production that works outside of the destructive marketplace characterizing most of Odets' previous plays.

The Flowering Peach looks back to the earliest plays in its hopeful ending, as Noah, his sons, and their wives set forth to begin the world anew after the flood. The image of the flowering fruit tree once more reappears as a symbol of bounty, seemingly freely offered. But there is, as Noah reminds us, a price to pay for this rebirth. The outside world is destroyed, and even on the ark, Esther dies on the journey. Her loss is an indication of how difficult it is to "be fruitful and multiply" (83), that plenty implies sacrifice and loss. Indeed, throughout the play, Esther has been the dominant symbol of bounty and abundance, the glue that holds the family together and provides it with material and spiritual sustenance. Like Bessie in *Awake and Sing!*, she is almost always involved in the preparation of meals and often uses food as a way to control situations; at one point, when Noah's visions become too much for her, she declares that "we'll eat supper—that's real" (19). Later, when they pack for the ark, she takes to wearing a hat with fruit on it (Noah jokes that "with such a hat, you couldn't go hungry" [45]), thus identifying her visually throughout the rest of the play with images of abundance. Indeed, they know she is dead finally because her hat has fallen off.

The Flowering Peach, in one sense, reads like an escape fantasy, the escape from a world where people are commodified. The world is washed clean; it is freed from all connections to a corrupt life, from the world where Noah is harassed in the town's market, where the businessman Shem bribes the tax collector. But Odets' hope is tempered by a realization that great effort is necessary to begin change and a recognition that change may in fact be minimal. There is an indication that everything will proceed within the family much as it did before the flood. Noah decides to live with his son Shem because "it's more comfortable" (83), and Shem, through hard work and careful planning, has acquired more cows and more material goods than all the others on the ark. It is in this tempered vision of a new paradise, one that recognizes the power of the marketplace and hopes rather to turn its benefit for good, that we see the greatest difference between early plays like *Waiting for Lefty* and *The Flowering Peach*. The radical message of Keller's "put fruit trees where our ashes are!," which seemed possible in the radical atmosphere of the 1930s, had become by the era of Eisenhower and HUAC a sentiment expressed quite differently: "I hope everyone gets everything their hearts desire" (83). Odets, the fiery political playwright of the 1930s who wanted audiences to "tear down the slaughter house of our old lives" (SP, 30) had become, with his last play, content to "tell you a mystery" (TFP, 85).

NOTES

1. Ralph Willett, "Odets and Popular Culture" *South Atlantic Quarterly* 27 (1970) 74.
2. James T. Patterson, *Grand Expectations: The United States, 1945-1974* (New York: Oxford UP, 1996) 348.
3. Pasi Falk. *The Consuming Body* (London: Sage, 1994) 178.
4. "Midcult" is a term coined by Dwight Macdonald to define the popularization of high culture for the benefit of the masses. Andrew Ross notes, "Midcult's institutions included the Book-of-The-Month Club, NBC radio's 'music appreciation' hours, the Great

Books series and many other self-educational programs that Macdonald satirized as How-toism" (*No Respect: Intellectuals and Popular Culture* [New York: Routledge, 1989] 57).

5.   Clement Greenberg, "Avant Garde and Kitsch," in *Mass Culture. The Popular Arts in America*, Bernard Rosenberg and David Manning White, eds. (London: The Free Press of Glencoe, 1957) 98-110.

6.   Greenberg, 102.

7.   Greenberg, 103.

8.   Leo Lowenthal, in *Mass Culture. The Popular Arts in America*, Bernard Rosenberg and David Manning White, eds. (London: The Free Press of Glencoe, 1957) 55. There was debate surrounding the use of the term "mass culture" as opposed to "popular culture" from the beginning. Critics such as Adorno and Greenberg, who saw the development of popular forms of culture as a system of control that fostered a largely unthinking audience, often referred to these forms as "mass" culture. Others tended to refer to popular forms as merely "popular" culture, emphasizing the democratic aspect of art, which was not produced for or by an elite ruling class. David Manning White, for example, argued that popular culture is a form that allows large audiences access to high culture. For White, it is not the technology, but how it is used, that is important. In Odets' case, his ambivalence toward popular culture and his frequently expressed hopes that it could, as White argues, reach large audiences with worthwhile art, undercuts the narcotizing effect of popular culture he describes in some of his plays.

9.   Dwight Macdonald, "A Theory of Mass Culture," in *Mass Culture. The Popular Arts in America*, Bernard Rosenberg and David Manning White, eds. (London: The Free Press of Glencoe, 1957) 72.

10.   Gilbert Seldes, "The People and the Arts" in *Mass Culture The Popular Arts in America*, Bernard Rosenberg and David Manning White, eds. (London: The Free Press of Glencoe, 1957) 87.

11.   T. W. Adorno, "Television and the Patterns of Mass Culture," in *Mass Culture: The Popular Arts in America*, Bernard Rosenberg and David Manning White, eds. (London: The Free Press of Glencoe, 1957) 474.

12.   Walter Benjamin, "The Work of Art in the Age of Mechanical Reproduction," in *Illuminations*, Harry Zohn, trans. (New York: Schocken, 1969) 224.

13.   Benjamin, 241. Frederic Jameson has argued, in fact, that advanced capitalism is a necessary historical condition for the development of popular culture. As mass production shifted the West toward a standardized and frenetic consumer capitalism, for the first time, it was possible for culture to become truly popular. As a result, the practices, if not the aims, of the advertiser and the artist were becoming more alike: "With the coming of the market, [the] institutional status of artistic consumption and production vanishes: art becomes one more branch of commodity production" ("Reification and Utopia in Mass Culture," *Social Text* 1 [1979]: 136-137).

14.   Ross, 35.

15.   Ross, 49.

16.   Ross, 62.

17.   Ellen Schrecker, *Many Are the Crimes: McCarthyism in America*. (Boston: Little, Brown, 1998) 317.

18.   Quoted in Gerald Mast, ed. The Movies in Our Midst: Documents in the Cultural History of Film America (Chicago: U of Chicago P, 1982) 322.

19.   The effects of the "blacklist" and the "graylist" against those in Hollywood who refused to cooperate with the committee are documented by Larry Ceplair and Steven Englund in their excellent book *Inquisition in Hollywood: Politics in the Film Community, 1930-1960* (Garden City, NY: Anchor /Doubleday, 1980). They note that the power of the committee to both find and punish suspected Communists was enormous

and suggest that while "virtually no Communists or former Communists escaped exposure, the lives and careers of the frequently named artists were even more lastingly blighted" (372). George Groman suggests, however, that even those witnesses who did cooperate suffered "loss of reputation and ability to make a living" ("Waiting for Odets: A Playwright Takes the Stand," in *Politics and the Muse: Studies in the Politics of Recent American Literature*, Adam J. Sorkin, ed. [Bowling Green, OH: Bowling Green State U Popular P, 1989] 65).

20. Harold Cantor emphasizes the influence of Steinbeck's *Of Mice and Men* in this scene in the character of a drunken man who has been paid to ignore his wife's affair and who wanders through the scene from time to time muttering "fat o' the land," Lennie and George's catchphrase in the Steinbeck novella. (*Clifford Odets: Playwright-Poet.* [Metuchen, NJ: Scarecrow, 1978] 118), and Gabriel Miller takes the analogy further, identifying Jerry as a sort of Lennie, "[a] strong, sweet, childlike man" (*Clifford Odets.* [New York: Continuum, 1989] 140). This seems in keeping with Odets' assertion, "Personally I am of the opinion that Steinbeck and myself are the two young American writers who see clearly what must be done and are doing it, each in our way" (TIR, 15).

21. Miller, *Clifford Odets*, 138.

22. Willett, 78.

23. Kenneth Tynan, *Curtains* (New York: Atheneum, 1961) 21.

24. Michael J. Mendelsohn, "Odets at Center Stage," interview with Odets. *Theatre Arts* (May 1963) 16-19, 74-76; (June 1963) 28-30, 78-80

25. Mendelsohn, "Center Stage," 19.

26. The idea of conformity and repression troubled Odets through the second half of his career. Even as late as 1961, in a speech before the National Women's Committee for Brandeis University, Odets argued that "our writers today seem conformists. They are afraid to offend. They have dropped their swords and . . . have gone to bed with the dragon they should have killed. They are in TV where the pay is fast and certain and where they are dominated completely by the advertising agency mentality that pays them their wages; they are there to sell merchandise and not much more" (LCA, January 30, 1961) Of course, by the next year, Odets himself would be writing for television. Still, his concern about conformity taps into an ongoing concern in American culture following the war. HUAC and McCarthy reflected a deepening distrust of difference, a repressive attitude that would eventually help to breed the discontents of the Beat Generation and, later, the social upheaval of the 1960s.

27. Michael Denning, "The End of Mass Culture," *International Labor and Working Class History* 37 (Spring 1990) 15.

28. Colin Schindler, *Hollywood in Crisis: Cinema and American Society, 1929-1939* (London and New York: Routledge, 1996) 77-78.

29. Mendelsohn, "Center Stage," 28.

30. John Gassner, *Theatre at the Crossroads* (New York: Holt, Rinehart, Winston, 1960) 155.

Chapter 6

"The Enemy with a Capital 'E'":
Odets' Final Years

RETURN TO HOLLYWOOD

After *The Flowering Peach* had opened in late December 1954, Odets returned to Hollywood. His ex-wife, Bette Grayson, had died during the year, leaving him with two young children to raise; he felt it would be best to raise them on the West Coast. For the last eight years of his life, Odets would remain there, working on and off in the film industry. He wrote a number of screenplays, including a "monumental" *Joseph and His Brethren* for Columbia in 1955 (never produced, perhaps because Harry Cohn had a hard time casting the role of Joseph),[1] *Sweet Smell of Success* in 1957, *The Story on Page One* in 1960, and *Wild in the Country* in 1961, as well as working as a dialogue writer on other screenplays and as an "advisor" for director Nicholas Ray on *Rebel Without A Cause*.[2] *The Story on Page One*, an original script that Odets also directed, is a conventional courtroom drama which, as Stanley Kauffmann argues, "plods along until it is finished, at which moment we ask ourselves why Odets bothered to write and direct it."[3]

Sweet Smell of Success is, by contrast, Odets at his screenwriting best. Based on a novella by Ernest Lehman, the screenplay stands alone in quality and style as Odets' best film work since *None but the Lonely Heart*—though in a very different vein. Taking Lehman's basic story of a corrupt press agent, Sidney Falco (Tony Curtis), who conspires with a Walter Winchell-like columnist, J. J. Hunsecker (Burt Lancaster), to break up a romance between the columnist's sister and a musician, Odets crafts sharp dialogue that illuminates a desolate world built on the shaky foundations of intrigue and innuendo. As the film progresses, Sidney's desperation to please forces him into murky moral territory, he prostitutes a girlfriend to further his plans, spreads rumors of Communism and plants drugs on the musician, and conspires at every level to gain access to the world of privilege represented by Hunsecker. Only fame, money, recognition, and power have value to Sidney. But by the end of the film, his elaborate

machinations have backfired. The sister leaves Hunsecker for the musician, turning the columnist's wrath upon Sidney. The last cry we hear from Sidney is the
vague threat to incriminate Hunsecker as well: "That fat cop can break my
bones, but he'll never stop me from telling what I know."

Gerald Weales has noted that the dialogue in the film is largely Odets'
work; at its best, it is undeniably powerful, metaphorical on the level of his best
work in *Awake and Sing!* and *Paradise Lost.*[4] "Watch me run a 50-yard dash
with my legs cut off," Sidney brags when confronted with a challenge. Even
more tellingly, the dialogue resurrects images of consumption that Odets had
used in his earlier plays, using them to identify a world horribly askew. "I'm not
a bowl of fruit, a tangerine that peels in a minute," the cigarette girl says as she
fights off Sidney's attempts to prostitute her. Returning to images of food and
consumption that had formed the bedrock of his best plays, *Sweet Smell of Success* shows a world almost completely separated from any vision of paradise.
Rather, the film is dominated by images of decay, corruption, parasitism, and
exploitation. Thus, the corrupt press agent confesses that the even more repre-
hensible columnist "uses any pepper to spice up his daily garbage" and defines
their relationship in terms of a perverse religion: "a press agent eats a columnist's dirt and is expected to call it manna," while the columnist responds by
calling the press agent "a cookie full of arsenic." Only the two lovers, innocent
to the point of sentimentality, are free of the corruption that engulfs this world—
their escape at the end seems a very dim ray of light in the hellish darkness of
the film.

After *Sweet Smell of Success*, Odets' output declined even further. He wrote
only two more films, spending most of his time on dialogue for other scripts or
in pursuing his newfound hobbies of art and stamp collecting. He became one of
the foremost collectors of Paul Klee paintings in the country. A number of his
friends tried to persuade him to write again for the stage, to put his numerous
outlines into a more concrete form, but Odets felt trapped by Hollywood and the
necessity of providing for his two children. As he wrote to Brenman-Gibson in
the early 1960s:

I am tired and miserable and my soul and all of its works follow behind two children and
their needs. . . . all of my plans to be working by now on the first and second of a series
of new plays have gone awry. And, willing to drudge for the mere living of it, I am unable at present to even find a movie job (B-G, 5)

Odets' inability to work on plays puzzled and concerned his friends, whom he
would avoid if possible.

Kazan and Clurman remember Odets in the early 1960s as a wounded man,
working on a musical version of *Golden Boy* to star Sammy Davis Jr., avoiding
contact with people who had known him when he was successful, dreaming of a
return to the theatre. As Kazan recalls: "Cliff wasn't 'shot.' Something was
wrong, but the mind and talent were alive in the man."[5] But despite Kazan's
urging, Odets could never shake himself free of Hollywood to write any of the
plays he had planned. Indeed, for the last months of his life, Odets worked as

head writer on NBC's *Richard Boone Show*, putting in long days of work. Under attack from those who saw this as the ultimate sellout, he defended this work on television as worthy of a craftsman and, at the same time, continued to criticize America for capitulating too easily to the powers of capitalism: "Madison Avenue has taken the enemy out of American life. We don't know who the enemy is with a capital E. This is a frightening thing. Who gives a goddamn about moon shots when you see zombies walking around with lost souls? This is why I have to write plays."[6] Even at the end of his life, working within the economic machine of television, Odets attempted to articulate the good fight against a common enemy—in this case, a debilitating conformity.

Odets worked feverishly on the television series; he would never write another play, however, despite being pressed repeatedly by his former theatre colleagues. During the summer of 1963, he began to grow ill, and on August 14, 1963, Odets died at the age of fifty-seven, a victim of stomach cancer. As he lay dying in Los Angeles, he called in his old Group friends, Clurman, Strasberg, and Kazan and others that he had known in Hollywood, including Cary Grant, Jean Renoir, Marlon Brando, and Danny Kaye. Kazan, convinced that "the tragedy of our time in the theatre is the tragedy of Clifford Odets," recounted Odets' sense of frustration at work uncompleted the final time he saw him: "[N]o longer able to avoid the tragedy he'd lived or the tragedy that he was or the thought of what he might have been, he beckoned me to lean closer, and he whispered—'Gadg! Imagine! Clifford Odets dying!'"[7] Odets' self-consciousness seems to reflect not only the dissipation of his early promise, but also his inordinate energy, his connection to life. Brenman-Gibson recounts the fervor with which he approached the last two weeks of his life, when he knew his cancer would kill him soon: "It was not enough for Odets simply to cling to the raw experience of these days. . . . he steadily tried to provide aesthetic form for his increasingly chaotic impressions" (B-G, 7).

Odets' fervor in death mirrored his energy in life. Clurman had once characterized his friend as possessing "[a] particular sense of gloomy fatality, one might also say an appetite for the broken and rundown, together with a bursting love for the beauty immanent in people, a burning belief in the day when this beauty would actually shape the external world" (TFY, 117). Odets was, at the core of his being, a generous man; there are countless stories of his gifts of money (he once gave Clurman a car and was loaning money to friends from his deathbed), time and energy. But even more importantly, his plays had been a gift: to the Group, to his family and friends, but ultimately to all those who believed in the hopeful future articulated in them.

At Odets' funeral, Danny Kaye delivered a eulogy Clurman had written, which stressed Odets' human concern for others, his openness:

The warmth which emanated from Clifford's person was not the fire of the fanatic but the comforting, healing glow of the lover. Clifford loved. . . His love was not abstract, not a response to a religious or philosophic injunction or commitment. It was a movement of his whole being . . . no one could long be angry with such a man. He overcame our reserves, he melted all coldness.[8]

Marlon Brando remembered Odets as "a wild man and a noble man" and remarked that "even when he talked about the price of bottle tops his eyes would
flash." Renoir saw in Odets' expression "a man thinking of profound things . . .
of creation" (B-G, 9-11).

Though obituaries would appear characterizing Odets as a failure or a sellout, he remained for many the embodiment of a theatre of social and political
importance and. more importantly, a symbol for something hopeful and open in
American life. His death was deeply felt; Alfred Kazin, who had never met
Odets, wept when he heard the news; Kim Stanley said that Odets' death dic-
tated "a reexamination of [her] whole life." Coming a few months before the
assassination of President Kennedy, Odets' death indicated on a smaller scale a
similar loss of innocence. Odets, who, as Brando said, "*was* the thirties," may
have offered more bright promises than he fulfilled. Nevertheless, his work on
Broadway and in Hollywood, his desire to secure the utopian plenty promised
by American democracy, and his deep sympathy for the struggles of everyday
life had offered a hope, as Ralph Berger put it in *Awake and Sing!*, that life
wouldn't always be "printed on dollar bills."

ODETS' LEGACY

Criticism of Odets is often as concerned with what he never wrote as with
what he did. By the time he died in 1963, the once "Golden Boy" of American
theatre had become for many a symbol of an entire generation's loss of commitment, failure of idealism, and capitulation to the forces of capital and conformity. Margaret Brenman-Gibson summarizes obituaries of Odets as generally
condemnatory for having sold out, characterizations that have continued in later
assessments. For example, Gerald Rabkin reduces Odets' work after *Night Music* to expressions virtually devoid of political commitment: "The rebel in Odets
had come to accept the futility of the radical gesture."[9] To be sure, there is a
lessening of political fervor in Odets' later plays. But to dismiss them for lacking ideology not only misses the political arguments that do exist in the plays
but also indicates a preconceived idea of what Odets should have written. It is,
in essence, to place the kind of demands on a writer that Odets struggled with
throughout his career, from the Group's demands for a hit to the pressures of the
Hollywood studios to create a commercial success. It is to make of Odets' jum-
bled, contradictory career a cautionary tale, a melodrama that etches sharp lines
between the acceptable and the unacceptable, the moral and the immoral.

To ignore what Odets did produce—including a number of plays (and at
least two screenplays) of indisputable quality—and concentrate on the "failed"
promise, then, is to wish away the paradoxes and contradictions. Furthermore,
the complexity of Odets' own career and the deep ambivalence revealed in his
plays about the promises and failures of American life point to the pivotal position Odets holds as a mirror of the times in which he lived. To misread Odets is
also to risk a partial misunderstanding of the era itself. He is a playwright centered in the depression, and his plays are a response to the cultural developments
he saw around him. From his work with the Group onward, his intuitive feeling
for the main currents of American life was always informed by a deep sympathy

with ordinary people and a desire to tell their stories. As he wrote in his notes, "In America all we hear about is the heaven of opportunity of success. No one seems ready or willing to talk of the hell of failures and perhaps lovingly comment on those who people that hell. Those blistered, lacerated and roasted" (LCA, no date).

Odets' reputation rests in the considerable achievement of his eleven produced plays, written over a twenty-year span on Broadway. Still, if Odets is a mirror of his times, it becomes necessary to understand how his work influenced writers who followed as well. While the influence of the Group acting style can readily be assessed by following the omnipresent graduates of schools set up by Group members Robert Lewis, Stella Adler, Lee Strasberg, and Sanford Meisner or the directing work of Elia Kazan, for writers, as Gerald Weales says, "the charting of influences is, at best, a chancy endeavor."[10] Odets' influence on Arthur Miller may be more readily apparent than on other playwrights, especially in the similarities of syntax, the Jewish protagonists, and the overtly political plots. A number of critics have noted a seed for *Death of a Salesman* in Odets' *Rocket to the Moon*, where Frenchy argues that in modern capitalism "the woman's not a wife. She's the dependent of a salesman who can't make sales and is ashamed to tell her so" (SP, 404), and see parallels between Ben Gordon of *Paradise Lost* and Biff Loman. Others who seem to have built upon Odets' successes are Tennessee Williams, Lorraine Hansberry, William Gibson, Sam Shepard, and David Mamet.

Dramaturgically, Odets' most lasting achievement is his unmistakably rich dialogue. Odets was, from beginning to end, a verbal volcano. His language is at once fervent, romantic, racy, and sharp, filled with wisecracks and heartbreaking expressions of longing; it is among the best dialogue American drama has to offer. Even his most vicious critic, George Jean Nathan, admitted that Odets wrote some of the best love scenes in American drama. The verbal power is what carries Odets' plays and sometimes what fails them. Every critic has a favorite line or two, and one or two they cite as an appalling lack of restraint, an inability to tame the gift to the task at hand. But there is no denying the power of the language, the life and immediacy it gives to its characters. It is a street argot heightened for dramatic purpose, the language of the living room shaped for a larger examination of American life. One of Odets' playwriting students at the Actor's Studio, playwright William Gibson, commented that Odets "invented a new kind of speech" that no one else could duplicate. Even more importantly, the dialogue was connected to "the most intimate knowledge of the ordinary lives of American people" (NYT, October 18, 1964). It reflected the longings and dreams of those with whom Odets always felt most in sympathy.

Harold Cantor gives the best and most thorough examination of Odets' dialogue, identifying the elements of hyperbole, wisecrack, Whitmanesque lyricism and, most importantly, of Yiddish English, that work in combination to give it its unique texture and power. Indeed, fed by his immigrant background, the memories of his Uncle Israel and Aunt Esther, the Jewish content and rhythms of Odets' work are hard to ignore. This content was readily familiar to the Jewish audiences who came to see themselves portrayed onstage. Alfred Kazin, for example, characterized *Awake and Sing!* as containing "a lyric uplifting of blunt Jewish speech, boiling over and explosive . . . brilliantly authentic, like no other theater speech on Broadway."[11]

Odets' Jewish background, therefore, serves as his starting point; his career truly began when he recognized that his personal experience as a second-generation American could be transmuted into art. His characters never stray far from their origins. There are numerous biblical references, some humorous (e.g., much of *The Flowering Peach*), some angry (Jacob's line in *Awake and Sing!* "In this boy's life a Red Sea will happen again!"), some tender (Georgie's admonition to Bernie at the end of *The Country Girl* to "wrestle. . . . you may win a blessing"). Yiddish expressions are woven seamlessly into his dialogue. In addition, the Edenic impulse of Odets' optimism is a powerful amalgam of Jewish-American experience, American romanticism, the social impulses of the Group Theatre, the economic guidance of Socialism, and the powerful seductions of commodity capitalism and popular culture. He seeks throughout his work to arrive at the epiphanic moment when illusion, despair, frustration, and suffering are thrown off to reveal the true human possibilities. This is what motivates the happy endings in the early plays and remains as a foundation of idealism beneath even the more somber late plays.

From his Russian-Jewish immigrant beginnings, Odets moved outward to examine the American marketplace in all of its manifestations, both Edenic and diabolic. His continuing ambivalence toward the culture of consumption and the world of popular culture surfaces in every corner of his plays, from the Caruso records in *Awake and Sing!* to the platinum cigarette case upon which the plot turns in *None but the Lonely Heart*, from the dark and menacing Hollywood of *The Big Knife* to the unreal wonder of the World's Fair in *Night Music*. Like Odets himself, his characters are trapped, fascinated, bullied, beguiled, rewarded, and punished by the marketplace. They can never, however, remain indifferent to it. Jean-Christophe Agnew has suggested that "to demand a 'thick' rather than 'thin' description of the world of goods is to open up vistas of interpretation that are almost vertiginous in their potential complexity."[12] Surely plays—like consumer goods—are not the simple things we often take them to be. A rereading of Odets' ambivalence toward the culture of abundance, then, thickens traditional interpretations of the plays in the same way as Agnew's examination of the world of goods. The world of goods is central to Odets' work and therefore to an understanding both of the work and of the culture in which it was produced. Always the most perceptive reader of Odets' work, Harold Clurman noted in the 1970s that the fierce power of Odets' work comes from "a perturbation of the soul which arises from the conflict between native idealism and a worshipful materialism" (SP, x). This conflict, central to Odets' career and work, is also undeniably central to American thought and culture, especially from the 1930s onward. Thus Odets, whom Clurman calls "literally a popular playwright, one close to the people, the most ordinary people" (x), lovingly captures for his audiences the difficult tension of a "life printed on dollar bills."

NOTES

1.   Bob Thomas, *King Cohn: The Life and Times of Harry Cohn* (New York: Putnam, 1967) 348.

2.   Paul Buhle and Dave Wagner, *Radical Hollywood: The Untold Story Behind America's Favorite Movies* (New York: The New Press, 2002) 376.

3.   Stanley Kauffmann, "Is Artistic Integrity Enough?" *The New Republic*. (February 8, 1960) 22.

4.   Gerald Weales, *Clifford Odets, Playwright* (New York: Pegasus, 1971) 181-182. In Lehman's story, Hunsecker is deliberately apolitical; Weales suggests that Odets made the character a right-wing columnist in order to indicate "the corruption is societal as well as personal" (182).

5.   Elia Kazan, *Elia Kazan: A Life* (New York: Knopf, 1988) 663. Both Kazan and Clurman recount similar stories about asking Odets to dinner at Chasen's, a popular Hollywood restaurant, and the unemployed Odets' profound embarrassment at being seen there.

6.   *Time*, December 14, 1962, 37.

7.   Kazan, *A Life*, 665.

8.   Quoted in Michael J. Mendelsohn, *Clifford Odets: Humane Dramatist* (Deland, FL: Everett Edwards, 1969) x-xi

9.   Gerald Rabkin, *Drama and Commitment* (Bloomington: Indiana UP, 1964) 211.

10.   Gerald Weales, "Clifford's Children: or It's a Wise Playwright Who Knows His Own Father" in *Critical Essays on Clifford Odets*, Gabriel Miller, ed. (Boston: G. K. Hall, 1991) 261

11.   Alfred Kazin, *Starting Out in the Thirties* (Boston: Little, Brown: 1962) 80-81.

12.   Jean-Christophe Agnew, "The Consuming Vision of Henry James" in *The Culture of Consumption: Critical Essays in American History, 1880-1930*, Richard Wightman Fox and T. J. Jackson Lears, eds. (New York: Pantheon Books, 1983) 69.

Chronology

Date	Events in Odets' Life	Theatre Events	U.S. and World Events
1906	July 18. Born in Philadelphia		
1908			Henry Ford introduces the Model T
1910	Sister Genevieve born		
1911		Irish Abbey Theatre Visits New York	
1912	Moves to New York with his family	George Pierce Baker begins 47 Workshop at Harvard	Woodrow Wilson elected president; Socialists get over 1 million votes
1913	Attends P.S. 52 in the Bronx		
1914			July 28. World War I begins
1915		Washington Square Players and Provincetown Players begin production	May 7. Sinking of the *Lusitania*
			Ku Klux Klan revived in the South and Midwest
1916	Sister Florence born	Susan Glaspell's *Trifles*	Wilson reelected

Date	Events in Odets' Life	Theatre Events	U.S. and World Events
1916		O'Neill's first play, *Bound East for Cardiff* *Theatre Arts Monthly* founded	
1917		Jacques Copeau's troupe visits New York	October. America enters World War I
1918			Passage of Sedition Act Armistice signed, ending World War I
1919	Prepares for *bar mitzvah*, but drops out	Washington Square Players reformed as Theatre Guild	Versailles Peace Conference
1920	First exposure to European drama	O'Neill's *Beyond the Horizon* wins Pulitzer O'Neill's *The Emperor Jones*	Warren G. Harding elected president Nineteenth Amendment gives women right to vote in United States
1921	September. Enters Morris High School	Glaspell's *Inheritors* O'Neill's *The Hairy Ape* Pirandello's *Six Characters in Search of an Author*	Prohibition begins Sacco and Vanzetti arrested and convicted
1922	Writes (unpublished) stories and poems; wins medal for declamation	O'Neill's *Anna Christie* wins Pulitzer	
1923	November. Leaves high school	Elmer Rice's *The Adding Machine* Moscow Art Theatre visits New York Shaw's *St. Joan* premieres at Theatre Guild	Harding dies in office; succeeded by Calvin Coolidge Stalin succeeds Lenin in Soviet Union
1924	Works odd jobs, including as a coat checker at Reinhardt's *The Miracle*	O'Neill's *Desire under the Elms* O'Casey's *Juno and the Paycock* Jean Cocteau's *Orpheus*	Coolidge elected president

Date	Events in Odets' Life	Theatre Events	U.S. and World Events
1925	Moves to Greenwich Village Works as disc jockey	Sidney Howard's *They Knew What They Wanted* John Howard Lawson's *Processional*	Scopes "monkey" trial in Tennessee
1926	Writes radio play, *At the Waterline*	O'Neill's *The Great God Brown* New Playwright's Theatre formed	
1927	Works with stock companies, including Mae Desmond Players		Sacco and Vanzetti executed
1928	Marriage to Roberta [?], birth of their baby, ends with death of both in 1929 murder/suicide	O'Neill's *Strange Interlude* Brecht and Weill's *The Threepenny Opera* Treadwell's *Machinal*	Herbert Hoover elected president
1929	Understudies Spencer Tracy in *Conflict* Tours as bit player with Theatre Guild	Rice's *Street Scene* wins Pulitzer	October. Black Tuesday stock market crash begins Great Depression
1930	Plays in Guild's *Midnight* and *Roar, China*	Group Theatre's organizational meetings begin	
1931	Joins Group Theatre	O'Neill's *Mourning Becomes Electra* Group's first production, *The House of Connelly*	Scottsboro trial of nine young African-Americans
1932	Understudies Luther Adler in *Success Story* Begins writing *I Got the Blues*		Franklin Delano Roosevelt elected president
1933	Parts of Awake and Sing! performed in Group's summer camp Teaches acting at the Theatre Union	Group's production of Sidney Kingsley's *Men in White* Gabriel Garcia Lorca's *Blood Wedding*	Screen Writer's Guild formed Prohibition repealed

Date	Events in Odets' Life	Theatre Events	U.S. and World Events
1934	Writes *Waiting for Lefty* Group agrees to produce *Awake and Sing!* Begins writing *Paradise Lost*	Paul Sklar's *Stevedore* Lillian Hellman's *The Children's Hour* Gabriel Garcia Lorca's *Yerma*	
1935	January. *Waiting for Lefty* opens at benefit for *New Theatre* magazine February. *Awake and Sing!* premieres March. Waiting for Lefty and Till the Day I Die move uptown April. *Three Plays* published May. Mother dies July. Travels to Cuba with fact-finding mission; arrested and deported December. *Paradise Lost* premieres.	Maxwell Anderson's *Winterset* Langston Hughes' *Mulatto* Kingsley's *Dead End* The Gershwins' *Porgy and Bess* Federal Theatre Project begun with Hallie Flanagan at head	Italy invades Ethiopia Stalin declares "Popular Front" against Fasicism CIO founded
1936	Goes to Hollywood for first time, writes *The General Died at Dawn* Meets Luise Rainer Begins work on *The Silent Partner*	Robert E. Sherwood's *Idiot's Delight* wins Pulitzer Irwin Shaw's *Bury the Dead* O'Neill wins Nobel Prize in Literature October. FTP's simultaneous production of Sinclair Lewis' *It Can't Happen Here* in 23 theatres Kaufman and Ferber's *Stage Door*	Spanish civil war begins Roosevelt reelected Germany occupies Rhineland
1937	January. Marries Luise Rainer in Hollywood Writes *Golden Boy* under pressure from Group November. *Golden Boy* premieres	Kaufman and Hart's *You Can't Take It with You* wins Pulitzer Playwright's Company founded	Violent "Little Steel" strike in Chicago leaves 10 dead Sino-Japanese War begins

Date	Events in Odets' Life	Theatre Events	U.S. and World Events
1937	Writes "Democratic Vistas in Drama" in *New York Times*	Reorganization of Group Theatre; Lee Strasberg and Cheryl Crawford leave	
1938	Writes *Rocket to the Moon*	Wilder's *Our Town* wins Pulitzer	Germany occupies Austria
	November. *Rocket to the Moon* premieres	Committee headed my Martin Dies investigates Communist influence in FTP and Hollywood	Munich agreement gives Germany Sudetenland
	December. Appears on cover of *Time*		
	London premiere of *Golden Boy*	Marc Blitzstein's *The Cradle Will Rock*	
1939	Separates from Luise Rainer	Sherwood's *Abe Lincoln in Illinois* wins Pulitzer	Soviet-German non-aggression pact signed
	Continues work on *The Silent Partner* March. *The Silent Partner* published in *New Theatre and Film*	Hellman's *The Little Foxes*	Germany invades Poland; World War II begins
		S. N. Behrman's *No Time for Comedy*	Fascists win civil war in Spain
	Six Plays by Clifford Odets published	Brecht's *Galileo* and *Mother Courage and Her Children*	World's Fair held in New York City
1940	February. *Night Music* premieres	Saroyan's *The Time of Your Life* wins Pulitzer, but he declines it	Roosevelt wins unprecedented third term
	Begins work on *Clash by Night*		United States begins Lend-Lease support to Britain
	Writes screenplay for *Night Music*		Peacetime military draft begins in United States
1941	December. *Clash by Night* premieres; first Odets play produced outside Group	May. Group Theatre ceases operation	December. United States enters World War II
		Sherwood's *There Shall Be No Night* wins Pulitzer	
1942	Writes *Rhapsody in Blue*, a screenplay about George Gershwin	Jean Anouilh's *Antigone*	Continued internment of Japanese-Americans on West Coast
	Adapts *The Russian People*, by Konstantin Simonov, for Theatre Guild		

Date	Events in Odets' Life	Theatre Events	U.S. and World Events
1943	Adapts *Jacobowsky and the Colonel* for the Guild but is removed from the project May. Marries Bette Grayson, his third marriage Writes screenplay, *None but the Lonely Heart*, directs the film with Cary Grant and Ethyl Barrymore	Wilder's *The Skin of Our Teeth* wins Pulitzer Rogers and Hammerstein's *Oklahoma!* Moss Hart's *Winged Victory*	Italy signs armistice with Allies
1944	Works on screenplays for RKO, MGM, and others	Sartre's *No Exit* and *The Flies* Tennessee Williams' *The Glass Menagerie*	Roosevelt wins fourth term as president June. Normandy invasion gains Allied foothold in Europe Roosevelt dies in office, succeeded by Harry Truman
1945	April. Daughter, Nora Odets, born	Arthur Laurents' *Home of the Brave* Brecht's *The Caucasian Chalk Circle* Jean Giradoux'*The Madwoman of Chaillot*	May. Victory on European front August. United States drops atomic bombs on Hiroshima and Nagasaki forcing Japanese surrender
1946	Writes screenplay, *Deadline at Dawn*; film is directed by Harold Clurman *Humoresque*, with screenplay by Odets and Zachary Gold, premieres	O'Neill's *The Iceman Cometh* American Repertory Theatre founded	November. Republicans gain control of House and Senate in midterm elections
1947	Named as participant in Communist activity by HUAC; attacks the committee in a letter to *Time* Son, Walt Whitman Odets, born	Williams' *A Streetcar Named Desire* Arthur Miller's *All My Sons* The Actor's Studio founded by former members of the Group Theatre	Declaration of Truman Doctrine aimed at stopping the spread of Communism National Security Act passed

Date	Events in Odets' Life	Theatre Events	U.S. and World Events
1947		Houston's Alley Theatre begins production	HUAC begins investigations of Communist activity in the film industry; trial of the "Hollywood Ten"
1948	Returns to New York Begins work on new play, *The Big Knife*	Williams' *Summer and Smoke*	Truman elected to full term as president
1949	Chairs panel, with Arthur Miller and Dmitri Shostakovich, at Congress for World Peace February. *The Big Knife* premieres	Lee Strasberg begins teaching at Actor's Studio Miller's *Death of a Salesman*	Mao-Tse-tung's Communists take control of China
1950	Begins work on *The Country Girl* November. *The Country Girl* opens	William Inge's *Come Back, Little Sheba* T. S. Eliot's *The Cocktail Party* Washington, DC's Arena Stage begins production	Senator Joseph McCarthy begins investigations into State Department Communism United States enters Korean War
1951	Divorced from Bette Grayson Teaches playwriting class at Actor's Studio	Williams' *The Rose Tattoo* Eugene Ionesco's *The Chairs*	Julius and Ethel Rosenberg convicted of espionage, sentenced to death
1952	Directs revival of *Golden Boy*, starring John Garfield May. Testifies in front of HUAC, naming names		United States successfully tests hydrogen bomb Dwight D. Eistenhower elected president
1953	Begins work on *The Flowering Peach*	Samuel Beckett's *Waiting for Godot*	End of Korean War
1954	November. Bette Grayson Odets dies December. *The Flowering Peach*, his last finished play, premieres		*Brown v. Topeka Board of Education* decision by United States Supreme Court

Date	Events in Odets' Life	Theatre Events	U.S. and World Events
1955	Returns to Hollywood, writes *Joseph and His Brethren* (shelved) for Columbia	Williams' *Cat on a Hot Tin Roof* wins Pulitzer Inge's *Bus Stop* Lawrence and Lee's *Inherit the Wind*	Montgomery bus boycott marks intensification of Civil Rights movement
1956		Jean Genet's *The Balcony* O'Neill's *Long Day's Journey into Night* John Osborne's *Look Back in Anger*	Eisenhower elected to second term Hungarian revolution crushed by Soviets
1957	Rewrites screenplay for *Sweet Smell of Success*	Friedrich Dürrenmatt's *The Visit* Beckett's *Endgame*	Sputnik I orbits the earth
1958		Ionesco's *Rhinoceros*	
1959	Writes and directs the film *The Story on Page One*		Fidel Castro takes control of Cuba
1960	Writes screenplay for *Wild in the Country*, starring Elvis Presley	Hellman's *Toys in the Attic*	John F. Kennedy elected president
1961	Awarded Gold Medal from American Academy of Arts and Sciences	Beckett's *Happy Days* Harold Pinter's *The Caretaker*	American presence in Vietnam escalates
1962	Begins a musical version of Golden Boy, for Sammy Davis Jr. Head writer for television's *The Richard Boone Show*; writes several original scripts	Edward Albee's *Who's Afraid of Virgina Woolf*	Cuban missle crisis
1963	August 14. Dies of stomach cancer in Los Angeles		March on Washington led by Martin Luther King Jr November. Kennedy assassinated, succeeded by Lyndon B. Johnson

Selected Bibliography

Aaron, Daniel. *Writers on the Left: Episodes in American Literary Communism.* New York: Harcourt Brace & World, 1961.

Adams, Henry. *The Education of Henry Adams.* New York: Penguin, 1995.

Adorno, T. W. "Television and the Patterns of Mass Culture." *Mass Culture: The Popular Arts in America.* Bernard Rosenberg and David Manning White, eds. London: The Free Press of Glencoe, 1957: 474-488.

Agee, James. *Agee on Film, Volume 1.* New York: McDowell Obolensky, 1958.

Agnew, Jean-Christophe. "The Consuming Vision of Henry James." *The Culture of Consumption: Critical Essays in American History, 1880-1930.* Richard Wightman Fox and T. J. Jackson Lears, eds. New York: Pantheon Books, 1983: 65-100.

Appel, Benjamin. *The People Talk: American Voices from the Great Depression.* New York: Touchstone, 1940.

Barnard, Rita. *The Great Depression and the Culture of Abundance.* Cambridge: Cambridge UP, 1995.

Barton, Bruce. *The Man Nobody Knows.* Indianapolis: Bobbs-Merrill, 1925.

Baskerville, Stephen J. and Ralph Willett, eds. "Introduction." *Nothing Else to Fear: New Perspectives on America in the Thirties.* Manchester: Manchester UP, 1985: 1-12.

Baudrillard, Jean. *America.* Chris Turner, trans. New York: Verso, 1988.

⸻. *The System of Objects.* James Benedict, trans. London: Verso, 1996.

Baumol, William J. and William G. Bowen. *Performing Arts—The Economic Dilemma.* New York: The Twentieth Century Fund, 1966.

Bell, Daniel. *The Cultural Contradictions of Capitalism.* New York: Basic, 1976.

Benjamin, Walter. "The Work of Art in the Age of Mechanical Reproduction." *Illuminations.* Harry Zohn, trans. New York: Schocken, 1969: 219-253.

Benson, Susan Porter. "Living on the Margin: Working Class Marriages and Family Survival Strategies in the U.S., 1919-1941." *The Sex of Things: Gender and Consumption in Historical Perspective.* Victoria de Grazia and Ellen Furlough, eds. Berkeley: U of California P, 1996: 212-243.

Bentley, Eric. *Thirty Years of Treason.* New York: Viking, 1971.

Bigsby, C. W. E. "*Awake and Sing!* and *Paradise Lost.*" *Critical Essays on Clifford Odets*, Gabriel Miller, ed. Boston: G.K. Hall, 1991: 153-164.

----------. *Twentieth Century American Drama, Volume One: 1910-1940.* Cambridge: Cambridge UP, 1982.

Blake, Ben. *The Awakening of the American Theatre.* New York: Tomorrow, 1935.

Block, Anita. *The Changing World in Plays and Theatre.* Boston: Little, Brown, 1939.

Bocock, Robert. *Consumption.* New York: Routledge, 1993.

Bonazzi, Tiziano. "Frederick Jackson Turner's Frontier Thesis and the Self-Consciousness of America." *Journal of American Studies* 27.2 (August 1993): 149-171.

Bordman, Gerald. *American Theatre: A Chronicle of Comedy and Drama, 1930-1969.* New York: Oxford UP, 1996.

Bordwell, David, Janet Staiger and Kristin Thompson. *The Classical Hollywood Cinema: Film Style and Mode of Production to 1960.* London: Routledge & Kegan Paul, 1985.

Bottomore, Tom and Patrick Goode, eds. *Readings in Marxist Sociology.* Oxford: Clarendon, 1983.

Bourdieu, Pierre. *Distinction: A Social Critique of the Study of Taste.* Richard Nice, trans. Cambridge, MA: Harvard UP, 1984.

Brady, John. *The Craft of the Screenwriter.* New York: Touchstone, 1981.

Brenman-Gibson, Margaret. *Clifford Odets, American Playwright: The Years From 1906-1940.* New York: Atheneum, 1981.

Brinkley, Alan. "The New Political Paradigm: World War II and American Liberalism." *The War in American Culture: Society and Consciousness During World War II.* Lewis A. Ehrenberg and Susan E. Hirsch, eds. Chicago: U of Chicago P, 1996: 313-330.

Bronner, Susan J. *Consuming Visions: Accumulation and Display of Goods in America, 1880-1920.* New York: W. W. Norton, 1989.

Brown, John Mason. *Broadway in Review.* New York: W. W. Norton, 1940.

----------. *Two on the Aisle.* New York: W. W. Norton, 1938.

Browne, Ray B. and Marshall W. Fishwick. *Symbiosis: Popular Culture and Other Fields.* Bowling Green, OH: Bowling Green State U Popular P, 1988.

Buhle, Paul and Dave Wagner. *Radical Hollywood: The Untold Story Behind America's Favorite Movies.* New York: The New Press, 2002.

Campbell, Colin. *The Romantic Ethic and the Spirit of Modern Consumption.* London: Basil Blackwell, 1987.

Cantor, Harold. *Clifford Odets: Playwright-Poet.* Metuchen, NJ: Scarecrow, 1978.

Carnegie, Andrew. *The Gospel of Wealth and Other Timely Essays.* Edward C. Kirkland, ed. Cambridge, MA: Harvard UP, 1962.

Catsy, Alan. "The Gangster and the Drama of the Thirties." *Challenges in American Culture.* Ray B. Browne, Larry L. Landrum, William K. Bottorff, eds. Bowling Green, OH. Bowling Green U Popular P, 1970: 224-233.

Ceplair, Larry and Steven Englund. *Inquisition in Hollywood: Politics in the Film Community, 1930-1960.* Garden City, NY: Anchor /Doubleday, 1980.

Chafe, William H. *The Unfinished Journey: America Since World War II.* New York: Oxford UP, 1999.

Chandler, Raymond. "Writers in Hollywood." *The Atlantic Monthly.* November, 1945. 50-54.

Clurman, Harold. *All People Are Famous.* New York: Harcourt Brace Jovanovich, 1974.

----------. *The Fervent Years: The Story of the Group Theatre and the Thirties.* New York: Hill and Wang, 1945.

----------. *Lies Like Truth*. New York: Macmillan, 1958

Cohen, Lizabeth. "The Class Experience of Mass Consumption: Workers as Consumers in Interwar America" *The Power of Culture: Critical Essays in American History*. Richard Wightman Fox and T. J. Jackson Lears, eds. Chicago: U of Chicago P, 1993: 135-160.

Cosgrove, Stuart. "The Living Newspaper: Strikes, Strategies and Solidarity." *Nothing Else to Fear: New Perspectives on America in the Thirties*. Stephen J. Baskerville and Ralph Willett, eds. Manchester: Manchester UP, 1985: 238-257.

Cowley, Malcolm. "While They Waited for Lefty." *Saturday Review*. June 6, 1944. 16-19, 61.

Crawford, Cheryl. *One Naked Individual: My Fifty Years in the Theatre*. Indianapolis: Bobbs-Merrill, 1977.

"Credo of a Wrong Living Man." *Time*. December 14, 1962. 37.

Cross, Gary. *Time and Money: The Making of Consumer Culture*. New York and London: Routledge, 1993.

Cunningham, Frank R. "*Night Music* and *Clash by Night*: Clifford Odets and Two Faces of Modernism." *Critical Essays on Clifford Odets*. Gabriel Miller, ed. Boston: G. K. Hall, 1991: 227-237.

Davis, Kenneth S. *FDR. A History*. 3 Volumes. *Volume 1: The New York Years, 1928-1933* [1985]; *Volume 2: The New Deal Years, 1933-1937* [1986]; *Volume 3: Into the Storm, 1937-1940* [1993]. New York: Random House.

Davis, Mike. *Prisoners of the American Dream: Politics and Economy in the History of the U.S. Working Class*. London: Verso, 1986.

Debord, Guy. *Society of the Spectacle*. Detroit: Black and Red, 1983.

DeMastes, William W. *Clifford Odets: A Resource and Production Sourcebook*. New York: Greenwood, 1991.

Denning, Michael. "The End of Mass Culture." *International Labor and Working Class History* 37 (Spring 1990): 4-18.

Denny, Reuel. "The Discovery of Popular Culture." *American Perspectives: The National Self-Image in the Twentieth Century*. Robert E. Spiller and Eric Larabee, eds. Cambridge, MA: Harvard UP, 1961: 154-77.

Dick, Bernard F. *Radical Innocence: A Critical Study of the Hollywood Ten*. Lexington: U of Kentucky P, 1989.

Dunne, Philip. *Take Two: A Life in Movies and Politics*. New York: Limelight Editions, 1992.

Dusenbury, Winifred L. *The Theme of Loneliness in Modern American Drama*. Gainesville: U of Florida P, 1960.

Eagleton, Terry. *Criticism and Ideology: A Study in Marxist Literary Theory*. London: Verso, 1978.

----------. *Marxism and Literary Criticism*. Berkeley: U of California P, 1976.

Eaton, Walter Prichard. *The Theatre Guild: The First Ten Years*. New York: Brentano's, 1929.

Ewen, Stuart and Elizabeth Ewen. *Channels of Desire: Mass Images and the Shaping of American Consciousness*. New York: McGraw-Hill, 1982.

Falk, Pasi. *The Consuming Body*. London: Sage, 1994.

Fearnow, Mark. *The American Stage and the Great Depression: A Cultural History of the Grotesque*. Cambridge: Cambridge UP, 1997.

----------. "Theatre Groups and Their Playwrights." *The Cambridge History of American Theatre, Volume II: 1870-1945*. Don B. Wilmeth and Christopher Bigsby, eds. Cambridge: Cambridge UP, 1999: 348-349.

Fine, Ben, and Ellen Leopold. *The World of Consumption*. New York: Routledge, 1993.

Fishwick, Marshall W. *Common Culture and the Great Tradition: The Case for Renewal*. Westport, CT: Greenwood, 1982.

Flanagan, Hallie. *Arena: The History of the Federal Theatre*. New York: Benjamin Blom, 1940.

Flexner, Eleanor. *American Playwrights, 1918-1938: The Theatre Retreats from Reality*. Freeport, NY: Books for Libraries, 1938.

Folsom, Franklin. *Days of Anger, Days of Hope: A Memoir of the League of American Writers 1937-1942*. Niwot, CO: UP of Colorado, 1994.

Fox, Richard Wightman. "Epitaph for Middletown." *The Culture of Consumption: Critical Essays in American History, 1880-1930*. Richard Wrightman Fox and T. J. Jackson Lears, eds. New York: Pantheon, 1983.

Freedman, Morris. *American Drama in Social Context*. Carbondale: Southern Illinois UP, 1971.

Gagey, Edmond. *Revolution in American Drama*. New York: Columbia UP, 1947.

Gans, Herbert. *Popular Culture and High Culture: An Analysis and Evaluation of Taste*. New York: Basic Books, 1974.

Gassner, John. "The American Galaxy." *Masters of the Drama*. New York: Random House, 1940. 662-99.

––––––––––. "The Long Journey of a Talent." *Theatre Arts* (July 1949). p25-30.

––––––––––. *Theatre at the Crossroads*. New York: Holt, Rinehart, Winston, 1960.

––––––––––. *The Theatre in Our Times*. New York: Crown, 1954.

Glenn, Susan A. *Daughters of the Shtetl: Life and Labor in the Immigrant Generation*. Ithaca, NY: Cornell UP, 1990.

Goldmann, Lucien. "Problems of a Sociology of the Novel." *Readings in Marxist Sociology*. Tom Bottomore and Patrick Goode, eds. Oxford: Clarendon, 1983: 178-188.

Goldstein, Malcolm. "Body and Soul on Broadway." *Modern Drama* 7 (1965): 411-421.

––––––––––. "Clifford Odets and the Found Generation." *American Drama and Its Critics*. Alan S. Downer, ed. Toronto: U of Toronto P, 1965: 133-146.

––––––––––. "The Playwrights of the Thirties." *American Theater Today*. Alan S. Downer, ed. New York: Basic, 1967. 25-37.

––––––––––. *The Political Stage: American Drama and Theater of the Great Depression*. New York: Oxford UP, 1974.

Gonzalez, Gilbert G. *Labor and Community: Mexican Citrus Worker Villages in a Southern California Community, 1900-1950*. Urbana: U of Illinois P, 1994.

Gorelik, Mordecai. *New Theatres for Old*. New York: E. P. Dutton, 1962.

Gorman, Paul R. *Left Intellectuals and Popular Culture in Twentieth Century America*. Chapel Hill, NC: U of North Carolina P, 1996.

Greenberg, Clement. "Avant Garde and Kitsch." *Mass Culture: The Popular Arts in America*. Bernard Rosenberg and David Manning White, eds. London: The Free Press of Glencoe, 1957: 98-110.

Griffin, Robert J. "On the Love Songs of Clifford Odets." *The Thirties: Fiction, Poetry, Drama*. Warren French, ed. Deland, FL: Everett Edwards, 1967: 193-200.

Groman, George L. "Waiting for Odets: A Playwright Takes the Stand." *Politics and the Muse: Studies in the Politics of Recent American Literature*. Adam J. Sorkin, ed. Bowling Green, OH: Bowling Green State U Popular P, 1989. 64-78.

Gurko, Leo. *The Angry Decade*. New York: Harper & Row, 1947.

Halberstam, David. *The Fifties*. New York: Fawecett Columbine, 1993.

Hamilton, Ian. *Writers in Hollywood, 1915-1951*. London: Heineman, 1990.

Hearn, Charles R. *The American Dream in the Great Depression*. Westport, CT: Greenwood, 1977.

Heilbrun, James and Charles M. Gray. *The Economics of the Performing Arts: An American Perspective*. Cambridge: Cambridge UP, 1993.

Heinze, Andrew R. *Adapting to Abundance: Jewish Immigrants, Mass Consumption and the Search for American Identity*. New York: Columbia UP, 1990.

Herr, Christopher J. "Writing the People: Political Theatre on Broadway in Interwar America." *Theatre Symposium* 9 (2001): 66-76.

Himelstein, Morgan. *Drama Was a Weapon: The Left Wing Theatre in New York, 1929-1941*. New Brunswick, NJ.: Rutgers UP, 1963.

Homberger, Eric. *American Writers and Radical Politics, 1900-39: Equivocal Commitments*. London: Macmillan, 1986.

Horkheimer, Max, and Theodor Adorno. "The Culture Industry: Enlightenment as Mass Deception." *The Dialectic of Enlightenment*. John Cumming, trans. New York: Continuum, 1972: 120-167.

Horowitz, Daniel. *The Morality of Spending: Attitudes Toward the Consumer Society in America, 1875-1940*. Baltimore: Johns Hopkins UP, 1985.

Horowitz, David A. *Beyond Left and Right: Insurgency and the Establishment*. Urbana: U of Illinois P, 1997.

Howe, Irving. "The Thirties in Retrospect." *Literature at the Barricades: The American Writer in the 1930's*. Ralph F. Bogardus and Fred Hobson, eds. Tuscaloosa, AL: U of Alabama P, 1982: 1-9.

Hughes, Glenn. *A History of the American Theater, 1700-1950*. London: Samuel French, 1951.

Issacs, Edith. "Clifford Odets: First Chapters." *Theatre Arts* (April 1939). 257-264.

Jameson, Frederic. "Reification and Utopia in Mass Culture." *Social Text* 1 (1979): 130-148.

Kael, Pauline. *5001 Nights at the Movies*. New York: Henry Holt, 1991.

——————. *For Keeps*. New York: Dutton, 1994.

Kaplan, Charles. "Two Depression Plays and Broadway's Popular Idealism." *American Quarterly* 15 (Winter 1963): 579-585.

Karp, Abraham J., ed. *Golden Door to America: The Jewish Immigrant Experience*. New York: Viking, 1976.

Karsh, Bernard and Phillips K. Garman. "The Impact of the Political Left." *Labor and the New Deal*. Milton Derber and Edwin Young, eds. Madison, WI: U of Wisconsin P, 1957: 79-119.

Kauffmann, Stanley. "Is Artistic Integrity Enough?" *The New Republic*. February 8, 1960. 22.

Kazan, Elia. *Elia Kazan: A Life*. New York: Knopf, 1988.

Kazin, Alfred. *Starting Out in the Thirties*. Boston: Little, Brown, 1962.

——————. *A Walker in the City*. New York: MJF Books, 1951.

Kempton, Murray. *Part of Our Time*. New York: Simon and Schuster, 1955.

Kline, Herbert, ed. *New Theatre and Film: 1934-1937, An Anthology*. New York: Harcourt Brace Jovanovich, 1985.

Koppes, Clayton R. "Regulating the Screen: The Office of War Information and the Production Code Administration." *Boom and Bust: The American Cinema in the 1940's*, Thomas Schatz, ed. New York: Scribner's, 1999: 262-281.

Krutch, Joseph Wood. *The American Drama Since 1918*. New York: Random House, 1939.

Laforse, Martin W. and James A. Drake. *Popular Culture and American Life*. Chicago: Nelson-Hall, 1981.

Lasch, Christopher. *The True and Only Heaven: Progress and Its Critics*. New York: W.W. Norton, 1991.

Lawson, John Howard. *Theory and Technique of Playwriting*. New York: Hill and Wang, 1960.

Leach, William R. "Transformations in a Culture of Consumption: Women and Department Stores, 1890-1925." *Journal of American History* 71.2 (September 1984): 319-42.

Lears, T. J. Jackson. *Fables of Abundance: A Cultural History of Advertising in America*. New York: Basic Books, 1994.

————. "From Salvation to Self-Realization: Advertising and the Therapeutic Roots of the Consumer Culture 1880-1930." *The Culture of Consumption: Critical Essays in American History, 1880-1930*. Richard Wightman Fox and T. J. Jackson Lears, eds. New York: Pantheon Books, 1983: 3-38.

Lebergott, Stanley. *Pursuing Happiness: American Consumers in the 20th Century*. Princeton, NJ: Princeton UP, 1993.

Lee, Brian. "Reel Life in the Dream Dump: Hollywood in the 1930's." *The Thirties: Politics and Culture in a Time of Broken Dreams*. Heinz Ickstadt, Rob Kroes, Brian Lee, eds. Amsterdam: Free UP, 1987: 248-266.

Leiss, William. *The Limits to Satisfaction: An Essay on the Problems of Needs and Commodities*. Toronto: U of Toronto P, 1976.

Levine, Ira. *Left Wing Dramatic Theory in the American Theatre*. Ann Arbor, MI: UMI Research Press, 1985.

Levine, Lawrence. *Highbrow/Lowbrow: The Emergence of Cultural Hierarchy in America*. Cambridge, MA: Harvard UP, 1988.

————. *The Unpredictable Past: Explorations in American Cultural History*. New York: Oxford UP, 1993.

Lynd, Robert S. and Helen Merrell Lynd. *Middletown: A Study in Contemporary American Culture*. New York: Harcourt Brace, 1929.

————. *Middletown in Transition: A Study in Cultural Conflicts*. New York: Harcourt Brace, 1937.

Macdonald, Dwight. "A Theory of Mass Culture." *Mass Culture. The Popular Arts in America*. Bernard Rosenberg and David Manning White, eds. London: The Free Press of Glencoe, 1957: 59-73.

Macherey, Pierre. *A Theory of Literary Production*. Geoffrey Wall, trans. London: Routledge, 1978.

Marchand, Roland. *Advertising the American Dream: Making Way for Modernity, 1920-1940*. Berkeley: U of California P, 1985.

Marquis, Alice. *Hopes and Ashes: The Birth of Modern Times, 1929-1939*. New York: The Free Press, 1986.

Marx, Samuel. *A Gaudy Spree: The Literary Life of Hollywood in the 1930's When the West Was Fun*. New York: Franklin Watts, 1987.

Mast, Gerald, ed. *The Movies in Our Midst: Documents in the Cultural History of Film America*. Chicago: U of Chicago P, 1982.

Mathews, Jane De Hart. *The Federal Theatre, 1935-1939: Plays, Relief, and Politics*. Princeton: Princeton UP, 1967.

May, Lary. "Making the American Consensus: The Narrative of Conversion and Subversion in World War II Films." *The War in American Culture: Society and Consciousness During World War II*. Lewis A. Ehrenberg and Susan E. Hirsch, eds. Chicago: U of Chicago P, 1996: 71-104.

McBride, Joseph. *Frank Capra: The Catastrophe of Success*. New York: Simon and Schuster, 1992.

McCann, Graham. *Cary Grant: A Class Apart*. New York: Columbia UP, 1996.

McCarten, John. "Revolution's Number One Boy." *The New Yorker*. January 22, 1938. 21-27.

McCarthy, Mary. *Mary McCarthy's Theatre Chronicles, 1937-62*. New York: Farrar, Strauss & Co., 1963.

McCracken, Grant. *Culture and Consumption: New Approaches to the Symbolic Character of Goods and Activities*. Bloomington: Indiana UP, 1988.

McElvaine, Robert S. *The Great Depression: America, 1929-1941*. New York: Times Books, 1984.

McLaughlin, Robert. *Broadway and Hollywood: A History of Economic Interaction*. New York: Arno, 1974.

Mendelsohn, Michael J. *Clifford Odets: Humane Dramatist*. Deland, FL: Everett Edwards, 1969.

————. "Clifford Odets: The Artist's Commitment." *Literature and Society*. Bernice Slote, ed. Lincoln, NE: U of Nebraska P, 1964: 142-152.

————. "Odets at Center Stage." Interview with Odets. *Theatre Arts* May 1963. 16-19, 74-76; June 1963. 28-30, 78-80.

————. "Odets: The Artist in Wonderland." *Drama Critique* 9 (1966): 31-34.

————. "The Social Critics on Stage." *Modern Drama* 6. (1963): 277-85.

Mersand, Joseph. "Clifford Odets: Dramatist of Young America." *The American Drama Since 1930: Essays on Playwrights and Plays*. Port Washington, NY: Kennikat, 1949: 61-90.

Miller, Gabriel. *Clifford Odets*. New York: Continuum, 1989.

————, ed. *Critical Essays on Clifford Odets*. Boston: G. K. Hall, 1991.

Mills, C. Wright. *White Collar: The American Middle Classes*. New York: Oxford UP, 1956.

Milner, Andrew. *Literature, Culture and Society*. London: UCL Press, 1996.

Moore, R. Laurence. *European Socialists and the American Promised Land*. New York: Oxford UP, 1970.

Moore, Thomas Gale. *The Economics of the American Theatre*. Durham, NC: Duke UP, 1968.

Mullen, Bill and Sherry Linkon, eds. *Radical Revisions: Rereading 1930's Culture*. Urbana: U of Illinois P, 1996.

Mumford, Lewis. *Technics and Civilization*. New York: Harcourt Brace, 1934.

Munslow, Alun. "Andrew Carnegie and the Discourse of Cultural Hegemony." *Journal of American Studies*. 22.2 (August 1988): 213-224.

Murphy, Brenda. "Plays and Playwrights, 1915-1945." *The Cambridge History of American Theatre, Volume II: 1870-1945*. Don B. Wilmeth and Christopher Bigsby, eds. Cambridge: Cambridge UP, 1999: 289-342.

Murray, Edward. *Clifford Odets: The Thirties and After*. New York: Frederick Ungar, 1968.

Nathan, George Jean. *Encyclopaedia of the Theatre*. New York: Alfred Knopf, 1940.

Navasky, Victor S. *Naming Names*. New York: Viking, 1980.

Odets, Clifford. *The Big Knife*. New York: Dramatists Play Service, 1949.

————. *Clash By Night*. New York: Random House, 1942.

————. *The Flowering Peach*. Dramatists Play Service, 1954.

————. "How a Playwright Triumphs." Based on an Interview with Arthur Wagner. *Harpers Magazine*. September 1966, 64-74.

————. *None but the Lonely Heart*. Screenplay. Dir. Clifford Odets. Perf. Cary Grant and Ethyl Barrymore. RKO, 1944. *In Best Film Plays—1945*. John Gassner and Dudley Nichols, eds. New York: Crown, 1946.

——————. *Six Plays*. New York: Methuen, 1982.

——————. *Sweet Smell of Success*. Screenplay. Dir. Alexander Mackendrick. Perf. Tony Curtis and Burt Lancaster. United Artists, 1957.

——————. *Three Plays*. London: Victor Gollancz, 1936.

——————. *The Time Is Ripe: The 1940 Journal of Clifford Odets*. New York: Grove, 1988.

——————. Billy Rose Theatre Collection, The New York Public Library for the Performing Arts. T-Mss 1981-008.

O'Reilly, Kenneth. *Hoover and the Un-Americans: The FBI, HUAC, and the Red Menace*. Philadelphia: Temple UP, 1983.

Orr, Clifford. "Around the Fair: Momentary Refuge." *The New Yorker* 15 September 19, 1939. 55.

Ostrander, Gilman M. *American Civilization in the First Machine Age, 1890-1940*. New York: Harper, 1970.

Parrish, Michael E. *Anxious Decades: America in Prosperity and Depression, 1920-1941*. New York: Norton, 1992.

Patterson, James T. *Grand Expectations: The United States, 1945-1974*. New York: Oxford UP, 1996.

Peary, Gerald. "Odets of Hollywood." *Sight and Sound* 56 (1986-1987): 59-63.

"People." *Time*. November 17, 1961. 38.

Perrett, Geoffrey. *America in the Twenties: A History*. New York: Simon and Schuster, 1982.

Phillips, Cabell. *From the Crash to the Blitz: 1929-1939. The New York Times Chronicle of Modern Life*. London: Macmillan, 1964.

Pinkston, C. Alex, Jr. "The Theatre Guild Acting Company." *American Theatre Companies, 1888-1930*, Weldon B. Durham, ed. New York: Greenwood, 1987: 433-442.

Poggi, Jack. *Theater in America: The Impact of Economic Forces, 1870-1967*. Ithaca, NY: Cornell UP, 1968.

Postlewait, Thomas. "The Heiroglyphic Stage: American Theatre and Society, Post-Civil War to 1945." *The Cambridge History of American Theatre, Volume II: 1870-1945*. Don B. Wilmeth and Christopher Bigsby, eds. Cambridge: Cambridge UP, 1999: 107-195.

Potter, David M. *People of Plenty: Economic Abundance and the American Character*. Chicago: U of Chicago P, 1954.

Powdermaker, Hortense. *Hollywood: The Dream Factory: An Anthropologist Looks at the Movie Makers*. Boston: Little, Brown, 1950.

Powers, Richard G. "Sports and American Culture." *Making America: The Society and Culture of the United States*. Luther S. Luedtke, ed. Chapel Hill, NC: U of North Carolina P, 1992: 272-288.

Precetaille, Edmond and Jean-Pierre Terrail. *Capitalism, Consumption and Needs*. Sarah Matthews, trans. London: Basil Blackwell, 1985.

Prover, Jora. *No One Knows Their Names: Screenwriters in Hollywood*. Bowling Green, OH: Bowling Green State U Popular P, 1994.

Rabkin, Gerald. *Drama and Commitment*. Bloomington: Indiana UP, 1964.

Ray, Robert B. *A Certain Tendency of the Hollywood Cinema, 1930-1980*. Princeton: Princeton UP, 1985.

Renoir, Jean. *My Life and Films*. Norman Denny, trans. New York: Atheneum, 1974.

Robertson, James Oliver. *American Myth, American Reality*. New York: Hill and Wang, 1980.

Rosenberg, Bernard and David Manning White, eds. *Mass Culture: The Popular Arts in America*. London: The Free Press of Glencoe, 1957.

Rosenberg, Bernard and David Manning White, eds. *Mass Culture Revisited*. New York: Van Nostrand Reinold, 1971.

Rosenberg, James L. "Situation Hopeless, Not Terminal: The Playwright in the Twenty First Century." *New Theatre Quarterly* 4 (1988): 226-231.

Ross, Andrew. *No Respect: Intellectuals and Popular Culture*. New York: Routledge, 1989.

Rubin, Joan Shelley. "Between Culture and Consumption: The Mediations of the Middlebrow." *The Power of Culture: Critical Essays in American History*. Richard Wrightman Fox and T. J. Jackson Lears, eds. Chicago: U of Chicago P, 1993: 163-191.

Sarlós, Robert Károly. *Jig Cook and the Provincetown Players*. Amherst: U of Massachusetts P, 1982.

Scharine, Richard. *From Class to Caste in American Drama: Political and Social Themes Since the 1930's*. New York: Greenwood, 1991.

Schatz, Thomas. *Boom and Bust: The American Cinema in the 1940's*. New York: Scribners, 1999.

Schlesinger, Arthur, Jr. *The Age of Roosevelt*. 3 Volumes. *Volume 1: The Crisis of the Old Order, 1919-1933* [1957]; *Volume 2: The Coming of the New Deal* [1958]; *Volume 3: The Politics of Upheaval* [1960]. Cambridge, MA: Riverside.

Schrecker, Ellen. *Many are the Crimes: McCarthyism in America*. Boston: Little, Brown, 1998.

Schwartz, Nancy Lynn. *The Hollywood Writers Wars*. New York: Knopf, 1982.

Seldes, Gilbert. "The People and the Arts." *Mass Culture: The Popular Arts in America*. Bernard Rosenberg and David Manning White, eds. London: The Free Press of Glencoe, 1957: 74-97.

Semple, Lorrenzo, Jr. "After Fifteen Years." *Theatre Arts*. December 1950. 30-31.

Shindler, Colin. *Hollywood in Crisis: Cinema and American Society, 1929-1939*. London: Routledge, 1996.

Shuman, R. Baird. *Clifford Odets*. Twayne United States Authors Series. New York: Twayne, 1962.

----------. "Clifford Odets and the Jewish Context" *From Hester Street to Hollywood: The Jewish American Stage and Screen*. Sarah Blacher Cohen, ed. Bloomington: Indiana UP, 1983: 85-105.

Slochower, Harry. "Through the Lower Depths: Clifford Odets." *No Voice Is Wholly Lost*. London: Dennis Dobson, 1946: 255-260.

Smiley, Sam. The Drama of Attack: Didactic Plays of the American Depression. Columbia: U of Missouri P, 1972.

Steinbeck, John. *The Grapes of Wrath*. New York: Modern Library, 1939.

----------. *Of Mice and Men*. New York: Collier, 1937.

Stempel, Tom. *Framework: A History of Screenwriting in the American Film*. New York: Continuum, 1988.

Stern, Robert A. M., Gregory Gilmartin and Thomas Mellins. Assisted by David Fishman and Raymond W. Gastil. *New York 1930: Architecture and Urbanism Between the Two World Wars*. New York: Rizzoli, 1987.

Susman, Warren. *Culture as History: The Transformation of American Society in the Twentieth Century*. New York: Pantheon, 1984.

----------, ed. *Culture and Commitment, 1929-1945*. New York: George Braziller, 1973.

Szostak, Rick. *Technological Innovation and the Great Depression*. Boulder, CO: Westview, 1995.

Thomas, Bob. *King Cohn: The Life and Times of Harry Cohn*. New York: Putnam, 1967.

Throsby, C. D. and G. A. Withers. *The Economics of the Performing Arts*. Melbourne: Edward Arnold, 1979.

Tomlinson, Alan. *Consumption, Identity and Style: Marketing, Meanings and the Psychology of Pleasure*. New York and London: Routledge, 1990.

Turner, Frederick Jackson. "The Significance of the Frontier in American History." *The Frontier in American History*. Cambridge, MA: Harvard UP, 1920.

Tynan, Kenneth. *Curtains*. New York: Atheneum, 1961.

Veblen, Thorstein. *The Theory of the Leisure Class: An Economic Study of Institutions*. London: Macmillan, 1908.

Vogel, Harold L. *Entertainment Industry Economics*. Cambridge: Cambridge UP, 1990.

Voigt, David Q. "No Sex Till Monday: The Fetish Phenomenon in American Sport." *Objects of Special Devotion: Fetishes and Fetishism in Popular Culture*. Ray B. Browne, ed. Bowling Green, OH: Bowling Green U Popular P, 1982: 115-135.

Waldau, Roy S. *Vintage Years of the Theatre Guild, 1929-1939*. Cleveland: Case Western Reserve Press, 1972.

Weales, Gerald. *Clifford Odets, Playwright*. New York: Pegasus, 1971.

----------. "Clifford's Children: or Its a Wise Playwright Who Knows His Own Father." *Critical Essays on Clifford Odets*, Gabriel Miller, ed. Boston: G. K. Hall, 1991: 261-73.

Wenger, Beth. *New York Jews and the Great Depression: Uncertain Promise*. New Haven: Yale UP, 1996.

White, David Manning. "Mass Culture in America: Another Point of View." *Mass Culture: The Popular Arts in America*. Bernard Rosenberg and David Manning White, eds. London: The Free Press of Glencoe, 1957: 13-21.

"White Hope." *Time*. December 5, 1938. 44-48.

Whitfield, Stephen J. *In Search of American Jewish Culture*. Boston: Brandeis UP, 1999.

Whitman, Walt. "Democratic Vistas." *Whitman. Poetry and Prose*. New York: Library of America, 1982: 929-994.

Willett, Ralph. "Odets and Popular Culture." *South Atlantic Quarterly* 27 (1970): 68-78.

Williams, Jay. *Stage Left*. New York: Scribners, 1974.

Williams, Raymond. *Marxism and Literature*. Oxford: Oxford UP, 1977.

Wilmeth, Don B. and Christopher Bigsby, eds. *The Cambridge History of American Theatre, Volume II: 1870-1945*. Cambridge: Cambridge UP, 1999.

Wilson, Garff B. *Three Hundred Years of American Drama and Theatre*. Englewood Cliffs, NJ: Prentice-Hall, 1982.

Ziegler, Joseph Wesley. *Regional Theatre: The Revolutionary Stage*. Minneapolis: U of Minnesota P, 1973.

Index

About the Author

CHRISTOPHER J. HERR is Assistant Professor at California State University, Los Angeles. He is a founding member of the North Coast Theatre in Toledo, Ohio. In addition to publishing or presenting papers on political theatre, he has also acted and directed for the stage.